FLORIDA ISLAND HOPPING

THE WEST COAST

Chelle Koster Walton

 PINEAPPLE PRESS, INC

SARASOTA, FLORIDA

T O R O B *My best island-hopping discovery yet*

ACKNOWLEDGMENTS

My first debt of gratitude goes to my family, who suffered through my absences and endured being dragged along on research trips (I'm not sure which was worse), and who share with me that mysterious island-lust gene.

A seaful of thanks to those islanders who helped me in my research with information, tolerance, kindness, and a benevolent sharing of their island home, especially Rose Drye on St. George Island, Quitman Hodges and Russel Brami on Cedar Key, Susan Phillips and Beth Cole on Long Key, Amy Bressler Drake on Longboat Key, Tom Brummitt on Keewaydin Island, "Uncle Joe" Wightman on Captiva Island, "Smoking Joe" Giordano on Marco Island, and Totch Brown on Chokoloskee Island.

Others to whom I am indebted for assistance include Lee Daniel, Tamara Laine, Kathleen Martin, Leslie Benz, Marcia Bush, Capt. Carl Johnson, Michael J. Kairalla, Allison Blankenship, Rosetta Land Stone, Jan Tully, Geiger & Associates, and the Zimmerman Agency.

Inquiries should be addressed to:
Pineapple Press, Inc.
P.O.Box 3899
Sarasota, Florida 34230

LIBRARY OF CONGRESS
CATALOGING IN PUBLICATION DATA

Walton, Chelle Koster. 1954-
       Florida island hopping: the west coast / Chelle Koster Walton.
                 p.   cm.
       Includes index.
       ISBN 1-56164-081-6 (pb : alk. paper)
              1. Gulf Coast (Fla.)—Tours. 2. Islands-Florida—Gulf Coast—Guidebooks. I. Title
F317.G9W35 1995   95-19837
914.5904—63—dc20   CIP

First Edition
10 9 8 7 6 5 4 3 2 1

Design by Carol Tornatore

CONTENTS

INTRODUCTION   1
Islands, Islanders, and Islandphiliacs   1
Using this Guide   4
Backflash   7
The Natural   11
Eco-Tourism   16
Aqua-Adventure   17
Stranded   18
Cultured Pearls   19
Table Hopping   20
Island Landings   22
Nitty-Gritty   24

I.   PANHANDLE   ISLANDS   29
Perdido Key   34
Santa Rosa Island   39
Okaloosa Island   46
Okaloosa/Walton Peninsula   53
Shell Island   65
Cape San Blas   68
St. Vincent Island   74
St. George Island   77
Dog Island   84

II.   CEDAR   KEYS   86

III. PINELLAS COAST 102

    Anclote Key 110
    Honeymoon & Caladesi Islands 111
    Clearwater Beach 116
    Sand Key 121
    Treasure Island 130
    Long Key 134
    Tierra Verde 143
    Fort DeSoto Park 145
    Egmont Key & Shell Key 149
    Terra Ceia Island 153

IV. SARSOTA/MANATEE COAST 155

    Anna Maria Island 159
    Longboat Key 166
    Lido Key/St. Armands 172
    Siesta Key 178
    Casey Key 184
    Venice 188
    Manasota Key 195

V. LEE ISLAND COAST 201

    Gasparilla Island 206
    Cabbage Key 217
    Useppa Island 220
    Cayo Costa 226
    Pine Island 231
    North Captiva 239
    Captiva Island 243
    Sanibel Island 252
    Estero Island 266
    Bonita Beach Area Islands 273

VI. TEN THOUSAND ISLANDS 282

    Key Island 286
    Marco Island & The Gulf Islands 293
    Chokoloskee & Ten Thousand Islands 307

"How wonderful are islands! Islands in space, like this one I have come to. . . . An island in time. . . . The past and the future are cut off; only the present remains. Existence in the present gives island living an extreme vividness and purity."

— Anne Morrow Lindbergh, *Gift From the Sea*

ISLANDS, ISLANDERS AND ISLANDPHILIACS

Anne Morrow Lindbergh stole these words from my heart before I was ever island-borne — indeed, before I was even born. She was my first islandphiliac read; I remember discovering her on a Jamaican beach and marveling that another shared my immediate and — to me, then — inexplicable, undeniable addiction to islands.

It took me many more years of traveling to, reading about, and living upon islands to realize that island infatuation is a universal emotion: universal in the sense that certain people around the world — not everyone, mind you — take to islands the way no-see-ums take to virgin flesh.

Why are some people drawn to islands while others aren't? It's

1

a question to which I have devoted much thought and research since I became a full-time and permanent islander myself 15 years ago. The psychology of an islander transcends any leather-couch analysis. I have found a few sources, nonetheless, mostly islanders themselves, who had something to offer on understanding this complex persona.

"Every one of these islanders is an island himself, safe, tranquil, incommunicable," Ralph Waldo Emerson wrote of the English. Island means security and peace to the islander. Which means, I suppose, that we're basically insecure, overwrought people looking for a chunk of land that — regardless of the fact that it could be wiped off the map with one good puff of wind — represents something stable.

Independence and freedom are what Lindbergh, in her poem "Back To the Islands," feels islanders seek. She likens island life to sailing. The analogy fits: Islanders often share a passion for sailing. Given our druthers, we would drift aimlessly at sea. Instead, we harbor on islands, waiting for our ship to come in and sail us forever away from this, liberation's halfway house.

With her famous aviator husband Charles, Lindbergh discovered the magic of islands as an escape hatch from the pressures of fame. Imagine how thrilled I was to discover one of her favorite island escapes to be Captiva Island, the sister island of my adopted homeland, Sanibel. There Lindbergh penned her famous *Gift From the Sea*, wherein she writes, "People [on islands], too, become like islands . . . self-contained, whole and serene; respecting other people's solitude, not intruding on their shores, standing back in reverence before the miracle of another individual."

Charles Lindbergh's writings elevate the power of islands to the cosmic: "mystical island where life and spirit could communicate," he wrote of one. "My mind worked best when I was not immersed in formal environments and paced by modern tempos."

Island love is a deep-seated emotion marked by fierce protectiveness. Is it because islands come in smaller packages, making

A great blue heron wades in Gulf waters.
(Lee County Visitor & Convention Bureau)

them seem more vulnerable? More possessable? Or more precious? In the end, it is the islanders who become possessed — possessed with a spirit that won't let them leave. I once had a car that would drag its feet whenever I tried to drive across the causeway. It was actually a case of bad brake shoes, but I was convinced the island gods had taken control.

Communion with nature and other higher forms, adventure, intimacy, independence, serenity, insularity — island infatuates crave it all.

The bevy of island beauties that parade along Florida's west coast perimeter send their siren's song on sea breezes to entice the island-blooded. Who can resist these, the state's most desirable destinations? Some are more desirable than others, of course. Sometimes it's the pristine environment of an island that makes it treasurable. Sometimes it's the people. Often it's an insular way of life that remains essentially unchanged by time and tourism.

My favorites have escaped condominium build-up, wildlife extinction, and other diseases to which islands seem extra susceptible. They are, as a rule, those islands unconnected to mainland, or at least somewhat at a distance from it. It's as though islands can contract mainland-itis by near contact. Those closest to the mainland are more prone to adopting a mainland personality and identity. This book favors Florida's natural island gems that have strong island identity, and focuses on their wildlife, heritage, culture, local life, and adventure.

USING THIS GUIDE

Since all island junkies have their specific needs, I comprehensively cover the total personality of every key, cay, cayo, and island upon which I hop. In a couple of instances, where a peninsula has given the area and its people island qualities, I include it as well. All are divided among six chapters by geographic area. Each chapter includes an overview of that region and a personal introduction to its major islands. Tiny or private islands are often omitted, unless some aspect of their history or make-up merits mention.

I introduce each chapter with the NITTY-GRITTY of sandspit travel. This includes land transportation to and on the island, climate, resources, and pointers on everything from hurricane routes and causeway crossing to love-bug season and tourist invasion.

Each island's section begins with a QUICK TOUR for the island hopper on a short outing who lacks the time to first get to know the island's history, people, and ecology. QUICK TOUR takes you on the best scoping route around the island according to a logical method of island exploration that I have developed. Island exploration, you see, is intrinsically satisfying because its boundaries are so well drawn. Exploring a new city, you never know when to stop. The more time you spend looking, the more distanced you become from the heart of the city. You move on to the residential neighborhoods, then the suburbs, then the environs and rural areas. Soon you've reached another city, never really knowing at what point you left the last.

The more you explore an island, however, the closer you come to the heart. You begin by skirting its edges, forming first impressions of its best sides, its most attractive face, its showpiece facade: the beaches and waterfront, its seaside character.

Time takes you spirally inward on an island, as it does when you're getting to know a new friend. Eventually you wander from the island's bayshore boulevards and best behavior. You work your way gradually to the heart, to the island's guarded spots and protected insecurities — to, alas, its darker moods and tendencies. Then you know the island.

My island dissertations take you deep into the island's psyche while I examine the natural and human history of each island, with an eye on how and how much the latter affects the former. BACK-FLASH sections deal with the island's human history. Under the heading of THE NATURAL, I explore the natural history, parks, wetlands, wildlife refuges, and beaches, followed by information on water and land adventure activities: canoe outfitters, cruises, tours, bike routes and paths, sailboarding lessons, scuba shops, snorkeling sites, shelling and fishing guides, surfing hotspots, in-line skating, golf courses, boat rentals, and other water and landlubber stuff to do. Specific docking and ramp information for boaters is included under the subheads *Touring* and *Boating, Sailing & Canoeing*.

The Intracoastal Waterway (ICW) — a system of buoys and channel markers — runs between the mainland and the islands. I have given water route instructions off the ICW to certain destinations when directions are easy to give. This is meant more for

Fishing charter boat from Treasure Island.
(St. Petersburg/Clearwater Area Convention & Visitors Bureau)

orientation when you are using an official sea chart. Whether you own or are renting a boat, you should have a chart of local waters. gulf coast island waters are tricky, fraught with shallowly submerged sandbars, oyster beds, and grass flats. If you're not a practiced boater and chart reader, it's best to hire someone with local knowledge to take you to sea.

Note: All motor-powered boats used in Florida must be registered at the tax collector's office. If currently registered out of state, boats need not be registered in Florida for stays of 90 days or less.

LOCAL CULTURE follows with a sketch of the islanders: Are the natives friendly? Do celebrities frequent? Where does the island fall on the spring-break barometer? Do homesteaders still live there? Mostly retirees? Predominantly a yuppie bedroom community? Ethnic enclave? Ferret-lover's haven? This section offers some casual and not-so-casual (i.e., demographic, where possible) observations. A few of the chapters give special insight into the island personality with profiles of longtime residents.

For the literate traveler, information on theater, art galleries, important authors and artists, literary works, music, and architecture come next. Folk culture is covered under subheads on fairs, festivals, and nightlife.

The guide's devotion to food, under the heading TABLE HOPPING, strays somewhat from normal guidebook treatment. I will offer restaurant recommendations when warranted by their fine representation of local cuisine, access to boaters, and islandness. But primarily, I deal with the overall type of cooking and local products, with perhaps a recipe here, a cookbook recommendation there, and a bit of food lore thrown in for un-dry measure.

The look at lodging in ISLAND LANDINGS focuses on inns and hotels that evoke a sense of island and avoids those types of resorts that sequester you from local life. Because seafaring plays such a major role in an island's character, I include accommodations with boat docking and launching facilities whenever possible. For each island, I also give an overview of the general types and availability of lodging you can expect to find.

Because they are inherent to many islands, I include a section on TOURIST TRAPS. *Sources & Resources* lists people, publications, organizations, and visitor services that have assisted me or can assist you with general information about Florida island travel. Other sources may be listed throughout each section as they relate to specific topics.

BACKFLASH

Florida claims the most islands — count 'em, 4,510 (and that's just those with ten acres or more) — of any state but Alaska. Only Alaska and Louisiana beat Florida's 840,727 acres of total island area. Most of Florida's islands measure under 100 acres (2,444 of them, to be exact); 837 spread out 100 to 499 acres; 1,112 are 500 to 999 acres, and 117 measure 1,000 acres and over. Those under ten acres in size are often labeled keys and, according to the U.S. Geological Survey, number 882. Anything smaller gets classified as a shoal, reef, or sandbar.

Millions of years ago, the Florida peninsula itself was but a scattering of volcanic islands akin to the Caribbean islands and unconnected to the American continental mainland. Even as Florida became solid land, shaped by ice age sea fluctuations, islands began to grow along its fringes. They did, indeed, literally grow —from a single grain of sand or mangrove tree sprout to stabilized sand masses and forests of matter-nabbing aerial roots. As sand and marine encrustations accumulated over the centuries, islands began to form into offshore homes for intrepid individuals.

Barrier islands made a perfect homeland for the state's aborigines. Unlike modern-day islanders, early native Amerindians selected these tribal sites not for their luxurious beaches and seafood restaurants, but for their strategic protection status and, yes, for their easy access to fish and the shells from which they fashioned their meals and tools.

Archaeological digs on many islands have unearthed shell mounds where early Amerindians deposited their dead and debris. Some, like Cabbage Key and Useppa Island on the southern Gulf coast, claim the highest Florida island elevations because of the height of these ancient dumps and tombs. Tribes with names such as Calusa, Tocobaga, and Timucua populated these islands long before the time of Christ, constructing intricate roadways and canal systems leading to and from the mounds. Despite their presumably advanced knowledge of engineering, agriculture, and art, and their dominance over the land today called Florida, they were no match for the Europeans who invaded their shores. Within three centuries, war and disease had decimated their way of life.

Juan Ponce de León was the first white island tourist in Florida. On his maiden expedition in 1513, he explored the Florida Keys and named the state *La Florida,* in celebration of the land's profuse flowers.

Ponce de León traveled to Florida seeking a fountain of youth and navigated the risky waters of Charlotte Harbor to meet his death at the hands of the Calusa Indians. Hernando de Soto made his first landfall at Longboat Key on the hot trail of gold. Pánfilo de Narváez explored the Panhandle coastline. Later, refugees from the law settled Florida's hidden Gulf coast islands. William Augustus "Billy Bowlegs" Bowles claimed much of the northern Gulf coast as part of his State of Muskogee in the late 18th and early 19th centuries. Legends of his sunken and buried treasure persist along the Panhandle.

Ever since, folks have been setting upon these shores in quest of treasure or escape. Many have come looking for buried or submerged pirate's booty, thanks to a rich legacy of buccaneering perpetuated by legends grown larger than life. Pirates have colored the pages of Florida history books in shades of blood red and doubloon gold. They have bequeathed to the state romantic nomenclature and theme — for everything from annual festivals and resorts to football teams and islands. Besides willing to its residents a certain cavalier spirit, these pirates have left Florida, if one believes the tales, millions of dollars in buried treasure.

On the west coast, legend was largely fabricated to romanticize pirate legacy. There, the name Gasparilla has come to mean more than just an island. A swashbuckling saga has grown up around a mostly fictional pirate assigned the name. It involves the swath of islands and keys from the Everglades' Ten Thousand Islands to St. Petersburg. Variations abound; the Gasparilla saga improves with each telling. All versions involve tales of bloodletting, innuendoes about buried treasure, and the right touch of romance. An annual pirate's gala takes place on Treasure Island, named for a chest of riches rumored to be buried there. Names such as Calico Jack Rackham, Anne Bonny, Jean LaFitte, and Bru Baker have sparked west-Floridian island tales of derring-do and social-don'ts for over a century.

Meanwhile, a new breed of Amerindians migrated south to replace those sacrificed to European greed, brutality, and insensitivity. Known as the Creeks in Georgia, they became the Seminoles — meaning wanderers — in Florida. They were joined by renegades from every land, who settled Florida in hopes of a better life. They all contributed their genes and ways to the cultural soup the state became.

War has played a major role in Florida's heritage, as the islands' many forts attest. Portions of the state changed hands and nationalities like most places change seasons. With each new government, the Seminoles were pushed farther and farther down the peninsula, a trend the tribe could finally no longer abide. Spain sold the peninsula to the United States after the first Amerindian uprising, termed the First Seminole War. And the shoving continued. Thousands of Seminoles were shipped out of the state to western wild lands. The rest eventually settled in the Everglades after 50 years of warring.

Statehood brought yet more strife as the Civil War ignited. Some Florida islands played a role that was to be repeated throughout modern history, that of smuggling camps. Others, such as Depot Key and Egmont Key, held lighthouses and strategic positions, and so became military stations. Floridians were generally split by or, by dint of distance, ambivalent about loyalty to either side. West coast islanders, a renegade bunch in those days, used the opportunity to buy arms and black-market goods from blockade busters. Cayo Costa harbored Yankee sympathizers fleeing Confederate vigilantes after the war.

By 1886, Cedar Key had stepped into the running for the state's four largest cities, along with Jacksonville, Pensacola, and Key West. Florida's less-populated islands began to know a more refined islander as railroads reached the secluded outposts. In 1913, the Charlotte Harbor and Northern Railway erected the Gasparilla Inn for its clientele of wealthy tarpon fishermen and visitors to Boca Grande on Gasparilla Island. Names such as du Pont, Crowninshield, Eastman, and J. P. Morgan splashed across the pages of the inn's guest book. In the 1920s, F. Scott Fitzgerald, Lou Gehrig, and their ilk propelled St. Pete Beach's Don CeSar to legendary status.

Word spread about this wondrous land of palm trees, sun, and fish galore. The boom sounded. Florida was *the* place to winter, especially if you possessed money and an adventurous spirit. The state's islands were the ultimate getaway for the wealthy.

Circa 1925, circus tycoon John Ringling put the islands off Sarasota's shores on the Social Register map. Farther south, agriculture and mariculture sustained the less-discovered islands around Fort Myers and Naples. Yet seclusion seekers and sportsmen such as Charles Lindbergh, Hedy Lamarr, Shirley Temple, and Teddy Roosevelt escaped to Captiva, Ten Thousand Islands, and others.

The boom deadened with a hurricane followed by the Great Depression. Still, Gulf coast Florida's population and tourism figures spiraled upward. In 1954, the Sunshine Skyway over Tampa Bay made St. Petersburg's Holiday Isles more accessible. Soon, a network of causeways and bridges reeled in Florida's islands, out of the hands of the extremely wealthy winterer and fiercely independent homesteader. Rampant development on most of the bridged islands heralded their new status as exotic playgrounds. Some tried to halt it, such as Sanibel with its incorporation and growth policies, and Gasparilla Island and Casey Key with their wealthy influence.

But popularity grows algebraically with each visitor to these pallets of sand and sun adrift upon balmy seas. Thanks to the forethought of the inspired, wildlife refuges on many islands preserve their natural heritage. And though escalating taxes and resort pressures often drive out the islands' "old breed" — the hardy homesteader and retired peace seeker — most retain the qualities that will always sate the island gourmet.

THE NATURAL

"We have been here a hundred years. In geological time the waters will again cover the peninsula and again recede, only to return again. So let us cherish this moment of paradise, relish these years of sun and beauty, and do what we can to keep it pristine" — John D. MacDonald, novelist and Siesta Key resident.

Whether sun-drenched beaches or sodden mangrove forests,

the natural attributes of an island attract its best fans. The amazing realm of Florida's wildlife has been preserved in its most natural state on several of its islands. Because Florida spans more than seven degrees in latitude, its islands possess the nation's greatest diversity of natural vegetation and animal life.

Aside from the ubiquitous sea oats, mangroves, and palmettos, island flora changes drastically on its island hop southward. Pine trees populate northern islands and gave Cedar Key its name. Live oak is more common and profuse in these parts, characteristically swaddled in its Spanish moss shawl. Mid-state, the palm trees become more profuse, especially sabal palms, Florida's state tree. More exotic and warmth-loving species occur down the line: royal palms, Washingtonias, coconuts, and date palms. Other tropical native varieties thrive in lower extremes: Gumbo-limbos, sea grapes, buttonwood, sea hibiscus, papayas, coffee bush, joewood. Honeymoon Island, north of Clearwater, is the northernmost island where many of the tropicals survive.

The citrus trees so highly associated with the state, though not native, abound on the islands, especially the trademark key lime along the southern coast. Their blossoms, along with those of the gardenia, frangipani, jasmine, and Hong Kong orchid, orchestrate a symphony for the nose. Practically every type of plant eventually blooms in Florida — even house plants you never suspected would. Hibiscus, bougainvillea, poinciana, blue porterweed, lily, and night-blooming cereus all affirm the state's flowery name. Rare tropical fruits grow, especially on the west coast's Pine Island, where unique geographical conditions insulate it from the cold. Mangoes, sapodillas, bananas, sapotes, pineapples, and guavas flourish here commercially and in the residential yards of neighboring islands.

Florida is home to myriad species of mammals. Many of these did not reach the islands until causeways and bridges allowed them on-foot passage. Today, sightings of an occasional Florida panther, bobcat, wild boar, and black bear are reported even on resort islands. On the Panhandle's St. Vincent Island, Asian sambar deer survive, the result of an erstwhile hunting preserve stocked with exotic animals. Raccoons and armadillos raid garbage bins and tear up yards on most islands. Often islands, sadly enough, wind up being dumping grounds for unwanted cats, which gives them a large population of feral felines. Florida's most precious mammal, the manatee, swims southern island waters for the benefit (and at the mercy) of attentive boaters.

Birds account for the island's most popular above-water fauna. Island refuges serve migrating bird flocks much as Florida's resorts do humans — as a warm and wonderful stopover on escape from northern chills. Sandhill cranes, wood storks, roseate spoonbills, white and brown pelicans, ibises, egrets, herons, ospreys,

Beachers commune with nature.
(Lee County Visitor & Convention Bureau)

hawks, bald eagles, cormorants, robins, seagulls, terns, sandpipers, pileated woodpeckers, cardinals and at least 280 other species have been logged on visits to, if not extended stays and permanent residency on, Florida islands.

One of Florida's favorite water creatures, the alligator, lives on freshwater islands. Sanibel, having first passed a no-feeding law after which the state finally modeled one of its own, is credited with the reptile's comeback from endangerment in recent years. A variety of snakes and lizards help the 'gator keep a natural balance on Florida islands. The black snake is most plentiful and completely harmless, as is the indigo. Rattlesnakes are found particularly in the off-islands of Cedar Key Wildlife Refuge, on Egmont Key, and on Caladesi Island, where they share nesting holes with gopher tortoises. Coral snakes, cottonmouths, dwarf rattlers, and other poisonous species are rare but existent. Anoles, skinks, geckos, and other lizards help keep the mosquito population down.

Florida's sea turtles receive utmost respect on many islands, where lights-off ordinances are often enforced to forestall interference with nesting. Florida hosts the largest population of nesting loggerheads in the Western Hemisphere. Gopher and box tortoises lumber around in secluded areas, occasionally ending up disoriented on a main island thoroughfare.

Not one of the island's greatest boasts, insects are nonetheless a major factor in island living. Abundance of sand and water often attracts the unloved sand flea — known locally as the no-see-um — especially in southern regions. Mosquitoes once made summertime outdoor activity impossible throughout most of Florida, but most places — with the exception of refuge islands — exert some measure of control today. Several varieties of cockroaches will always survive, they tell us, in Florida. One type flies, and has been euphemistically pet-named the palmetto bug. Ants come in every size and dietary preference, along with their destructive termite cousins. Love bugs get their name from their characteristic wedlocked state and cause problems only when they conspire to splatter car windows and clog radiators. A huge grasshopper named lubber can make a night's work of an entire marginata plant. The spiders grow big too. The golden orb weaves intricate webs to background her shiny torso. The zippy housekeeper spider has the leg span the size of a child's hand and is considered good luck in the home. The less lovable black widow and brown recluse lurk in dark places. A battalion of pests from white flies to mites make Florida gardening a challenge. Who said life in paradise was problem-free?

Fortunately, more desirable creatures outnumber the bad. One need merely consider island marine life. Mollusks found elsewhere only in the Caribbean provide beachers and serious collectors a pastime and passion. The west coast especially attracts malacologists, conchologists, and casual shellers to sandy shores in search of lightning whelks, conchs, olives, sanddollars, junonias, murex, tulips, angel wings, and hundreds of other species.

Shelling is best at low tide and after storms. Most shells found on beaches in fair weather have been abandoned by their mollusk inhabitants and have suffered the assault of wind, sun, and waves. Serious shellers hunt under less favorable conditions for live specimens whose shells remain intact. Before you attack the beaches and their shell life, you should educate yourself, especially if you plan to hunt live shells. Get a good book that will help you find, identify, and clean shells. A fishing license is required for collecting live shells.

No matter how you clean your live shells, the experience falls far short of being the highlight of the hobby. Keep this in mind when you are collecting. Do not gather more than you need or care to clean. The place to throw back unwanted shells is at the beach, not at the hotel when you are cleaning them, or back home with the rest of the smelled-up contents of your suitcase. Sanibel Island and Florida's national and state parks prohibit the collection of live shells.

Dolphin and mullet perform free acrobatics for beachers and boaters. Majestic tarpon boil waters with feisty activity, especially around Gasparilla and Useppa Islands, where the first tarpon fishing clubs formed. Sharks serve their ecological purpose, despite their bad reputation. Rare sports catches such as the snook, redfish, and triple-tail delight tastebuds. Waters once teemed with grouper, snapper, sheepshead, mackerel, redfish, tuna, dolphinfish, mullet, cobia, pompano, shrimp, stone crab, and lobster. Today commercial and environmental pressure has endangered Florida's waterlife legacy. Recently, a law went into effect banning commercial net fishing. Most charter guides support catch-and-release for certain species, especially small or inedible fish. Strict laws regulate size, number and season for catching, and licensing hopes to help reverse damages.

The state of Florida requires that nonresidents purchase a license for freshwater and saltwater fishing. Check with local bait shops, marinas, K-Marts, Wal-Marts, or the Department of Natural Resources, Florida Marine Patrol, Support Services, 3900 Commonwealth Blvd., Tallahassee 32303; 904-488-5757.

ECO-TOURISM

Without controls, Florida's most valuable asset lies in the balance. The state makes steady advances toward eco-tourism — the conservation of our tourist-attracting natural environment — mostly through education.

"Brochures and ads include more of a 'help us take care of the environment' message instead of just giving people carte blanche to come down and rape, pillage, and plunder while they're here," according to Dwaine Raynor, administrator of Florida's environmental education program.

Communities where tourism prevails have set their own eco-tourism policies without any mandate from the state. In some places, public trash cans are labeled "Recyclables" and "Non-Recyclables." Many hotels and restaurants encourage water conservation with signs in the rooms and water-upon-request-only policies.

The Gulf of Mexico Program involves representatives from five states whose target is citizen involvement and training. Its boater's pledge program, for instance, offers incentives for commercial fishermen to haul their trash back to shore.

"People come to Florida and want to catch fish and enjoy our beaches and see the Florida they see in the picture books," said Barbara Sheen Todd, a member of both the Florida Advisory Council and the Gulf of Mexico Program. "If we don't protect that, then what Florida has that is different from Chicago or Detroit will be destroyed."

AQUA-ADVENTURE

Coastal waterways account for the state's most popular venue of sports and adventure activities, preventing any need for Disney-like development to keep visitors occupied.

All watery whims are satisfied in island seas and rivers, from kayaking to wreck diving. Certain islands hold a reputation for one activity or another. Ten Thousand Islands are known more for wilderness camping, treasure hunting and pontooning. Sanibel and Captiva excel in sailboarding and shelling, Gasparilla Island in tarpon fishing, and Clearwater Beach in volleyball.

Biking, hiking, archaeological excavation, in-line skating, and turtle-tracking opportunities add an active dimension to island vacationing.

Sea kayaking, a favorite gulf coast sport.
(Lee County Visitor & Convention Bureau)

Many islands provide paved bike paths or bike lanes for cyclists. On a bike path, a bicycle operator must follow the same rules and safety guidelines as pedestrians. That means yielding right-of-way to cars entering and exiting driveways. Under Florida law, bicycle riders using the roadway carry the same responsibilities as motorized vehicle drivers.

STRANDED

All very interesting and fascinating, this talk about wildlife and adventure, but where are the beaches? This is probably the most-asked question on any Florida island.

Florida beaches have a reputation, and most of the best are found on islands. Some earned their fame by carpeting their sands in layers of shells. Others boast their sailboard breezes or whiter-than-white sand. Seclusion, wildlife, and powdery moguls of dunes earn other strands their popularity. No matter what the attraction, being stranded rates as the number one alfresco activity of choice on the sandy turf of West Florida islands.

Nothing is quite as mentally and physically therapeutic. My beach therapy routine always begins with the coquina foot massage. I search along the sea's edge for the perfect spot. I watch the surf closely, and as a wave ebbs, I look for jumping jelly beans in its wake. As the wave sweeps away their top layer of sand protection, the coquinas suddenly and magically appear, like a handful of colored dice the sea tosses up on the beach. The tiny bivalves then break out in a race back to the cool damp womb of the sand. Upended, they bubble and squirm, opening and closing their shells, slickly escaping the sun's glare and providing your planted feet with delightful stimulation.

Next on the beach therapy regiment is the whirlpool. This involves no equipment whatsoever. You simply lie there and let the waves and their sand entourage wash over you. Sand is by nature therapeutic, especially sea sand, with its inherent salts and minerals. Not only does it sandpaper away dead skin and hard-to-escape realities, it provides healthful properties recognized by the early Greeks and their modern-day descendants: spas with their thalasso-therapy regimes.

Of course, the therapeutic value of beach-potatoeing does not end with coquina massages and sandblasting. There's that relaxing attitude people ask to be submerged in tanks of water to achieve. There's the skin coloring for which folks pay parlors. And there's that natural henna women gook up their hair to attain.

Unfortunately, like Florida's other cherished assets, beaches have become endangered by development. Beaches by nature are impermanent formations that shift with the whims of nature. Add sky-high condos, bridges, and cosmetic changes, and something's got to give. Communities pay billions of dollars to renourish their beaches, only to have them wash away within seven years. Scientists are finding now that the renourishment is environmentally detrimental and could be killing our rivers and streams.

It's an issue yet unresolved; a problem everyone is taking very seriously these days. The solutions are not easy, but ignoring the problems could prove fatal to our islands.

CULTURED PEARLS

Some Florida islands and archipelagoes boast their cultural aspects. Cedar Key's resident artisans have created a name and annual fair for their crafts. Sarasota's islands equate with art galleries; Sanibel with professional theater. Florida islands have inspired authors from Anne Morrow Lindbergh to John D. MacDonald, artists from Jimmy Ernst to Robert Rauschenberg to Dik Browne.

These and other islands combine to combat Florida's bad rap as a state devoid of culture. This reputation stems partially, ironically enough, from Florida's melting-pot role. Closer inspection reveals that Florida islands' appeal to all nationalities has provided the cultural textures that give many of the islands their unique character. The Miccosukee and Seminole Amerindian tribes bring colorful patterns and ways to the area of Ten Thousand Islands. In the Panhandle, Deep South culture prevails. African-Americans, Puerto

Ricans, Cubans, Jamaicans, Haitians, Crackers, and Yankees have all woven their diverse traditions into the fabric of island life to create a culture both rich and complex. Partially, the cultureless label stems from the old brand of tourist who came here with the intention of not thinking for seven days. In response to the sophistication of today's traveler, islanders are honing their crafts and building theaters, museums, and galleries galore.

Aside from such cultural hauteur, homier beach and folk cultures endure to lend certain islands a timeless appeal. This materializes in its most concentrated form at annual festivals that home in on the sea and its treasures. Since farming has long been abandoned on most islands (with the notable exception of Pine Island and Cedar Key), fishing remains the anchor to old island heritage. There's nothing like a peeling fishing boat basking on the beach to evoke a rich sense of the past. Festivals throughout the state's islands celebrate this legacy with fishing contests, fleet blessings, and seafood feeds.

TABLE HOPPING

The Florida table holds a smorgasbord of regional and ethnic cuisine. Few influences have fallen short of the state's lengthy shoreline.

Of course, seafood is the most highly associated and highly demanded commodity, and rightly so. In times past, fish and shellfish seemed infinitely abundant and incredibly inexpensive here, tantalizingly rare and costly up there. Refrigeration and overnight shipping has diminished visitors' collective craving for seafood upon island arrival. Indeed, many complain that they can buy grouper or shrimp as cheaply at home. Aside from the fact that "at home" fish often means a brush with below-30-degree temperatures, fish just ain't so cheap anymore because we've eaten it all up. Or killed it off in attempts to net other catches, or through environmental pressures.

You'll never guess this by island restaurant menus, however.

They swim with grouper, snapper, and shrimp year-round. Seasonally, stone crab ("a treat as rare as nightingales' tongue," as decribed by novelist Marjorie Kinnan Rawlings), pompano, crayfish, spiny lobster, bulldozer lobster, cobia, and mahi-mahi delight. Certain restaurants, especially in the Panhandle, employ Florida's underutilized fish to temper escalating seafood costs. For instance, the rock shrimp: So-named for its hard shell, it harbors flesh many liken to the taste of lobster. Triggerfish, amberjack, and monkfish get netted incidentally, which makes them more affordable than the main catch of the day.

Its long growing season makes Florida a double-whammy breadbasket. Tomatoes, melons, peppers, and cucumbers are often harvested twice a year. Oranges, grapefruit, limes, lemons, calamondin, sapodillas, avocados, mangoes, coconuts, carambola (star fruit), blueberries, and strawberries fill the basket with fruit all year long.

As a leader in cattle farming, Florida has a long legacy of beef eating. Early Spanish conquistadores left animals on shore, the descendants of which became known as today's scrub cattle. Legend has it, they contributed not only to Florida cuisine but also to its heritage by assigning the name Cracker to the cowhunters who once drove them cross-state with long cracking whips. The lighthouse on Sanibel Island was built specifically to assist the brisk cattle-shipping trade out of nearby Punta Rassa.

The basis of Florida island cuisine is the native foods prepared by the Seminoles. They subsisted on wild fowl, fish, roots, berries, sea grapes, and swamp cabbage. The latter, come to be known as hearts of palm, survives most popularly, particularly on Cedar Key. It is harvested from the bud of the cabbage palm, a process that kills the tree and has thereby killed some of its popularity in this environmentally aware day and age.

Deep South cuisine was the second major influence on how Floridians eat, because many early pioneers settled by way of Georgia and Alabama. Into the melting pot, they anted sweet potatoes, greens, peanuts, and cornbread. Southern heritage survives most strongly on the islands of the Panhandle.

Hispanic, Creole, Mediterranean, and Yankee foodways all brought their contributions to the Florida potluck. That's why it's not unusual to find, all on the same island restaurant menu, black beans 'n rice, hearts of palm salad, blackened grouper, Cuban bread, Jamaican pork, shrimp curry, and key lime pie.

New Florida cuisine is described as a cross between Cajun, Caribbean, and California influences. It marries fresh local produce to spicy tropical methods. It lightens "down-home" without sacrificing the goodness.

For the best, most comprehensive, and most modern definition of this upcoming regional cuisine, read Joyce LaFray Young's *Tropic Cooking* (Ten Speed Press, 1987). It contains some restaurant recipes as well as folk favorites of Florida and the Caribbean.

For an excellent compendium of Florida recipes, spiced with bits of history and lore, buy *The Florida Cookbook* by Jeanne Voltz and Caroline Stuart (Alfred A. Knopf, 1993).

ISLAND LANDINGS

Throughout history, Florida tourists holed up in thatch huts, "tin cans" (the not-so-flattering name for early RVs), fish camps, safe harbors, mom-pop motels, inns, hunting lodges, condominiums and fantasy resorts. Florida island lodgings still span the spectrum, but most commonly you will find the latter two. Island real estate has become prime real estate, and only the devoted hold on to commercial island property developed for a few.

Cedar Key's vintage Island Hotel remembers the island's pre-comfort era with mosquito netting over the beds and antique furniture. Sanibel's Island Inn celebrates 100 years of gracious, unpretentious beach lodging. One bed-and-breakfast stands tenacious ground among Anna Maria Island's luxury beach resorts. And Boca Grande's Gasparilla Inn still stands as a bastion of vintage privileged vacationing. With a bit of searching, away from the anonymous high-rises, old Florida can still be found in island accommodations.

The great egret pauses among the pilings at a marina along the Lee Island Coast.
(Lee County Visitor & Convention Bureau)

Each section will broadly overview the type and range of accommodations you can expect to find. I will specifically name special island places — the historic inns, charming B&Bs, sportsmen's havens, docking-available resorts and simply islandy places.

NITTY-GRITTY

Transportation

Hourly flights fire visitors into Florida hub airports, from where they disperse to islands via charter plane, rental car, taxi, shuttle, public transportation, ferry, or private boat.

On some islands, cars are rare to nonexistent. Feet, bikes, and golf carts are the only way to go. Many islands have built bike paths, accessible to all nonmotorized traffic including in-line skaters and baby strollers. Trolleys and trams run on some islands, sometimes as the only means of transport, and sometimes to alleviate the congestion endemic to seabound landmass.

For true island hopping, boat is my preferred vehicle. If time is of no essence, sailing is the quintessential hop mode. Motoring saves time but sacrifices peace. Jet-skiing and waverunning are actually forbidden off some island shores. Tours, rentals, ferries, charters, and shuttles off the mainland or other bridged islands provide infinite options.

Changes in latitudes

The mental Florida slide show is filled with images of sunshine, sweat, sea, sand, shores, and all those other "s" words — excluding snow. But remember, with a span of seven latitudinal degrees, Florida encompasses all weather patterns from snow (albeit extremely rare) to sleet to swelter. And did I mention hurricanes, tornadoes, waterspouts, and drought? Florida is rightfully called the Sunshine State, but be mentally and physically prepared for otherwise.

Winter months are high tourist season in West Florida's southern islands, and yet the islands of the Panhandle enjoy a brisk spring/summer trade. Island climes, fortunately, stay warmer than those of the mainland in the winter, thanks to the thermal waterbed upon which they float. Of course, the farther south you travel, the more likely you are to find balmy. Unfortunately, however, the likelihood of finding crowds also increases. Spring and fall are usually the quietest island times. I always recommend October, when crowds and bugs are at their minimum and summer swelter has desisted.

In the summer, island heat is tempered by sea breezes and insulation. That's good, because summers are hot and seem to go on longer than a Canadian winter. Summer island visitors are wise to stay in the northern regions, or in the swimming pool from time of arrival until departure. Humidity tickles 100 percent regularly. Electric storms are prevalent throughout the state, and rain comes almost every summer afternoon. It's the season for tornadoes and waterspouts, all of which curb boating activity.

Hurricane and tropical storm season opens in June and runs through October. Most activity occurs in the fall, sometimes even as late as November. Forewarnings normally come well in advance, giving islanders and island visitors plenty of time to evacuate when necessary.

Island living

It's said that once you get Florida sand between your toes, you will never be able to resist the impulse to return. I believe that once you have island sand in your scalp, it never washes out. It just seeps into cranial cavities to short-circuit certain functions having to do with good judgment and logic.

How does one keep sand exportation to a minimum? The best advice I can offer, other than staying on the mainland, is to shake out beach towels and paraphernalia with the wind, rather than against it. Really the best advice is to revel in sand. Sit right in it, roll around in the stuff, let the waves pound it into every gap in your swim apparel, let the wind sandblast you. In other words, get used to it.

Ingrained sand is a small inconvenience when it comes to

island living. Black-outs, brown-outs, pink skin, and red bumps are the more colorful problems. To forestall inconvenience, pack flashlights, candles, matches, strong sunscreen, hats, sunglasses, DEET products, and Avon Skin-So-Soft for any island vacation. The last two are the recommended deterrents for mosquitoes and no-see-ums, respectively. Relief from bites can be had from a bottle of rum (or any alcohol) — applied externally, of course. Aloe and cortisone are also effective.

Chapters

If you were to stretch out Florida's coast in a straight line, it would reach from Louisiana to Nicaragua. Florida island hopping could become a career. Heaven knows, I've tried to make it mine.

For those who don't have a lifetime to devote to island exploring, I have divided the islands of Florida's Gulf Coast into neat little packages, full of fun surprises. This I have done geographically, starting with the northwesternmost reaches, commonly known as **The Panhandle**. Islands in this area appeal to the summer family traveler who counts exploration as agenda priority number one. Shockingly white beaches, amusement parks, and underdevelopment typify the Panhandle's gift to island addicts.

Cedar Keys comprise some of the state's most hidden and unknown destinations. Way Key, the only bridged island (and thus the most visited), has reverted from its bustling mid-century industrial heyday to a laid-back artisan's haven and wildlife reserve core.

Known as **Pinellas Coast**, the barrier islands of St. Petersburg/ Clearwater plunge you directly into resort madness, complete with blaring Buffett, sandcastle-building contests, and hotel-lined sands. Some of the islands in this family, such as Caladesi and and those at Fort deSoto Park, win awards for their secluded beaches.

The islands of the **Sarasota/Manatee Coast** cast a more exclusive spell over visitors. Boasting the world's whitest beach and the coast's poshest shopping, it is a land of superlatives.

Pace slows steadily upon descent to the **Lee Island Coast**, where you can experience the wide variety of island life from total seclusion to wet-T-shirt contests.

Life comes almost to a halt in the world of **Ten Thousand Islands**. The most exciting thing to do on some of these land spits is to watch the mangroves grow. Outdoor life beckons the adventuresome islandite.

Sources & Resources

For general travel information about Florida, contact the **Florida Division of Tourism**, 432 Collins Bldg., 107 W. Gaines St., Tallahassee, FL 32399-2000; 904-487-1462.

To learn more about preserving Florida's environment, contact the **Florida Advisory Council on Environmental Education**, 237 Holland Bldg., Tallahassee, FL 32399-1400; 904-487-0123.

For information on boating, look for Tom Lenfestey's *A Gunkholer's Cruising Guide To Florida's West Coast* (Great Outdoors Publishing, revised annually) or *Cruising Guide to Western Florida* by Claiborne S. Young (Pelican Publishing, 1992). They both are directed at sailing vessels, but offer general information valuable to all recreational boaters regarding marinas, hotels, restaurants, and other water-accessible facilities.

Fish & Dive Florida and The Keys, by M. Timothy O'Keefe and Larry Larsen (Larsen's Outdoor Publishing, 1992), is another sportsperson's must-own.

To learn more about Florida literary history, find *The Book Lover's Guide to Florida*, edited by Kevin M. McCarthy (Pineapple Press, 1992).

See the last page in this book for other titles about the Florida outdoors.

PANHANDLE ISLANDS

The sand drifts like snow and actually crunches when you walk across it. Only wisps of seaweed and a few broken shells interrupt the sheer whiteness. Dunes look like first snowfall in the mountains when vegetation still protrudes. Here the vegetation is sea oats, planted for their anchoring root systems, and what looks like bonsai magnolias. The salt air dwarfs the trees as they are buried continually by the sands of time.

The white sands traveled far to make this one of the world's whitest beaches. It started in the Appalachian Mountains millions of years ago. Rivers brought the pinkish quartz into Gulf waters to be pulverized, salted, and blanched. Who but Nature would have thought of importing Appalachian quartz to process into the world's finest sand?

Along this westward arm lie 200 miles of coastal sands, lapped by calm, clear waters whose color has been compared to various gems: emerald, jade, aquamarine. The water gets its precious color from a shallow shelf of offshore waters carpeted with seaweed dust. (You'll see the name Emerald Coast used widely in these parts; the nomenclature rightly belongs, those in public relations tell me, only to the Okaloosa County portion of the coastline, i.e., Fort Walton Beach and Destin.)

This is last landfall for many migrating birds; some 280 species have been counted. Not so well loved are the rattlesnakes that live on the islands of the eastern Panhandle. Hikers, beware.

Marlin is the prize catch of the region, especially come July. But it doesn't end then and there. The Panhandle means variety to fishermen in the know — more variety than any other coastal region.

The quality of the islands also varies in these parts. Some are so developed, they seem part of the mainland. Part of the peninsular mainland is so secluded, it feels like an island. Islands far offshore or unbridged remain lost in the soft sentiments of sea breezes and cloistered from civilization.

At Pensacola, the Gulf Coast becomes Florida as it makes its gentle transition from Alabama. Here **Perdido Key** threads the two states together and to landscapes long gone on some Gulf Coast islands. The Gulf Islands National Seashore ensures that primeval beaches are left alone here, and on **Santa Rosa Island**, a long formation that exhibits several disparate personalities.

Okaloosa Island, really part of Santa Rosa, is home to funky Fort Walton Beach. A narrow pass separates Okaloosa Island from **Okaloosa/Walton Peninsula**, which I include in this book because of its insular character.

Panama City ends the developed resort stretch of the Panhandle with the region's optimum commercialization. Its **Shell Island** is the antithesis of Panama City Beach's amusement parks and spring-break bars.

The Emerald Coast redefines white sand beaches.
(Emerald Coast Tourist Development Council)

East of Panama City, life takes a turn toward porch sitting and line casting. The islands, themselves a front porch for fishing-famous Apalachicola, each reflect a different facet of this other Florida, hardly related to most other of the state's coastlines.

Cape San Blas, though not technically an island, would be the porch's hammock: primitive in design, relaxed, low-slung, tethered. **St. Vincent Island,** an unbridged national wildlife preserve, is a flower box gone wild. The most built-up, **St. George Island,** is the porch's door to a carefully planned residential development. Easygoing **Little St. George Island** sways to island tempos like a porch swing suspended in time. Laid-back **Dog Island** sits and chews on a rosemary twig at a rocking chair pace.

THE NITTY-GRITTY

Land Routes

Pensacola Regional Airport, Fort Walton Beach-Destin Airport, and **Panama City Bay County Airport** serve the Panhandle.

Highway 98 is the best way to travel along the coast. It's scenic and closest to the islands. Interstate 10 runs along the Panhandle's northern border.

PERDIDO KEY: From Pensacola Airport, follow Airport Boulevard and turn left on Ninth Avenue (Route 289). Turn left on Cervantes Street (Highway 98) and follow Highway 98 west to Bauer Road (Route 293). (Highway 98 contorts between Routes 289 and 293, so pay close attention to signs.) Turn right on Sorrento Road (Route 292) and cross the bridge to Perdido Key.

SANTA ROSA ISLAND: From the Pensacola Airport, follow Airport Boulevard and turn left on Route 289 (Ninth Avenue). Follow it until you see the sign for Highway 98. Turn left on Highway 98 and cross the Pensacola Bay Bridge (also called Three-Mile Bridge) to the town of Gulf Breeze, then the Bob Sikes Bridge ($1 toll), which takes you to Pensacola Beach.

Yellow Cab-Taxi (904-433-3333) serves Perdido Key and Santa Rosa Island.

FORT WALTON BEACH: From the Fort Walton Beach airport, follow Route 85 South into town until you reach Highway 98, and veer left to cross Santa Rosa Sound.

OKALOOSA/WALTON PENINSULA: The easiest way to get from the Fort Walton Beach Airport to the peninsula is to cross from Fort Walton Beach's Okaloosa Island into Destin via Highway 98 (see directions above).

SHELL ISLAND: You must take a boat from Panama City Beach. To get there from the Panama City Airport, follow Airport Road. Turn right on Route 390 and again on Highway 98/Route 30. Cross the Hathaway Bridge and turn left on Thomas Drive to **Treasure Island Marina,** or continue to **St. Andrews State Park.** Both places offer lifts to the island. (See Shell Island section for more details.)

CAPE SAN BLAS: From Panama City Airport, follow Airport Road to Highway 98 and turn left. Follow 98 east. After Port St. Joe, turn right on C-30. Take another right on C-30E.

ST. VINCENT ISLAND: Accessible only by private or charter boat. Inquire in Apalachicola. To get to Apalachicola from Panama City Airport, follow Airport Road to Highway 98, turn left and head east.

LITTLE ST. GEORGE ISLAND: Charters out of Apalachicola will take you there. To get to Apalachicola from Panama City Airport, follow Airport Road to Highway 98, turn left and head east.

ST. GEORGE ISLAND: From Panama City Airport, follow Airport Road to Highway 98 and turn left. Follow 98 east to Eastpoint. Turn right on Island Drive (watch for signs to St. George Island) and continue across the Franklin Bridge.

For taxi limo to Cape San Blas and St. George Island, try **Crooms Transportation** in Apalachicola (904-653-8132).

There's a 3,800-foot paved runway at St. George Plantation for private planes (with no runway lights).

DOG ISLAND: A ferry runs from Carrabelle to the island almost daily. To get to Carrabelle from the Panama City Airport, follow Airport Road to Highway 98, turn left and continue east.

Water Routes

The Intracoastal Waterway, known as the Gulf Intracoastal Waterway (GIWW), runs between the mainland and the Panhandle islands from Santa Rosa Island east, connecting to wide and roomy Apalachicola Bay. Look for more information in individual island sections below.

Island Life

The Panhandle is so different from the rest of Florida that much of it lies in a time zone separate from the rest of the state's Eastern Standard Time. West of the Apalachicola River you will be on Central Standard Time.

Pensacola claims an average of 343 days of sunshine annually and an average temperature of 75. (All temperatures are given in Fahrenheit.) This climatic profile remains fairly steady along the coast, dropping to a mean annual temperature in Gulf County of 68 in some places. Temperatures reach a high of around 81 in July and a low of about 55 in January. Gulf temperatures, normally warmer than land readings, dip into the mid-60s in winter and reach 84 in summer. For current weather conditions, call (904) 432-7411 for Pensacola, (941) 763-1701 for Panama City, and (904) 227-1135 for Port St. Joe.

"Bank blink" is an unusual natural phenomenon endemic to the white sands of the Panhandle. Something like the green flash in reverse, it manifests as a hazy mirage or a bright light reflection over white sandbanks. Boaters are most susceptible.

Hikers are more susceptible to soft-sand fatigue. Like walking in deep, soft snow, Panhandle sand hiking tires you out more quickly than terra firma hiking.

Although some snowbirds from Canada and the U.S.'s coldest parts nest along the Panhandle for the winter, most of the region's seasonal visitors first arrive in spring during kids' vacation days. Summer brings tourists from neighboring states, particularly Georgia, for whom this is the nearest coastline.

Fall is preferred by connoisseurs who will notice that the water is often clearer, not clouded by summer's algae blooms and storm churnings. It's also when the monarch butterflies and several bird species begin their migrations south, passing through the Panhandle en route.

When we visited Cape San Blas in late October, however, after a summer of severe storm battering, low spots along the Cape were flooded, particularly at Salinas Park, which meant lots of mosquitoes. No-see-ums and sandspurs were also biting. The latter are abundant year-round, so watch where you step off the beach.

Here's a tip for removing the prickly vegetative burrs from feet, shoes, or clothing: First lick your fingers, then lightly grasp and pull firmly. Check shoes before getting into your car or room. These little devils love to jump out and grab your bare feet later.

The especially bright sand of the Emerald Coast makes sunscreen, sunglasses, and hats tantamount to enjoying your vacation.

Sources & Resources

Noted Florida naturalist Jack Rudloe encourages protection of the Panhandle coastline in his *The Wilderness Coast: Adventures of a Gulf Coast Naturalist* (Dutton, 1988).

The Gulf Coast Taste Great cookbook reveals secrets to Panhandle-style Southern and seafood cookery. It includes a guide to selecting seafood. Send $19.95 plus $2.50 handling to P.O. Box 321, Sunnyside, FL 32461.

 PERDIDO KEY

QUICK TOUR

This feels like the end of the world. It is the end of Florida — its western extreme, anyway. Part of the 16-mile island lies in Alabama and goes under the name Orange Beach.

Approach Perdido Key from Route 292 and go left on Johnson Beach Road. Pass pastel Victorian homes and towering condos until you come to the Gulf Islands National Seashore. Certain times of the year you must pay $4 to enter; $1 if you're on foot or bike. The road ends and a beach access lets you onto nearly six miles of deserted, preserved sands. On the way you'll see recent battery installations to 19th-century Fort McRee, which has slid into the water. A nature trail on the left side of the road loops around to the bay side.

Returning to Route 292 and headed straight, you reach Perdido's lightly developed commercial section: a few hotels and restaurants, a small but pretty shopping complex, beach shops, and many condos. Those that tower are at least spaced well apart, many with low-rises in between. A couple of miles further on, you enter Perdido Key State Recreation Area, which affords two beach accesses. The Chamber of Commerce is less than a mile away. Three miles later, you're in Alabama.

On the way back off the island, turn left on River Road and circle around the bayside, azalea-brightened, residential area of the island — a low-density neighborhood of large houses. We're talking big houses. There's a watersports concession on the way. Off on Canal-A-Way is an old but functioning marina. Continue under the bridge to a newer model, complete with stylish restaurant. Follow the driveway back up the road to Route 292 for exiting the island.

BACKFLASH

Perdido Key means "Lost Land," named after Perdido Bay, a body of water that eluded Spanish explorers for many years. Pirates and ghosts haunt the legends of this once-mysterious land. Perdido Key's modern history can be mostly summed up in a span of 15 years. The island really didn't develop until the 1980s, which explains why much of the building is either fantastic homes or multi-unit structures. By that time, waterfront land prices had risen, albeit not as much as on other area islands. Only the very wealthy or the entrepreneurial could apply.

Before that, the island held a few fishing camps and homes. But once this lost land was found, its riches were quickly claimed. Fortunately, development reins have been kept tightly pulled to retain the island's quiet demeanor.

Historical Attractions

All of the original 19th-century **Fort McRee** has been buried at sea, thanks to migrating sands. A couple of latter-day batteries still survive in the National Seashore Park.

THE NATURAL

First, there's the sand. Beach-revelers can't help but think that's the island's greatest natural achievement. It drifts like powdered sugar into awesome dunes with seaside grass cowlicks. Only recently built up, the island has shifted, as barrier islands do when unchecked by human anxieties. Like a masterpiece of performance art, its beauty has lain in its fluidity. It has been allowed to shift freely, like an unruly child. Now, development will want to chain it in. At least development is careful to preserve the several layers of barrier island ecology evident here: the coastline, the primary and secondary dunes, the uplands studded with pines and oaks, and the bay sloshed with marsh.

Natural Attractions

The good news: 64 percent of Perdido's beachfront rests in the guardianship of governmental hands.

The Perdido Key Area of the Gulf Islands National Seashore

protects nearly eight miles of pristine shoreline extending to Pensacola Pass. The road ends about six miles short of the pass, so you must hike the soft, dunes-buttressed beach from there. Public facilities are located at the road's end. A nature trail explores bayside ecology. More beachscape is set aside for posterity at **Perdido Key State Recreation Area** in the midst of a housing development.

A Q U A - A D V E N T U R E

Touring

Several bodies of water are accessible from Perdido Key. Old River, which runs between Perdido and Ono Island (property of Alabama), is connected to the once-elusive Perdido Bay. Big Lagoon separates Perdido Key's eastern end from Big Lagoon State Recreation Area on Pensacola's mainland.

A favorite beaching spot for boaters is the east end of Gulf Islands National Seashore. Since the road ends six miles to the west, this area stays secluded. Leeside, come ashore the island at either Oyster Bar Marina on the east side of the bridge or Holiday Harbor Marina on the west. Tour charters depart from **Oyster Bar Marina** (13700 River Rd.; 904-492-0555).

Fishing

The grass flats of Perdido Key are known for their cache of speckled trout. The western end of the island produces the biggest specimens. For both bottom and deep-sea fishing charters, go to **Oyster Bar Marina** (13700 River Rd.; 904-492-0555). **Holiday Harbor Marina** (14050 Canal-A-Way; 904-492-0555) sells tackle, bait, and other necessities.

Swimming

Though prone to undercurrents, the beaches of Perdido Key generally beg you to swim them. Their waters can be incredibly clear, calm, and inviting. Avoid waters in Pensacola Pass.

Boating, Sailing & Canoeing

Edgewater Rentals (Oyster Bar Marina, 13700 River Rd.; 904-492-0192) rents pontoons and center-console powerboats.

ISLAND ADVENTURE

Hiking

The Gulf Islands National Seashore gives you six miles of beach hiking off the beaten sand. Be cognizant that soft sand at least doubles the exertion level of hiking when compared to hard surfaces. Allow enough time and take plenty of water and skin protection. You may want to try the quarter-mile nature loop on the bay side first.

Shelling & Beachcombing

The quartz sands of the western Panhandle are, by definition, devoid of shells. Quartz-based beaches are composed, of course, of quartz. The carbonate-based beaches of the southern Gulf Coast, on the other hand, are made up of ground coral and shell.

You may find a few shells on Panhandle beaches, especially after a storm. But the Panhandle's wide coastal shelf denies the great shell-collecting potential of other beaches. Which just goes to show: you can't have it all.

CULTURE

The People

I couldn't get a good read on islanders here. Maybe they're too new to the island, not settled into any sense of place. I did meet one old-time character who knew his island like an islander should, with intimacy and pride.

Fairs & Festivals

For local fun, try the **Interstate Mullet Toss** at the Flora-Bama Lounge (904-492-0611) and the **Great Gulf Coast Beach Party**, both in April.

Island Shopping

I need no other reason to love the shopping center called **Colours on the Key** (14110 Perdido Key Dr.) than its charming paint job — like an architect's sidewalk chalk etching. I liked what I found at several of Colours' shops, especially **Frazier's Gifts** (904-492-1671) with beach-themed souvenirs and **White Wolf Emporium** (904-492-2008) emphasizing Native American crafts and arts. There are other places to shop on the island, most of them spread out here and there.

Architecture

Newer homes affect a Victorian style. The Caribbean motif, articulated so succinctly at the Colours shopping center, is also popular.

Nightlife

With the yee-haw influence of Alabama nearby, nightlife on the island is limited to country-type bars across the border. **Flora-Bama Lounge** (17401 Perdido Key Dr.; 904-492-0611) straddles the state line and features country music most regularly, with blues, jazz, and rock bands for special parties.

TABLE HOPPING

Oyster Bar Restaurant (13700 River Rd.; 904-492-0192) overlooks the marina, where you can dock to dine. Not your typical "oyster bar," which often connotes a casual fish-house atmosphere in certain parts of Florida, this one is done up with wood, plush carpeting, and lots of windows on the water.

ISLAND LANDINGS

The few resorts on the island are chain types — reasonably priced but without much character. Most visitors rent condominiums that range from high-rises to six-plex units. Contact one of the local real estate rental agents, such as **Century 21 Leib & Associates** (14620 Perdido Key Dr., Pensacola, FL 32507; 800-553-1223 or 904-492-0744).

Sources & Resources

Perdido Key Area Chamber of Commerce, 15500 Perdido Key Dr., P.O. Box 34052, Perdido Key, FL 32507; 904-492-4660. **The Pensacola Convention & Visitor Bureau,** 1401 E. Gregory St., Pensacola, FL 32501; 800-343-4321 or 904-434-1234.

 SANTA ROSA ISLAND

QUICK TOUR

Cross Bob Sikes Bridge from Gulf Breeze (observe the speed limit; police cars are everywhere) and land at Pensacola Beach. Alongside the bridge, fishermen will be dropping their lines from the parallel pier. At the end of the bridge and extending to the first major intersection, Quietwater Beach and its boardwalk shopping center occupy bay shores. The Chamber of Commerce and more shops are to the right.

Turn right on Fort Pickens Road at the stoplight. Follow the road as the dunes grow mountainous on the left and development thins out. A white cross atop one of the dunes marks the first religious service held in Pensacola in August, 1559. A marina, some commercial areas, and tall hotels, new homes in clapboard South Florida style, and condo villages eventually give way to the naturalness of Gulf Islands National Seashore/Fort Pickens National Park. Pay a fee to enter ($4 per car for one to seven days; $1 for bike- or walk-ins).

Now you've crossed a time zone into the past. The landscaping becomes that of prehistoric Florida, lonely, with simulcast views of the Gulf and Santa Rosa Sound. Dunes and vegetation — grasses and wild flowers — are low to the ground. Fishermen cast from the shore. Churned-up waters necessitate constant windshield rinsing some days. Dunes walkovers with paved parking provide access to the beach (no facilities). Campground registration and the ranger's station is on the right.

About five miles into the park, Langdon Beach lies to the left, a picnic area with bike trail to the right. You begin to see remnants of Fort Pickens batteries. The island widens and vegetation grows loftier. Nearby is the entrance to a campground on the right, and the boardwalked Dune Nature Trail to the left. The latter leads to the beach while signs interpret maritime vegetation.

More fortification ruins are scattered along the bay and Gulf, plus other oddities such as a range-finding tower and a plantation gravesite moved to the park. At last, about eight miles from the park entrance, you pass through the yellow-brick walls of nearly 170-year-old Fort Pickens. Among the ruins and white clapboard, trimmed-in-green military buildings, you'll find a museum, a gift/book shop, a fishing pier into the sound, and trails through the ruins.

Backtracking eastward, there's a public beach picnic area outside the park. At Via de Luna, Casino Beach shows off its recent improvements. Turn right on Via de Luna and proceed past newer resorts and other commercial enterprises. To the left are old-style shops, bars, and restaurants. A couple of shopping strips with storybook facades change the tone. Past the resorts, old, plain island homes run roadside. Take one of the "avenidas" to Ariola Drive, where upscale building is upcropping. (Signposts stuck into the ground serve as street signs.)

Down the road, a series of public beach accesses offer solitude, but no facilities. The route begins to feel other-worldly here. Few cars pass. No buildings are in sight. Dunes undulate like the moon's surface. (No, that is not the reason the road is named Via de Luna — literally, "Moon Way" — it's a historic allusion to Don Tristan de Luna, who established the first colony there in 1559.)

Seven miles east of the Via de Luna stoplight, you again enter The National Seashore, here called the Santa Rosa Area Seashore. Wind-sculpted dunes continue their surrealistic ripple effect. Several Gulfside and one bayside public access area allow entrance into this eerie, sandy world.

Back to civilization, you enter Navarre Beach, quieter than Pensacola Beach. Its beaches are less attractive, but popular.

The eastern end of the island belongs to Eglin Air Force Base, with radar facilities to scan the Gulf and the Caribbean. The road ends shortly past the Navarre Beach bridge. Fort Walton Beach sits at the other end of the base, but promoters choose to call that segment Okaloosa Island.

B A C K F L A S H

Pensacola Bay was settled early in the history of Florida — four years before St. Augustine, in fact. Tristan de Luna's short-lived Spanish settlement, established in 1559, lasted only two years. In 1698, another attempt was made, but by 1719 the colony moved to Santa Rosa Island in hopes of better defending the harbor during the wars between Spain and France. Soon after, a hurricane wiped out the settlement of Santa Rosa Punta de Siguenza. In 1826, the U.S. Army took the next stab at taming the island when it began work on Fort Pickens, at Santa Rosa's westernmost point, to protect Pensacola's mainland deepwater port.

During the Civil War, Pensacola-area residents were divided in their sympathies. The territory itself was divided. Fort Pickens on Santa Rosa Island was held by Union forces, while the South took over Fort McRee across the pass on Perdido Key. Fort Pickens later became notorious for its most famous prisoner: Geronimo. He was incarcerated along with fellow Apache warriors in 1886, and attracted seagoing sightseers who hoped to score a glimpse of the aging legend.

In later years, the fort was reoutfitted for both world wars. It became a state park in 1949, and later was taken under the auspices of the National Park Service as part of Gulf Islands Seashore.

Historical Attractions

Fort Pickens's long and sensational history is preserved within a national park. The visitor's center has a small museum that relates the natural and military history of the park.

T H E   N A T U R A L

One of Santa Rosa's most remarkable features is its luxuriously white sands. Mounds of it. Lengths and widths of it. As if it were some sand-Midas's private stash.

Thanks to its protected areas, the island attracts birds in great numbers during their migrations. Other animals are of the small variety: skunks, lizards, ghost crabs, box turtles, and Eastern ribbon snakes.

Natural Attractions

The Gulf Islands National Seashore (904-934-2600) encompasses 150 miles of barrier islands — 100,000 acres of land and sea — most of it in and around Pensacola. On Santa Rosa Island, there are two appendages, one at **Fort Pickens National Park** at the west end, the other mid-island, called the **Santa Rosa Day-Use Area.** Birdwatchers have logged more than 280 different species of birds sighted in these areas.

AQUA-ADVENTURE

Touring

Boaters can explore the Gulf (though waters get rough at certain times), Santa Rosa Sound (part of the Intracoastal Waterway, between the island and Gulf Breeze peninsula) and Pensacola Bay (between Gulf Breeze peninsula and the mainland). On the island's west end, Pensacola Pass gives wide and easy entrance to the very deep port and to exploring Perdido Key. Small boaters should watch out for large-vessel traffic.

Santa Rosa Island's marinas cluster around the Bob Sikes bridge.

Fishing

The **Bob Sikes Bridge Fishing Pier** crosses Santa Rosa Sound. There are three other piers on the island: Casino Beach, Fort Pickens, and Navarre Beach.

Swimming

Pay attention to the sign at the toll booth on the bridge. It warns when waters are too rough for safe swimming. This happens often enough. One day the water can be calm as a pond, the next day rough as the Atlantic. Undercurrents are a problem, particularly in Pensacola Pass at the west end of Fort Pickens Park.

Snorkeling/Scuba

The Pensacola area is one of Gulf Coast Florida's richest diving destinations. Visibility ranges from 30 feet inshore to a maximum of 100 offshore. Artificial reefs attract dolphins, turtles, and a great variety of marine life. The battleship USS *Massachusetts* makes a popular dive site, a little more than a mile off the Fort Pickens jetties. The same jetties provide a beach dive, but currents can get tricky here. Other dive sites are reachable from the beach to the east, including two wrecks. There's much more in up to 75 feet of water, from one to 22 miles offshore.

Boating, Sailing & Canoeing
Key Sailing (400 Quietwater Beach, Pensacola Beach; 904 932-5520) rents pontoons and Hobie Cats.

Sailboarding & Surfing
Surf & Sail Boardsailing (15 Via de Luna, Pensacola Beach; 904-932-7873).

ISLAND ADVENTURE

Hiking
Fort Pickens National Park affords hiking opportunities along its 1,600-foot boardwalk Dune Nature Trail and along bike trails through the woods.

Biking
About seven miles of bike paths run roadside in Pensacola Beach. Fort Pickens has two unpaved, backwoods paths. One connects a battery ruins site to the fort ruins.

CULTURE

The People
Not at all by choice, I ended up on Panhandle beaches during spring break. The college students on Pensacola Beach were well-mannered compared to those I later encountered at Panama City Beach. According to officials, spring breakers aren't discouraged from coming to Pensacola Beach, but they're not encouraged either. Pensacola Beach likes to position itself to families with kids on spring break, not necessarily to college students traveling in droves.

Island Inspirations

American painter **George Catlin** was perhaps the first to capture the white sands of Pensacola Bay in his painting "Seminole drying fish, Santa Rosa Island," circa 1841. In the literary world, Santa Rosa Island surfaces in many a history on Amerindians and the Civil War. An 1890 thriller titled *The Boy Spy,* by Joseph Orton Kerbey, is set at Civil War-era Fort Pickens.

Fairs & Festivals

Pensacola Beach hosts several big functions every year. **Mardi Gras on the Island** is one of the wildest. In June, the town celebrates its discovery by Spaniard Tristan de Luna in 1559 with the **De Luna Landing Festival**. April brings **Jazz Fest**; October, **Beatles to the Beach Fall Festival**. The **Pensacola Beach Seafood Festival** takes place in September.

Island Shopping

The **Quietwater Beach Boardwalk** (400 Quietwater Beach Blvd., Pensacola Beach) has the best shops. **Island Graffiti** (904-934-8464) and **Go Fish T-Shirt & Sole Co.** (904-934-5251) sell the unusual and artistic in clothing and jewelry. Check out the **Fort Pickens Park** gift shop (1400 Fort Pickens Rd., Pensacola Beach; 904-934-2600). It's full of books specializing in Civil War history and cooking, and local history.

Architecture

Every period style of island construction is represented here. Older sections are built with plain, concrete-block homes. The architectural time line stretches to today's trendy fashions — lots in the Victorian stilt style. Pensacola Beach has a few odd specimens besides, which fit into no specific era. There's one dome home, for example, and another that looks as if a flying saucer has landed atop it.

Music

The Panhandle loves country music. Pensacola Beach seems partial to Caribbean styles, too.

Nightlife

A lot of the night life is geared to the college crowd, such as at **Flounder's Chowder and Ale House** (800 Quietwater Beach Rd., Pensacola Beach; 904-932-2003). Not exactly on the beach, it makes its own within its courtyard, where you can dance barefoot to reggae bands. **Under Where? Bar** (below Peg Leg Pete's Oyster Bar, 1010 Fort Pickens Rd., Pensacola Beach; 904-932-4139) does nearly the same thing, plus it has a lighted sand volleyball court. Live musicians entertain weekends. Weeknights, plenty of socializing goes on upstairs and down.

TABLE HOPPING
Amberjack is a popular catch in these parts. Meaty like tuna, but oilier, its season falls in summer and autumn. It's an economical option in most restaurants and seafood marts.

Jubilee (400 Quietwater Beach Rd., Pensacola Beach; 904-934-3108) serves casual downstairs and candlelit upstairs. It char-grills steaks, grouper, and other seafood. You can dock at the public pier or anchor your boat ashore.

Flounder's Chowder and Ale House (800 Quietwater Beach Rd., Pensacola Beach; 904-932-2003) is nearby. This place is pure fun. It specializes in all the trademark Panhandle foods: char-grilled amberjack, shrimp, fried oysters, and blue crab. There are several dining rooms to choose from, plus alfresco seating.

Peg Leg Pete's Oyster Bar (1010 Fort Pickens Rd., Pensacola Beach; 904-932-4139) is a little bit country and a lot of seafood. Oysters come nine different ways, shrimp figures importantly, and Cajun breathes its fire on several dishes. The rice and beans makes a meal in itself. The place uses its own trademark hot sauce: Peg Leg Pete's Pirate Sauce, actually bottled in Louisiana, smacks of cinnamon, cloves, and mild peppers. The atmosphere is youthful and local — big-screen TV, picnic tables, and country music on the juke box. Docking is available at the nearby marina.

Home cooking comes with a Southern accent here. At the Fort Pickens gift shop, you can find books on Civil War cookery (such as an appetite-suppressing one titled *Yanks, Rebels, Rats & Rations:*

Scratchin for Food in Civil War Prison Camps by Patricia B. Mitchell).

ISLAND LANDINGS

Most resorts are franchised and/or high-rise types. **Clarion Suites Resort** (20 Via De Luna, Pensacola Beach, FL 32561; 904-932-4300) puts character into its pastel suites and townhouses. Plus, it's right on the beach.

Sources & Resources

The Islander (P.O. Box 292, Gulf Breeze, FL 32562; 904-934-3417) concentrates on Pensacola Beach events and lifestyle. *Pensacola: Spaniards to Space Age,* by Virginia Parks (Pensacola Historical Society, 1986), cruises local history. *Pensacola, The Deep Water City* (Continental Heritage Press, 1982), by Lucius and Linda Ellsworth, provides excellent historic coverage in photos (black and white and color) and text.

Pensacola Beach Visitor Information Center & Chamber of Commerce, Hwy 399; 800-635-4803 or 904-932-1500. **The Pensacola Convention & Visitor Bureau** 1401 E. Gregory St., Pensacola, FL 32501; 800-343-4321 or 904-434-1234.

 OKALOOSA ISLAND

QUICK TOUR

Fort Walton Beach's Gulf front occupies a long, tall island across Santa Rosa Sound. Cross Brooks Bridge on Highway 98 to get there. You immediately come to a major intersection; take Santa Rosa Boulevard to the right and head west past the high-rise hotels and male dancer joints to the island's quieter residential section. On the way, you'll pass a couple of public beach access points, but I recommend holding out for the east-end beaches. When you reach the dead end, return to 98, where most of the activity clusters. Eglin Air Force Base claims a portion of the island to the west, saving it at least from plundering.

Things start out pretty tacky on this branch of 98: shell-junk emporiums, go-cart racing, a miniature golf castle, a water theme park, and the main attraction, the Gulfarium sealife show. A brand-new boardwalk complex next door, called Okaloosa Island Park, dresses up the area with shopping, dining, and a view of amazingly white sands and the Okaloosa Fishing Pier. Past the Ramada, the frenzy tapers off. Towering dunes sidle up to the road. Eglin Air Force Base installations nestle among the moguls. Beasley County Park makes for secluded beaching. On the other side of the road, the Gulf Islands National Seashore park fronts sheltered waters where they widen into Choctawhatchee Bay, but the beach doesn't compare to the Gulf-front: it's oriented more toward locals and boating, with waverunning and parasailing concessions nearby.

The bridge at the island's west end connects to Destin and its peninsula. In the pass floats Crab Island. Once a true island, today it is a shallowly submerged sandbar where local boaters and concessioners like to gather and party on weekends.

BACKFLASH

Local legend says that when Spanish explorer Pánfilo de Narváez landed here in 1628 to quench his sea-driven thirst, he was chased away by local Creek Amerindians before he had a chance to sip. They'd been here, after all, since 7 A.D. The colonizers eventually won out, and by the 1600s, the area was on its way to becoming a community.

William Augustus Bowles, better known as Billy Bowlegs, is the resident pirate of Okaloosa and its environs. In 1778, he formed the State of Muskogee, which controlled the Gulf shores, to the envy of Spain, England, and America. He led the Creeks against their European enemies. Legends of his sunken gold-laden ship and buried treasure persist.

Despite its name, no fort was ever built in Fort Walton Beach, only a mainland Civil War campsite with tall ambitions.

During the 1920s, Chicago entrepreneurs brought gambling, prostitution, and bootleg liquor to the Emerald Coast. Okaloosa experienced its greatest growth circa 1960, after the building of the Gulfarium sparked tourism along desolate sands. The island more or less remained stalled in that era of family amusement parks until county commissioners recently took action to change the resort's image. Once considered by area residents as the local "dump" frequented by spring breakers and Alabama summer beachers, today new beach structures and walkovers restore the natural beauty of the snow-white dune drifts.

THE NATURAL

Promoters like to stress that 60 percent of the beaches in Okaloosa County (which includes Destin) are protected and will always remain pristine. In effect, this means there's a setback rule for those beaches that remained undeveloped before the law was passed.

The beaches are Okaloosa's only treasure, so thank goodness they're being protected. Especially at the island's east end, the gleaming white drifts with vegetation poking through never fail to mentally transport you to snowy climes or otherworldly destinations. The sand even squeaks when you walk on it, like snow. Supposedly it's because the quartz grains have been polished round, not rough-edged like other sand. Pelicans, gulls, and friendly herons remind you you're in Florida.

Vegetation is sparse on Okaloosa. Sand and slash pines dominate the skyline at the east end. Cabbage palms survive, and even an occasional struggling banana tree.

The Gulf is the most fertile milieu for fauna, hosting dolphins, rays, and loggerhead turtles, which make their nests where they can hide from beach lights.

Natural Attractions

Beasley County Park (Hwy. 98 E.) frames a bed of Okaloosa's famous fluffy sands between huge dunes and that indescribable green sea. It's Okaloosa's cleanest, nicest beach, with a new Florida-style shelter, picnic facilities, showers, and lifeguards.

AQUA-ADVENTURE

Touring

You'll have to go to Destin Harbor to rent boats or find touring charters. Arriving with your own boat, you can dock on the island's north side at **Lee Side Inn** around Marker 15 or **Marina Bay Resort** at #10.

Fishing

The lighted **Okaloosa Island Fishing Pier** (Hwy. 98 E., 904-244-1023), 1,260 feet long, is open 24 hours. There's a small admission fee. It's known for its tarpon catches in summer.

Swimming

Okaloosa's long shelf makes its beach perfect for young waders. The water is conceivably swimmable year-round, though you'll rarely find a Floridian in the water past October.

Snorkeling/Scuba

The water is extra clear, and one can explore off the beach for shells and coral clusters. Locals compare their water to the Caribbean, but they overstate a bit. It provides, however, some of Florida's best visibility.

Boating, Sailing & Canoeing

Fort Walton Beach hosts the **Spring Splash Sailing Regatta** at the Gulf Islands National Seashore every April. Besides all the luffing and coming about, a lot of Southern barbecuing and dancing to live music go on.

Other

Parasailing and waverunning are big on Okaloosa in the Sound. **Paradise Parasail Water Sports** has a few locations on the island. Call 904-664-7872.

ISLAND ADVENTURE

Hiking

You rarely find folks walking the streets on Florida islands. I suppose that's because it's too hot to walk anywhere too far from the beach. But I felt particularly peculiar walking around Okaloosa, mainly because there are few sidewalks and I didn't see anyone else doing it.

Shelling & Beachcombing

The only thing you find on Okaloosa's beaches are a few stray strands of seaweed washed up. Some crumbled shells collect at the tide line. The wide shelf precludes good shelling, and I suppose beach-grooming further buries finds. The county claims it is among the top five shelling destinations in the world based on what's findable in offshore waters and sandbars.

Sand Dollar City is a sandbar named for its layers of sea bucks. The encircling limestone edge three miles from shore hides lion's paws, tulips, queen helmets, and large horse conchs.

Golfing

Brush up on your putting at one of the island's miniature golf courses. **Island Golf Center** (Hwy. 98 E.; 904-244-1612) has nine lighted holes of golf and a nine-hole pitch-and-putt course.

C U L T U R E

The People

Only geographically is Okaloosa a part of Florida. Culturally, it belongs to Alabama, and is sometimes referred to as the Redneck Riviera. Natives talk with a twang, many drive pick-up trucks, and they love their fish deep-fried, with hush puppies on the side. Another large segment of the local population is detectable by their haircuts: service personnel from Eglin AFB, the largest Air Force base in the world.

Even the tourists on Okaloosa are Southerners for the most part, especially in summer, when vacationers from Georgia head to the nearest beach. The season begins late March as spring breakers descend en masse. In winter, Canadians find it relatively warm, and enjoy the off-season rates.

Island Inspirations

One claim to fame: The filming site for *Jaws II* in 1978.

Fairs & Festivals
Fort Walton Beach Seafood Festival celebrates the sea's bounty every April. Shrimp-on-a-stick and steamed crab claws by the bucketful are trademark.

Island Shopping
Alvin's is a household name along Panhandle beaches. It calls itself a Tropical Department Store. Buy your beach trinkets here. The one in Fort Walton Beach is at 1204 Hwy. 98 E.; 904-244-3913.

Architecture
One local used the word "ugly" to describe his island's residential architecture. Perhaps "funky" would be kinder. Concrete best describes commercial development. The county's new neo-Victorian-style structures at beach access entrances help relieve the island's honky-tonk feel.

Music
Australian singers were popular when I've visited. Country music also rates high, and Jimmy Buffett remains the universal beach sound.

Nightlife
Nightlife caters to the spring break crowd in March and April. Standards are set by wet-T-shirt contests and male dancers. **Fudpucker's** (Santa Rosa Blvd.; 904-243-3833) provides relief, with Caribbean-type live bands. Then there's **Hog's Breath Saloon** (1239 Siebert Ave.; 904-243-4646), motto: "Hog's breath is better than no breath." The **Pelican Roost** at the Ramada (Hwy. 98 E., 904-243-9161) sits on stilts overlooking the beach, which also raises it above college level.

TABLE HOPPING
See a restaurant? Seafood. The finfish is mostly local. Restaurants in these parts serve what snootier restaurants throw back: triggerfish, amberjack, mackerel, mullet, and so on. They taste good, so go ahead and try them. You'll most commonly find them wrapped in a jacket of Southern breading and toasted in a deep

fryer. Cajun and chargrilled preparations are also gaining favor. Most of the island's restaurants are extremely casual. **Fudpucker's** (Santa Rosa. Blvd.; 904-243-3833) looks like a shipwreck inside. Don't confuse it with the more recent Fudrucker's hamburger chain. This is an original (although there is another in Destin). Food is typically Panhandle casual, with a comprehensive menu of faddish munchies, lunches, and dinners. **The Seagull** (at the foot of the Brooks Bridge; 904-243-3413) has slips for dinner guests. Its menu offers a variety of seafood and steaks.

ISLAND LANDINGS

The brassy, flashy **Ramada Beach Resort** (Hwy. 98 E., 800-874-8962 or 904-243-9161) and high-rise **Holiday Inn** comprise the biggest lodging options. Other hotels may be smaller, but they won't have much more character. Hotels cater to families and spring breakers with less than five-star aspirations. More tasteful condominiums on the island's west end are reasonable, considering they preclude eating out for every meal.

Marina Motel, near the Lee Side Inn, accommodates overnight boat-ins.

TOURIST TRAPS

Your kids are going to love this island. Away from the beach, it's more like a carnival than an island. This was Florida vacationing before Disney made it obsolete. I actually prefer it to Disney, because you can do it in bite-size pieces: Go to the beach, then do some go-carting one day. Go to the beach, then putt-putt golf another. **Gulfarium** (1010 Hwy. 98 E.; 904-244-5169), the nation's second-oldest aquarium show, shows its age. It touts its rehabilitation and education efforts, but I can't help feeling uncomfortable wherever healthy dolphins live in tanks and sing "Happy birthday." Call me an environmental romantic, but I much preferred the show we got free of charge out in the Gulf when a pod followed our fishing boat out to sea.

Some local so-called ecological charters hand-feed dolphins. It is not in the best interests of wildlife to cause creatures to lose their ability to hunt their own food.

Sources & Resources
History and folkloric recollections are gathered in *Camp Walton to Fort Walton Beach* (The Service League, 1987). Contact the **Emerald Coast Tourist Development Council and Convention and Visitors Bureau**, P.O. Box 609, Fort Walton Beach, FL 32549-0609; 800-322-3319 or 904-651-7131.

 OKALOOSA/WALTON PENINSULA

QUICK TOUR
Not technically an island, this 40-mile-long peninsula has island characteristics, however, given its lengthy stretch of watery separation from the mainland. People on Destin refer to it as "the island." And things are still laid-back and small enough there that many addresses have no street numbers.

Destin is the starting point of this island drive. It connects to the mainland via a bridge that crosses over to Okaloosa Island to the west. Highway 98 is the four-lane main drag through town. It skims the city's commercial section, at first along the Destin Harbor waterfront that separates it from Holiday Isle. At its onset it will take you past Destin's fish houses, marinas, and local color. Exit on Gulf Shore Drive to detour to Holiday Isle, mostly a posh residential area.

Farther east on 98, the line-up of chain-store malls and tourist attractions begins. Scenic Highway 98 or Emerald Coast Highway (via Matthew Boulevard) takes you away from it all to Crystal Beach, home of Henderson Beach State Recreation Area, a bed and breakfast, and James Lee Park beach access.

As you cross the line into Walton County, the scenic highway continues through the low-key resort towns of Frangista Beach and Miramar Beach. It joins again with Highway 98 at the upscale resort community of Sandestin.

Seaside's Victorian architecture.
(Chelle Koster Walton)

Cut off on Route C-30A to head back along the litany of colorful beach towns: Dune Allen Beach, Santa Rosa Beach, Blue Mountain Beach, and Grayton Beach. Stop at the beach parks for sunning or follow the twisting roads through the quirky communities. On Route 283, Grayton Beach, with its artsy temperament and antique shops, allows terrific off-the-beaten-path exploration.

Continue on C-30A to Grayton Beach State Recreation Area (entrance fee $3.25 per car, $1 per bike or pedestrian) and the avant-garde town of Seaside. This planned community has made a splash with its Victorian-style pastel architecture, artist's community, and yuppie appeal. Approaching from the west, you round a bend and there it magically appears, like a cache of colored eggs in an Easter hunt.

Return to the main highway via Route 283 and head back west. To leave the peninsula along this route, turn north on Highway 331 at Blue Mountain Beach or Mid Bay Bridge just east of Destin.

BACKFLASH

The Choctaw and Euchee tribes used the area as hunting and ceremonial grounds from 1000 B.C. to the late 1700s, when Spaniards and other European settlers chased them away. The first settlement in the area was in the vicinity of Santa Rosa, where the supporting industry was timber harvesting.

In 1824, Walton County, which encompassed today's Destin and Fort Walton Beach, was formed. Destin got its name from Captain Len Destin, an 1830s settler. He founded a fishing settlement originally known as East Pass.

Willis Herbert Butler developed Grayton Beach in 1920, the first beach community between Pensacola and Apalachicola. The paving of Highway 98 and building of the East Pass Bridge in the 1930s sparked growth in Destin and its adjacent beaches. During World War II, the U.S. used the deserted coastlines along the Panhandle to test bombs and train soldiers. After the war, many veterans returned with their families to settle amongst the beauty they remembered. The peninsula developed with vacation communities during the 1960s. Later, grand destination resorts, like 2,400-acre Sandestin, popped up.

Much of this area's history is recent, reflecting rapid growth and change in the past decade. Destin did not incorporate until 1984.

"When I grew up, there wasn't a single house on this stretch," a youngish Destin resident told me. In most cases, the growth has been strictly controlled to avoid repetition of what happened to Fort Walton Beach.

Other coastal communities emerged slowly. Seaside, on the other hand, was an overnight sensation. In an effort to preserve what was pure and simple about beach vacation towns, Robert Davis conceived a modernized Victorian prototype of front porches and pastels in 1981. Today, more than 180 cottages line brick-paved streets, and building is ever ongoing according to strict guidelines. It's a place almost too pretty and too perfect to believe.

Historical Attractions

Destin has a few small museums that explore its seafaring and prehistoric past. **Museum of the Sea and Indian** (Old Hwy. 98 E.; 904-837-6625) displays shells from around the world, Amerindian artifacts and some live animals. The **Destin Fishing Museum** (Harborwalk Plaza; 904-654-1011) uses videos, mounted fish, a hands-on tidal pool, maritime memorabilia, and a dry aquarium walk adorned with coral reef, sponges, sea fans, sea turtles, and blacktip sharks to explore Destin's fishy reputation. For some flavor of Destin past, visit the **Old Destin Post Office Museum** (Stahlman Ave.; 904-837-8572). It's open Wednesdays and whenever it can find volunteers to open it.

THE NATURAL

The Emerald Coast's snowy sands continue their ethereal stretch along the peninsula, paling to their whitest ever. The beaches get more natural the farther east you go. In newly developed Destin, efforts only recently restore what development stole. The county has planted sea oats to rebuild dunes worn down by foot traffic (higher dunes have been used for tobogganing in the past). In Seaside, they surely reach their plushest and whitest, for everything in Seaside abides by superlative standards.

What's not occupied by moguls of sand is claimed by stands of slash pine. At the east end, the dunes climb higher and scenery gets more wooded: a lovely and unusual blend of beach and forest feel. Banana trees and palms give way to flatwoods and scrub. Endangered plants found on the peninsula include Cruise's golden aster, large-leaved jointweed, conradina, and Godfrey's blazing star.

The monarch butterfly reigns as the most worshipped natural entity. In Seaside, there are "Monarch Crossing" signs among the dunes. In October, the whole coastal area of Walton County celebrates the butterflies' brief flit through their lives as the monarchs migrate to Mexico. Along with musical festivities, there are nature walks and seminars on butterfly behavior.

Natural Attractions

Henderson Beach State Recreation Area (Hwy. 98 E.; 904-837-7550) captures a patch of predevelopment Destin in a time-stilled hourglass of alabaster sand. There's lots of parking, wood pavilions, long dune walkovers, and privacy bought at $2 per car.

Small but highly touted **Grayton Beach State Recreation Area** (Rte. 2 Box 6600, Santa Rosa Beach, FL 32459; 904-231-4210) converges the best of the area's scenery: pine-studded brackish lake, salt marshes, and beaches trimmed in dunes rickrack. Enjoy camping, fishing, and walking trails.

AQUA-ADVENTURE

Touring

Choctawhatchee Bay, nearly 25 miles long, separates Okaloosa Island and the Okaloosa/Walton peninsula from the mainland. Watersports are popular here. Restaurants and marinas lie on both side of the bay, providing boaters with plenty of luncheon destinations.

The most popular thing going on water in Destin is fishing. There are sightseeing and other specialty charters that take you offshore in search of birds, dolphins, sunset, and such.

Blackbeard Sailing Charters (behind A.J's Restaurant, Destin; 904-837-2793) sails twice daily, once at sunset, for three-hour tours with a pirate theme. **Sweet Jody 5** (Destin Harbor; 800-531-9386 or 904-837-2222) does half-day party boat tours. **Glass Bottom Boat** (at Capt. Dave's Marina; 904-654-7787) provides education with its sealife peek. Grayton Beach State Recreation Area has a public boat ramp. Others can be found in local marinas.

Fishing

Destin has been tagged The World's Luckiest Fishing Village because of its great angling past the offshore shelf dropoff, where the 100-fathom curve comes closest to shore. The town has, it says, the largest fleet in Florida. I recommend **Moody's** (194 Hwy. 98 E.,

Destin; 904-837-1293), where they also clean your catch. (Then take it next door to A.J.'s to be cooked; mention Moody's for a discount.)

Amberjack, triggerfish, snapper, and grunts are common catches. Billfishing is good spring through fall for sailfish, marlin, and wahoo. The town promotes its piscean good fortune with shark, king mackerel, billfish, and cobia tournaments throughout the year, and an October **Fishing Rodeo.**

The 3,000-foot **Destin Bridge Catwalk** is a good place to catch redfish. Try in the bay for bass, bluefish and sheepshead. **Grayton Beach State Recreation Area's Western Lake** supplies both fresh and saltwater species: redfish, trout, bass, bluegill.

Swimming

With their slow-slope bottom, the peninsula's beaches are ideal for kids.

Snorkeling/Scuba

The bottom slopes ever so gradually off the beach, so most dive sites require boat transport at least a mile offshore. Sealife abounds in deep, clear water. Timber Hole reveals a submerged petrified forest known for its lobsters and sponges. Reeflike ledges, rocks, and sunken ships, railroad boxcars, and airplanes diversify bottom time. Snorkeling excursions with **Kokomo Snorkeling**

At Destin Harbor, the World's Luckiest Fishing Village.
(Chelle Koster Walton)

Headquarters (500 Hwy. 98, Destin; 904-837-9029) take you to live shell finds in clear waters. **Aquanaut Scuba Center** (Hwy. 98; 904-837-0359) arranges snorkeling and Scuba charters, and offers snorkeling rentals and instructions. **Emerald Coast Scuba School** (127 Hwy. 98 #10A, Destin; 904-837-0955) teaches certification and specialty courses.

Boating, Sailing & Canoeing
Rent powerboats for full and half days at **Premier Powerboat Rentals** (Hwy. 98, Destin; 904-837-7755). Memorial Day regattas are held in Seaside and Sandestin.

Sailboarding & Surfing
Grayton Beach is the coast's "surf's up" haven. A sign outside the Grayton Corner Café reads "Hours may vary depending on the quality of the surf." Summertime's best.

ISLAND ADVENTURE

Hiking
A 30-minute Barrier Dune Nature Trail at Grayton Beach Park lets you observe scrub oak thickets, migrating dunes and traces of ghost crabs, raccoons and lizards. Interpretative signs educate along the way. Stop in at the Seaside rental office for a Walking Tour of Seaside folder.

Biking
You can rent bikes at Sandestin (guests only: 904-267-7077) and Seaside (904-231-2214). Folks cycle around the peninsula's backroads and around its resort communities.

Golfing
Golf courses along the peninsula are plentiful, many of them semiprivate. In Destin, there's **Indian Bayou** (Country Club Dr.; 904-837-6191), a 27-hole course; the highly rated **Emerald Bay** (40001 Emerald Coast Pkwy.; 904-837-5197), with 18 holes; and **Seascape** (100 Seascape Dr., 904-837-9181), with 18 holes. Dune Allen's **Santa Rosa Golf & Beach Club** (Rte. C-30; 904-267-2229) has 18 holes. **The Southern Golf School** (Santa Rosa Beach;

800-889-4126 or 904-267-3745) gives personalized instruction and private lessons.

Tennis

Tops'l Resort's Pro Shop (904-267-9263) near Sandestin sponsors a slate of year-round events, including women's, men's, and team invitational competitions.

Courts are open to the public at **Buck Destin Park** (724 Legion Dr., Destin; 904-654-6060), **Sandestin** (5500 Hwy. 98 E., Destin; 904-267-7110), **Seascape** (100 Seascape Dr., Destin; 904-837-9181), and **Seaside** (Rte. C30A; 904-231-2214).

Other

Seaside offers croquet playing, lessons, and tournaments. Along the peninsula, resorts and towns sponsor triathlons, duathlons, and runs throughout the year.

C U L T U R E

The People

Destin residents are sea oriented by birth. Tourism turns them landward for profit. The number of spring breakers is limited by a regulation prohibiting anyone 25 or younger from renting a room in Destin.

Grayton Beach used to be an old surfer's and artist's haven, but in recent years, the yuppies have discovered it. In it and many of the nearby communities, populations are largely seasonal.

In Seaside, you find street people. Although the progenitor of this project envisioned a town where people would do a lot of porch sitting, walking or biking the brick streets has become a much more popular pastime. It's fun to read the names of the houses and the names and origination of the people who own them. The majority hail from south of the Mason-Dixon line.

As in many regional coastal communities, Seaside seems to lack a sense of community, despite its high ideals to recreate the old-fashioned hometown. Children are held in high respect, however, and the average age seems younger than in many Florida "wintering" communities. And wealthier than most in the Panhandle.

Island Inspirations

Vivian Foster Mettee wrote *And the Roots Run Deep* (1993), an early history of the area and its people, which is available at the Old Destin Post Office Museum. Seaside attracts writers and artists. **Sundog Books** (Rte. C-30A; 904-231-5481) is the nucleus of the town's literati. **The Seaside Institute** (904-231-2421) annually co-hosts the **Florida International University Seaside Writers Conference** in October.

Fairs & Festivals

Destin holds several not-to-miss occasions for revelry. **Billy Bowlegs Festival** celebrates the town's swashbuckling spirit in June. **Destin Seafood Festival** comes in October, and **Destin Mayfest** (guess when) pays homage to the culture of its Cajun neighbors with tasty jazz and jambalaya.

Grayton Beach Fine Arts Festival in May brings artists downtown.

Seaside, too, is big on festivals. For **The Seaside October Weekend** (The Seaside Institute, 904-231-2421; or Downtown Seaside Association, 904-231-5424), the tag line reads: A celebration of wine, music, food, and art with world-class winemakers and chefs and local artists and musicians. **Seaside Jazz By the Sea Festival** features top-name artists in November. Seaside's **Gatsby Garden Party** in August combines croquet, big-band music, and Gatsby attire.

Monarch Festival of South Walton centers in Seaside, with environmental, horticultural, and invertebrate educational seminars and live concerts. The highlights of **South Walton Sportsfest Weekend**, October and November, include a triathlon, a duathlon, runs, water ski tournaments, a bike race, and a beach to bay volksmarch.

Museums & Galleries

Grayton Beach has an artistic tint to its soul. **Patrone's**, the local artists' colony, specializes in handcrafted Floridiana. **Magnolia House** (Magnolia St.; 904-231-5859) is a pretty, old, tin-roofed home full of nostalgic gifts and home furnishings.

Seaside is the peninsula's artistic heart and soul. **The Ruskin Place Artist Colony** is a cobbled open-air plaza lined with galleries and artsy places around open-air workshop and exhibition space. **The Forsythe House Workshops** hold classes for kids, teens, and adults.

Visit **Artz by Donna Burgess** (Hwy. C-30A; 904-231-5781). She's locally famous for her pastels and watercolors depicting seaside scenes. She also has a gallery in Destin (120-B Highway 98; 904-837-1887).

Island Shopping

On the beach side of Route C-30A in Seaside, a Caribbean-like marketplace convenes, decorated in primitive-style paint jobs. The tiny shops and outdoor tin-roofed stalls of **Per-spi-cas-ity** (Rte. C-30A; 904-231-5829) sell all manner of gifts, crafts, and clothing.

Sundog Books (Rte. C-30A; 904-231-5481) at Seaside — small, properly cluttered with kid's stuff, bestsellers, Southern literature, local guides, transcendental meditation books — is a browser's delight. There always seems to be a stimulating conversation going on.

Architecture

The bridge at East Pass crosses a great gap in Florida architecture. Everything's newer, more upscale in Destin than in Fort Walton Beach. New England maritime architecture heavily influences the area, with its telltale cupolas, gables, and wood-shake siding.

Seaside, at the peninsula's other extreme, has had the greatest influence on the area's architecture. This planned development community gave new meaning to cookie-cutter architecture. Buildings may be cut from the same dough — predominantly gingerbread — but each Victorian structure claims a separate personality with lacy embellishments and soft-to-vibrant pastel paint jobs. Codes mandate picket fences, and that they each be cut from a different pattern. The town has won several architectural awards, including the Governor's Design Award in 1986, and *Time* magazine's Design of the Decade in 1990.

The **Seaside Institute** (904-231-2421) regularly presents lectures on architecture and its social impact, including a work/study program for student architects. Seaside's forward-looking philosophy of community and architecture takes on the importance of religion in many ways. The town/resort has initiated an architecture camp for kids on a trial basis. **Architectural House Tour** and **archiCamp** take place in October.

Recent discovery of laid-back little Grayton Beach has juxtaposed made-to-look-old Florida houses with sweet and authentic Cracker-style homes.

Music

The **Northwest Florida Symphony Orchestra** makes occasional appearances at the Sandestin Beach Hilton (5540 Hwy. 98 E., Destin; 904-267-9500). Jazz is the favored style of the coast. Major artists are featured during various festivals, concerts, and events throughout the year. Seaside especially goes well with jazz.

Nightlife

Destin's nightlife scene stays lively and island-flavored around the harbor at **A.J.'s** (Destin Harbor, 904-837-1913) and **Lucky Snapper** (Destin Harbor, 904-654-0900). **Bud & Alley's** (Seaside, 904-231-5900) hosts live jazz and rhythm and blues Friday and Saturday evenings. On clear nights, watch sunset from the upstairs bar.

TABLE   HOPPING

Fried seafood still dominates the cuisine scene in these parts, though you'll find a more cosmopolitan influence as well. Destin Harbor gathers up a slough of waterfront restaurants heavily salted on flavor. Most provide docking. **Lucky Snapper** (Destin Harbor,

904-654-0900) excels in waterfront views and fresh fish pan-fried or char-grilled with creative toppings and preparations. **A.J. Seafood & Oyster Bar** (Destin Harbor, 904-837-1913) looks very islandy with its harbor stance and chickee hat. Try the smoked yellowfin tuna dip for an appetizer. The menu, again, concentrates on fried food done fish-house style. The twist at **Harbor Docks** (538 Hwy. 98 E.; 904-837-2506) is Thai dishes and influence (my shrimp chowder had a nice chile bite to it, for instance). It's also famous for its sushi. The restaurant is decorated in antique rods and reels, with indoor and outdoor seating.

In Grayton Beach, **Criolla's** (Rte. C-30A; 904-267-1267) is the venerated name in fine dining. Originally Creole/Caribbean in cuisine, it has recently flexed to include other global styles. Go for a special occasion: it's expensive.

Seaside's eateries are quite sophisticated. Stop at **Modica Market** (904-231-1214) for a to-go bite from the deli. You'll not get out of there without a basketful of gourmet goodies from its white cubicled floor-to-ceiling shelves.

Bud & Alley's (Rte. C-30A; 904-231-5900) is Seaside's best-known restaurant, and with good reason. Try to get a seat in the gazebo around sunset time. It adds so much to the wonderfully successful eclecticism of the menu. A cat brushes against your leg. People at tables talk to each other.

ISLAND LANDINGS

Henderson Park Inn (35000 Emerald Coast Pkwy., Destin, FL 32541; 800-336-4853 or 904-837-4853) looks like a quaint, New England-style B&B. It's quaint enough, and definitely inspired by the gabled, wood-shake-sided Queen Anne architecture of the north Atlantic Coast. But it's new (opened April, 1993) and lacking the patina that age brings — its antique furniture pieces are all reproductions. Its greatest feature is its beachfront. It borders Henderson Beach State Recreation Area, which means it will never have to worry about neighbors.

Sandestin (5500 Hwy. 98 E., Destin, FL 32541; 800-277-0800 or 904-267-8000) is a 2,400-acre resort community featuring both a beach front and a full-service marina. Accommodations come in various shapes, sizes, and price ranges. Just be careful not to get so caught up in all that's offered here that you never leave and explore the wonderful countryside.

Camping is permitted at **Grayton Beach State Recreation Area** (Rte. 2 Box 6600, Santa Rosa Beach, FL 32459; 904-231-4210). Many of the sites are wooded, some lakeside. Reservations are accepted in season, beginning in March.

Josephine's Bed & Breakfast (Monarch Realty at Seaside, Inc., P.O. Box 4767, 101 Seaside Ave., Seaside FL 32459; 800-848-1840 or 904-231-1940) is one of the many options in Seaside. There are also honeymoon cottages, regular cottages, and the "motor inn." Contact Seaside Cottage Rental Agency (P.O. Box 4730, Seaside, FL 32459; 800-277-8696 or 904-231-1320).

TOURIST TRAPS

Destin repeats Fort Walton Beach's predilection for amusement-park entertainment, just with newer, more grandiose settings. **Big Kahuna's** (1007 Hwy. 98 E.; 904-837-4061), for example, has giant monkey sculptures and other special effects to advertise it. Inside, you'll find bungee jumping (à deux, no less), dune buggies, go-carts, stock cars, a water theme park, and midway games.

Sources & Resources

The Seaside Times (P.O. Box 4730, Seaside, FL 32459), more P.R. than news, predicts "Weather: Fabulous" and has the slogan "All the News That Washes Up On The Beach." **The Beaches of South Walton, South Walton Tourist Development Council**, P.O. Box 1248, Santa Rosa Beach, FL 32459; 800-822-6877.

SHELL ISLAND

QUICK TOUR

A man-made island, this oasis from Panama City Beach's "Where the Boys Are" scene offers refuge to birds and crowd-weary travelers. You need a boat to get there.

Mostly state-owned Shell Island is long and thin. At its widest end to the west, there are pine trees, a freshwater pond, and alligators. At Spanish Shanty Cove leeside, a few docks allow specially permitted charter boats to tie up and put their customers ashore. Private boaters anchor offshore. The hike via boardwalk to the Gulf is a short one. At its east end, the island grows. One charter drops you here to find the best shells.

BACKFLASH

Shell Island came into this world in the early 1930s when a pass was cut through the east end of a then-peninsula occupied by Panama City Beach. The area, known up until that time as Land's End, extended southeast into St. Andrews Bay, leaving only a narrow opening for the ships of early Spanish explorers. The point's 40-foot bluffs and narrow pass led navigators to believe the bay was only a river. Later sailors discovered the error. Of course its secretive harbor was a magnet for the unscrupulous. Spanish Shanty Point, they say, holds the buried profits from Land's End's pirate days. By 1868, a hurricane had changed its bluffy profile.

Before the Civil War, an engineer named Robert E. Lee surveyed St. Andrews Bay as a possible fort locale. It was used instead as a temporary prison for men captured during raids on nearby salt works. At the turn of the century, with the arrival of the railroad to Panama City, what is today Shell Island was built with a beach pavilion to serve sand-destined boat excursions. Besides dressing rooms, it had a dance floor upstairs. Later it was moved to another beach by ox cart. A private club for boaters grew up around it, where food and drink were served for a minimal joiner's fee. It was later burned down by a campfire.

Captain Carl Johnson remembers when his daddy was in the shark-fishing business and would hang the fins out to dry on Shell Island and two other small islands in the pass.

At Spanish Shanty Cove, some vacation homes were later built, although they had no electricity or water. Plans were made to develop an island community, until the state waltzed in and bought out property owners. A few still privately hold land on the island. The state has plans to build a new shelter, but the project has no disclosed timetable.

THE NATURAL

Before the mid-1800s, four islands punctuated Land's End peninsula: Sand, Hummock, Hurricane, and Crooked Islands. Hurricane became part of Shell Island. Crooked Island still exists. Sand and Hummock got erased by the great hurricane of 1868.

Seven miles of undisturbed beach edge Shell Island. The island continually expands at its eastern end with the shifting of sands. New islands are sprouting. "I can see it change yearly," one longtime tour captain told me. Its older, west end is wide and supports various degrees of habitat, including a freshwater pond with alligators, and woodlands with deer. Older residents remember duck-hunting expeditions to the island.

Natural Attractions

In 1968, a tiny island sprang into existence in St. Andrews Bay, created from dredge sand. Within two years, gulls and blackwing skimmers set up housekeeping. Brown pelicans made it their only nesting sight between Cedar Key and Mobile Bay. The local Audubon Society fought for the island's designation as Audubon Island Wilderness Preserve. It is co-managed by the Audubon Society and the Florida Department of Natural Resources.

Today, more than 150 pairs of pelicans nest each year on Audubon Island, birthing about 300 chicks annually. I'm told you don't want to get downwind of the island because of the stench this produces.

AQUA-ADVENTURE

Touring

Several Panama City and Panama City Beach charters go daily to Shell Island. The best and most knowledgeable operation is **The Glass Bottom Boat** (Treasure Island Marina, 3605 Thomas Dr.; 904-234-8944). **St. Andrews State Park** does daily shuttles every half hour from the Jetty Dive Store. Call 904-233-0504.

Private boaters anchor their vessels along bayside shores in great numbers on weekends. Gulf waters are often too rough to pull ashore on the windward side of the island. Avoid waters at the island's east end. The sands are shifty.

Fishing

Best from the west pass at the jetties between Shell Island and St. Andrews State Park.

Snorkeling/Scuba

Snorkel around the pass jetties (beware of strong currents on incoming tides) to see the best of the region's fish life. St. Andrews State Park (904-233-0504) offers a snorkel shuttle to Shell Island.

Scuba diving is big business and one of Panama City Beach's best attractions. Sites and charters are plentiful.

Shelling & Beachcombing

On an island named Shell, people expect to find an abundance of beachcombing treasures. In winter, this is true, but the supply is becoming depleted. Best shelling is at the east-end flats and sandbars just offshore. Olives, cockles, and scallops are common finds.

Sources & Resources

Panama City Beach Convention & Visitors Bureau/Bay County Tourist Development Council, P.O. Box 9473, Panama City Beach, FL 32417; 800-722-3224 or 904-233-5070.

 CAPE SAN BLAS

QUICK TOUR

Another insular peninsula with a tenuous connection to the mainland, Cape San Blas springs from Gulf County shores like an open safety pin. Barely a mile wide in places, its skinniness keeps it from overdevelopment. Resorts are low-key and of low density, thanks to lack of a sewer system. Quite off the road-more- traveled, it harbors seclusion and an old-Florida environment within its safe-ty-pin shape.

Route 30A off of Highway 98 takes you past a small sign announcing Cape San Blas (when locals pronounce it, it sounds like Cape Sandblast). Turn on 30E and continue past the small housing and resort developments sprinkled among the dunes. They range from camping enclaves to ritzy neighborhoods. One of the first such communities you reach is the Old Salt Works, with a historic marker and museum to go along with its cabins. Salinas Park on the left, Gulf side, has parking, beach walkovers, picnicking, a terrific playground, and a web of boardwalks that wind to a gazebo with a fabulous view at a dunes high point.

Another unobtrusively marked left turn takes you to the Cape San Blas Lighthouse, a modern skeletal structure that lacks the romance one normally associates with lighthouses. It hides among Eglin Air Force Base facilities. More light development, a restaurant, and a couple of general stores line the road before you reach St. Joseph Peninsula State Park ($3.25 entrance fee for cars, $1 for bikers or pedestrians).

Here is Cape San Blas's showpiece, a 2,500-acre refuge for birds, ghost crabs, dunes ecology, and recreaters. There's a public beach access near the entrance, with a boat launch and playground across the road. You can see Black's Island from here. Last inhabited by Amerindians, today it serves as an environmental summer camp for boys. Tours can be prearranged by calling 904-229-6330.

Where the road ends five miles short of the point, undisturbed wilderness occupies 1,650 acres.

BACKFLASH

Named for a Spanish Bishop of Sebaste, Cape San Blas proved an impediment to early sailors. Legends say rebel William Augustus Bowles buried his treasure at the base of the Cape, around an area known as Money Bayou.

In the 1830s, the coastal region fronted by Cape San Blas was one of the nation's fastest growing as squatters on nearby timber company territory were forced from their homes. The town of St. Joseph boomed and became a major shipping port and the selected site of the state's Constitutional Convention. The glow of success attracted wealthy planters and merchants. All went well until financial hardship, yellow fever, and a hurricane hit within a span of a few years.

Cape San Blas's beaming lighthouse lit its way to becoming an important Civil War site. The first structure was built in 1847. Storms caused the toppling of it and another before a brick tower went up in 1859. That one collapsed in 1882 from erosion. The next one, a movable iron tower, was modeled after one built in southwestern Florida on Sanibel Island. Erosion has twice caused the latest lighthouse's relocation.

During World War II, the U.S. Army used St. Joseph peninsula for a training base. St. Joseph Peninsula Park opened in 1967, officially named T.H. Stone, for a local settler and community leader.

Historical Attractions

Old Salt Works (Rte. C-30E; 904-229-6097), today a cabin resort on the Cape, holds remnants of the Confederate Salt Works that operated there until 1862. It processed bushels of salt from the waters of St. Joseph Bay. Union troops destroyed the facility during the Civil War.

THE NATURAL

Geologists believe that 5,000 years ago Cape San Blas was actually two barrier islands. They joined together and to the mainland about a thousand years ago.

The entire peninsula is sand. Dunes of sand. The Badlands of sand, supporting the scrubby-looking pines, reindeer moss, and wildflowers that survive salt assaults. The fine sand on the 17 miles of beach is a bit more tannish than the glare of its neighbors to the west. It spans wide at low tide. At the lower end of the Cape, the sand is harder packed and widest. To the north, the dunes look chiseled off, a result of 1994's summer storms. Rubble from a demolished building litters one stretch.

Ghost crabs, some bigger than a man's hand, perforate the

beach with their holes and scuff marks. Pelicans and shorebirds come to peck at the smaller specimens and at the coquinas embedded at shoreline. More than 200 species of birds have been sighted at St. Joseph Park, which is considered a prime location in the eastern U.S. for spotting migratory hawks in the fall. The endangered peregrine falcon is another visitor. Armadillos, gray foxes, skunks, bobcats, and white-tailed deer hide in remote wildlife areas.

Natural Attractions

T. H. Stone Memorial/St. Joseph Peninsula Park (904-227-1327) encompasses more than 2,500 acres of recreational and wildlife area.

The northernmost five miles and 1,650 acres of the Wilderness Preserve protect some of Florida's tallest sand dunes and more than 200 species of resident and migratory birds. The best bird-spotting area is along the beach and bay shoreline and in the sand pine scrub and pine flatwoods.

Flocks of monarch butterflies also stop here in late October as they make their way to Mexico. The park offers naturalists opportunity for primitive camping, hiking, and nature study.

AQUA-ADVENTURE

Touring

There's a public boat launch inside St. Joseph State Park, near the entrance.

Fishing

Surfcasting yields sea trout on the St. Joseph Bay side. Offshore, redfish, mackerel, flounder, dolphin, cobia, wahoo, shark, and sailfish are plentiful.

Snorkeling/Scuba

Nearby Port St. Joe has a reputation for wreck diving. Sites include galleons of the Spanish Armada and German U-boats. Around Cape San Blas, explore the brick base of its submerged lighthouse (it was the third of four to be built). A sunken World War II British tanker, the *Empire Mica*, rates as one of Florida's top wreck

Sand dunes give way to alabaster beach at Cape San Blas.
(Chelle Koster Walton)

dive sites. Clams and other sea life collect underneath a long shelf of limestone ledges about eight miles offshore.

Boating, Sailing & Canoeing

Canoe rentals are available at St. Joseph Peninsula Park.

ISLAND ADVENTURE

Hiking

You'll find nature trailheads at the parking lot just south of the park's entrance on the bay, at campground #1 along the Gulf, and at the picnic grounds on Eagle Harbor. Trails explore beach, bay, and interior environment, with occasional opportunity to glimpse rare birds and mammals.

While I was visiting Cape San Blas, I met a threesome from Pensacola who had decided to see the Panhandle by foot. They'd been hoofing along beaches, and roads when necessary, for three weeks. They talked as though they'd had a special religious experience. I believe they did.

Shelling & Beachcombing

The beaches are well cluttered with vacated shells, most of them wave-abused clams, cockles, and other bivalves.

CULTURE

The People

The best news about the people is that they are few. This is one of the quietest beaches I've ever walked. Even the birds are quiet, and the white ghost crabs practically invisible. From the road, you get almost a ghostly feeling as the sea breeze whips across the dunes. The eerie silence is periodically broken by an Air Force jet or two scrambling the air waves.

Many "islanders" are part-timers, most with Southern accents. The Cape does get visitors, primarily in summer. The state park counts 100,000 coming through its gates each year.

Architecture

Most buildings have a modern look, with Victorian and old-Florida tendencies. Older homes copy New England style and assimilate earth tones, with a settled-in, weather-whipped look. Newer ones adopt the modern pastel color scheme. There's a bit of sameness to some developments.

Log and wood cabins and cottages look more in place. The new places stand rather starkly, without vegetation cover, atop dunes, tippy-toeing on their stilts.

TABLE HOPPING

Nearby Port St. Joe is known for its freshly scooped-from-the-bay scallops. Catch your own or buy them fresh or cooked from local houses off-island. You'll also want to taste the other indigenous food fish: Apalachicola Bay oysters, bulldozer lobsters, grouper, and shrimp.

There's only one restaurant in Cape San Blas. The food at **Cape Café** (Rte. C-30E; 904-229-8688) is okay, but the place is just too modern and deli-like for the location. I prefer the more authentically fishy atmosphere of mainland eateries in Mexico Beach and Apalachicola. Or try nearby **Indian Pass Raw Bar** (C-30, 904-227-1670), which serves oysters, crawfish, shrimp, clams, and seafood gumbo in an old roadside country store.

Sweet **tupelo honey**, which has inspired song lyrics, is a product of nearby Wewahitchka. Look for it in stores.

ISLAND LANDINGS

Lodging spans the spectrum from tent camping and cabins to upscale condominium and home rentals. **St. Joseph Peninsula State Park** (SR 1, Box 200, Port St. Joe, FL 32456; 904-227-1327) has some of the nicest furnished cabins on the cape, actually more like lofted townhouses in the woods. But reserve early, up to a year ahead of time; there are only eight.

Old Salt Works Cabins (P.O. Box 526, Port St. Joe, FL 32456; 904-229-6097) occupy a Civil War historical site, with a museum and pleasant little units that front either the bay or Gulf near the entrance to Cape San Blas.

Cape Cottages (SR 1, Box 351, Port St. Joe, FL 32456; 800-556-1322 or 904-229-8775) ride the dunes near the beach at the northern end, near the state park. Fully equipped with kitchen needs; linen costs extra.

For condo and beach rentals, contact **Anchor Realty & Mortgage Co.** (SR1, Box 223, Port St. Joe, 32456; 800-624-3964 or 904-229-2770).

Sources & Resources

Gulf County Chamber of Commerce, P.O. Box 964, Port St. Joe, FL 32456; 904-227-1223.

ST. VINCENT ISLAND

QUICK TOUR

One of Florida's most primitively preserved barrier islands, St. Vincent holds 12,358 acres of raw nature. It is rare among Florida islands for its natural freshwater sources and its size: It forms a rough triangle nine miles long by four at its widest. Eighty miles of sand road and 14 miles of beaches lure explorers and nature lovers. The east-west sand roads follow the island's inner ridge formations. Roads are marked. Numbers indicate roads running north-south; letters label east-west roads. The island is accessible by boat only during daylight hours, except by special permit.

BACKFLASH

Pottery shards found on St. Vincent date early inhabitants to the year 240. The first record of human habitation was in 1633, when Franciscan monks visited the Apalache tribes in residence there. The good friars gave the island its modern-day name. The Apalaches were succeeded by Creek and Seminole Amerindians moving down from the north.

In 1868, George Hatch purchased the island in an auction for $3,000. Next a private hunting and fishing preserve belonging to patent medicine mogul C. W. Pierce, St. Vincent became home, in the early 1900s, to the 500-pound sambar deer (indigenous to Southeast Asia), which Dr. Pierce introduced. The exotic deer joined native white-tailed deer, bald eagles, and loggerhead turtles on the island. A later owner went even further and imported zebras, elands, Asian jungle fowl, black bucks, and pheasants.

Before the federal government took over in 1968, St. Vincent served the industries of cattle raising, oyster fishing, and pine logging. The U.S. removed all foreign species, except sambar deer and black bucks, which had acclimatized. The sambars are frequently seen in herds; the black bucks are more reclusive.

THE NATURAL

Fourteen miles of beach line St. Vincent Island's southern and eastern shores. Dune ridges run down its middle, mapping out past geological fluctuations in sea level and beach location. Between the dunes, explorers will find freshwater lakes and sloughs on the east end and dry, elevated forests on the west. All together, biologists identify ten types of wildlife habitat, from wetlands to hardwood dunes to beaches.

Among the island's most cherished natural endowments are the white-tailed deer, the turkey, and the endangered bald eagle. The native white-tailed deer coexists with its much larger exotic relative, the sambar deer. Each keep to their own corner: the white-taileds to the uplands, the sambars to the wetlands. Originally established to protect bird life, the sanctuary has expanded its role as protector of deer, turtles, alligators, and snakes. Wood storks and peregrine falcons are the rarest of its migrating visitors. Vireos and warblers also pass through. In 1990, the sanctuary began breeding the endangered red wolf for reintroduction into woodlands in northern states of the Southeast.

AQUA-ADVENTURE

Touring

For passage to the island, contact private charters in Apalachicola.

Fishing

The island's small lakes, ponds and creeks are open for fishing between March 1 and October 31. Freshwater fish include bream, shellcracker, speckled perch, catfish, and bass.

Boating, Sailing & Canoeing

A public boat ramp at Indian Pass on Route C-30B gets you closest to the island.

ISLAND ADVENTURE

Hiking

You've got 80 miles of sand road and 14 miles of beach to wear yourself out. Just remember, soft sand slows you down, and affects different leg muscles than does hard-surface hiking.

Other

To manage the populations of deer and feral hogs, controlled annual hunts are held. Camping is allowed in conjunction with the hunts. All participants must be approved by the refuge manager.

Sources & Resources

For information, contact Refuge Manager, **St. Vincent National Wildlife Refuge**, P.O. Box 447, Apalachicola, FL 32329; 904-653-8808.

 ST. GEORGE ISLAND

QUICK TOUR

Too slim for much else, St. George is a mostly residential island with state parks like parentheses at each end. You approach the island via the five-mile-long Bryant Patton Bridge from Eastpoint on Route G1A (Island Drive). The doormat is made up of the island's commercial section, a cluster of convenience stores, gas stations, and restaurants primmed up by the Victorian, blue-shutter prettiness of the St. George Inn to the left.

Go right on Gulf Beach Drive West to have a look at the older part of the island. Halfway to the end, a security gate at St George's Plantation development impedes progress to the western tip. Across Bob Sikes Cut, Little St. George Island, accessible by boat only, is home to a 19th-century lighthouse. The island is shaped like a crooked arm and contains almost three square miles.

As you return on Gulf Beach Drive, head right toward the Gulf and follow West Gorrie along the waterfront and through to the East End, marked by newer, grander residential buildings. When Gorrie ends, jog left, then right to Gulf Beach Drive, which takes you the St. George Island State Park entrance. It costs $3.25 per car ($1 per biker or pedestrian) to enter this primeval world of sand, dunes, pines, and birds. Several boardwalks cross the dunes for beach access. Two parking lots with facilities lie along the road. At the end, four-wheel-drive vehicles can continue toward the east-end pass, where fishing is best.

From the park entrance, return down the center of the island along Pine Street back to the bridge at Franklin Boulevard.

BACKFLASH

Human habitation has been fairly recent on this over-3,000-year-old island. Creek Amerindians lived here in the tenth century A.D., leaving behind proof of their existence in bayside middens. They were probably scattered by the arrival of Spaniards in 1528.

Pirate legends in these parts center around William Augustus Bowles, a.k.a. Billy Bowlegs, who led the Creek Amerindians in defense of their land. He is said to have buried treasure on St. George and Little St. George Islands.

The 1900s saw the turpentine industry tapping into St. George's pine forests. Army training exercises brought temporary residents during World War II. In 1954, after much debate, the federal government cut a pass through St. George Island's west end, thus creating the new island of Little St. George. The Sikes Cut got fishermen to shore from the Gulf more quickly, but may have hurt the oyster industry by increasing Apalachicola Bay's salt content.

The purchase of state parklands in 1963, followed by causeway construction in 1965, put St. George on the map. The park opened for use in 1980. Development since then has been closely restricted by minimum lot size and building codes.

Historical Attractions

In 1933, Cape St. George Lighthouse was built at the elbow of what is today Little St. George Island to guide boat traffic passing from the Gulf into Apalachicola Bay. A new model, built two miles away, replaced it in 1847. Wind damage caused another to be built in 1852; it still stands today — barely.

THE NATURAL

"It's a long, skinny island, and that's the way we deal with it," says Roy Ogles, park ranger at St. George Island State Park.

St. George Island is estimated at between 3,000 and 5,000 years old. At first glance, the island looks like one big sandbar, with 28 miles of beach and scrubby dunes sandwiched between waterfronts. There's little vegetation; the stilt homes look to be all that grows above knee-high in some places.

Typical of a skinny barrier island, St. George's profile is ever changing. Currently it grows at its east end as it rolls inward toward the mainland. At the peak of its shifting dunes, the island measures 12 feet above sea level.

Variety is found in the state park and at other older parts of the island, where 16 different biological communities have been identified, including live oak hammocks, slash pine stands, and small freshwater ponds and sloughs. Bay- side marsh tracts flourish with black needlerush.

St. George's most celebrated wildlife thrives in the water. At the front door to Apalachicola's oyster industry, and caught in a crosswalk of marine life, the island has a reputation for fishing equal to Destin's. Birds on the wing to southern destinations make an annual visit to St. George Island. Osprey, bald eagles, and a variety of shorebirds, including the blackwing skimmer and willet, call the island home. Raccoons, ghost crabs, sea turtles and snakes favor the state park.

Natural Attractions

Nine miles of dune-edged beach wrap from the Gulf of Mexico to the Apalachicola waterfronts of **St. George Island State Park** (Box 62, Eastpoint, FL 32328; 904-927-2111). Within its 1,800 acres, pines and oaks grow. Sand and salt marshes cover much of its terrain. Hiking trails and boardwalks accommodate hoofers. Beaching and swimming are the most popular pastimes. The quartz sand here takes on a golden glow due to minerals in the earth.

AQUA-ADVENTURE

Touring

Sightseeing and photography excursions can be arranged through **Jeanni's Journeys** (E. Pine St.; 904-927-3259). Environmental camp for kids is another specialty.

Fishing

Selected as the number one fishing beach by coastal geographer Stephen Leatherman, St. George's waters yield speckled trout, pompano, redfish, flounder, red snapper, mackerel, sheepshead, amberjack, and tarpon. The best place for big redfish is **Bob Sikes Cut** between St. George and Little St. George and at the pass at St. George Island State Park's east end.

Jeanni's Journeys (E. Pine St.; 904-927-3259) arranges fishing charters. For tackle and bait, visit **Fisherman's Headquarters** (W. Bayshore Dr., 904-927-9817).

Swimming

An offshore sandbar reduces undercurrents at St. George Island. You won't see much water play in the winter months, but waters warm up nicely come late spring.

Snorkeling/Scuba

Jeanni's Journeys (E. Pine St.; 904-927-3259) arranges charters for snorkeling and diving. Residents find antique bottles along the bay shoreline, some dating back to the mid-19th century.

Boating, Sailing & Canoeing

Boat ramps can be found at two locations in **St. George Island State Park**. In summer, you can rent Hobie Cats from **Sailboat Dave**, near the Blue Parrot Restaurant.

ISLAND ADVENTURE

Hiking

In St. George Island State Park, a 2.5-mile trail penetrates pine flatwoods to reach Gap Point, a primitive campground on the bay.

Biking

Rent bikes at **Fisherman's Headquarters** (W. Bayshore Dr., 904-927-9817) or **Island Bike Rental** (904-927-3544), which delivers.

Shelling & Beachcombing

Especially at the east end, you'll find periwinkles, moon snails, and crown conchs in abundance. Rarer finds include sundials, horse conchs, and junonias. Shelling gets best in winter.

Other

Dove and duck hunting by permit only is allowed on Little St. George Island.

CULTURE

The People

About 600 people stick it out on the island year-round. Most of them are newcomers, within the last ten years — professionals,

Frolicking among the dunes.
(Emerald Coast Tourist Development Council)

retirees, lots of realtors. A quarter million people visit the state park each year.

Island Inspirations

Island Light by Alexander Key (Bobbs-Merrill, 1950) is a novel about the difficult life that the St. George Lighthouse keepers' families suffered. **Sallie Mandell Hyslop** is an emerging artist on St. George. She portrays local sea life and is especially known for her residential and commercial murals.

Fairs & Festivals

St. George Island Chili Cook-Off is held the first Saturday in March. Besides the cooking competition, take part in the Red Fish Run and auction. The first Saturday in November is **Seafood Festival**, with food booths, an oyster-eating contest, crab races, crafts, and auctions. Between Thanksgiving and Christmas, **St. George Island Arts Festival** brings artisans to Oyster Cove Restaurant (904-927-2600).

Island Shopping

Two Gulls (E. Pine St.; 904-927-2044) sells cards, gifts, and clothing with a beach motif.

Architecture

Just about everything is new — even St. George Inn, which looks old and Victorian.

Music

Country music gets lots of play here.

Nightlife

Harry A's (904-927-9810) has a one-man band on weekends, and a pool table every night of the week. Locals love it here, and it has a reputation for good partying.

TABLE   HOPPING

Docked right offshore from famous oyster center Apalachicola, St. George Island is as good a place as any around to try sweet **Apalachicola Bay oysters**. More than 90 percent of Florida's oyster harvest comes from these waters, a blend of salt and fresh. In 1992, that amounted to 1.8 million pounds of meat. The local variety is small, sweet, and juicy, known as either "American" or "Eastern" oyster. Scientific circles know them as *Crassostrea virginica*.

In recent years, pollution northward in the Apalachicola River has threatened oyster populations, and there was a recent bacteria scare. Today, restaurants must give notice that raw oysters can pose danger to consumers with certain health problems. Cooking kills bacteria. Seasons have been cut back to further ensure safety, reverting, in essence, to the old "r"-month rule, which restricts oyster ingestion to months ending in the letter "r."

Flounder, grouper, shrimp, blue crab, pompano and red snapper also come from local waters to local tables. Some island restaurants thankfully break away from local deep-fried tradition. The **St. George Inn** (Franklin Blvd.; 904-927-2903), for example, fries food only upon request, and even then begrudgingly.

Oyster Cove Seafood Bar & Grill (E. Pine St. & E. Second St.; 904-927-2600) is another. Its style merges the influences of Cajun and Greek cuisine with delicious results. The view of the bay enhances the epicurean experience.

Happy Pelican (W. Pine St.; 904-927-9826) adheres to old-Florida-style cookery for the most part, in a purely local atmosphere. Try the oysterburger. For fresh catches, go to the Apalachicola or Eastpoint Fisherman's Wharf, or any of the seafood markets along Route 98 in Eastpoint.

ISLAND LANDINGS

Most people rent homes for their stay on St. George Island. Contact **Accommodations St. George** (HCR Box 108, St. George Island, FL 32328; 800-332-5196 or 904-927-2666).

Hotel accommodations on the island are limited. **St. George Inn** (Franklin Blvd.; 904-927-2903) has eight rooms with views of the Gulf or bay. Each has French doors opening to a wraparound second-story porch.

St. George Island State Park (904-927-2111) allows camping in its forested sites and primitive camp. You can also camp on Little St. George Island with advance permission.

Sources & Resources

Making Waves (904-927-3511) is a self-proclaimed lifestyle magazine published on the island and filled monthly with chatty news, locally written fiction, and historical information on the Apalachicola area.

Outposts on the Gulf: Saint George Island and Apalachicola

(University of West Florida Press, 1986) by William Warren Rogerts covers the history of the island from early exploration to World War II.

 DOG ISLAND

QUICK TOUR

Catch the daily ferry out of Carrabelle at 11 A.M. It returns at noon. By foot is the mode of exploration, but only by day — there are no street lights. A single sand road meanders around the three-square-mile island, past about 100 private homes (most of them vacation getaways), deserted beach, pine forest, tall dunes, and bayside marshes. Three-quarters of the 7.5-mile-long island is devoted to a nature preserve.

BACKFLASH

A gruesome chapter of Florida history was written on Dog Island, and later became the subject of controversy and two books. The event took place in 1766 when the ship *Le Tigre* wrecked on a reef near the island. Fifteen survivors made it to Dog Island, where Native Americans were living. Of the 15, only three survived. The others died due to drowning, illness, or cannibalism. When one of the survivors related the tale in book form, fraught with untoward sexual activity, it shocked European readers. Recently verified, the facts were again revealed in *Shipwreck and Adventures of Monsieur Pierre Viaud* by Robin Fabel (University of West Florida Press, 1990).

During World War II, soldiers trained on Dog Island. At one time, someone tried to upgrade the island's image by fancifying the name to Isles de Chien, but it never took. It's just not a fancy kind of island.

THE NATURAL

Dog Island is home to 30 species of endangered wildlife,

including loggerhead turtles and certain birds. Between mangroved and duned shores, sand pines, live oaks, rosemary, reindeer moss, and sea lavender proliferate.

ISLAND ADVENTURE

Hiking

A 3.5-mile sand road hugs forests and dunes. Other trails delve into the little island's diverse terrain.

CULTURE

The People

Only 20 residents live on the island full-time.

ISLAND LANDINGS

Pelican Inn (Box 1351, Fairhope, AL 36532; 800-451-5294) is the one option for overnighters on Dog Island. It has eight beachside efficiencies blessed with no phones or televisions. Bring your own food.

CEDAR KEYS

R ecently, the seven-county area from Wakulla to Hernando, formerly loosely designated as The Big Bend (or, more unkindly, The Armpit), has followed the lead of other Florida coastal areas and adopted its own descriptive handle: The Nature Coast.

Islands are few along this crescent-shaped coastline. The shoreline is marshy and mangrove lined. A small island here and there has been turned into a recreational area, such as Fort Island off the coast of Crystal River and Pine Island near Brooksville.

The Cedar Keys group in Levy County is all that's worth considering for this book's purposes. It gains its importance from numbers and its role in sustaining wildlife. The main island, Way Key, is an island unlike any other in Florida. In many ways, it's an island in the truest sense of the word, regarding character and attitude.

Holding Cedar Key — one of the state's earliest communities — it has historic significance; bearing a heritage of artistic inspiration, it also has cultural importance. Lacking beaches and tourist hordes, it maintains a rural way of life uncommon to Gulf coast islands. The town and its first pencil factory originally resided on Depot Key, now called **Atsena Otie** (from the Creek Amerindian expression for Cedar Island). A lighthouse and military installations occupied Seahorse Key. Several other of the archipelago's islands make popular boating destinations, including **Snake Key**, once the site of a quarantine hospital. Seahorse and Snake, along with **Bird (Deadman's)** and **North Keys**, are part of Cedar Keys National Wildlife Refuge.

THE NITTY-GRITTY

Land Routes

The closest major airport is **Tampa International.** The quickest route to Cedar Key from there is Interstate 4 to Interstate 75 north. Highway 19 runs closer to the coast, but it gets very clogged between Clearwater and Port Richey. North of there, it's a great drive along old-Florida forested profiles. At times, only the "Watch For Bear" signs interrupt the forested landscape. Route 24 connects Cedar Key to both I-75 and Highway 19.

The **Gainesville Airport** is about 60 miles from the island, and hosts a couple of major airlines. Most people prefer to rent a car at the airport so they have transportation on and off the island. There are, however, charter plane and taxi services that will deliver you to Cedar Key.

On Cedar Key, a 2,300-foot lighted runway accepts small planes.

Water Routes

The Intracoastal Waterway ends north of Anclote Key (between Tarpon Springs and New Port Richey). Boaters must take to the Gulf from there. The Big Bend buoyage system outlines the coast about five to ten nautical miles offshore. The snaky channel to

Cedar Keys lies northeast of marker #2. Waters around the keys are extremely skinny in places, and require local knowledge and high tides to navigate.

Island Life

Cedar Key lies at about 29 degrees 8 minutes latitude and 83 degrees 2 minutes longitude. The average year-round temperature is 80 degrees.

No matter what the season, the pace of Cedar Key doesn't change by time of year so much as by time of week. Fluctuation comes on weekends, when tourists visit the island for a taste of its seafood restaurant specialties and a look around the galleries and shops.

 CEDAR KEYS

QUICK TOUR

The long, wilderness-fraught approach to Cedar Key on Route 24 foreshadows the island's end-of-the-world isolation. Along the causeway, you first begin to see a few homes on spits of land among the salt marshes, then an RV park and small motels, a couple of restaurants, and some old Cracker houses holding people or shops.

Route 24 turns into D Street. Finding your way around downtown is as easy as 1-2-3, A-B-C. East-west streets are numbered, north-south streets have letter names.

Norwood's Marina is on D Street around Fifth. Fourth Street holds some historic and architectural structures. The Cedar Key B&B sits on the corner of Third Street and F. Second Street is the heart of the historic district. To the left, you'll find a string of colonial-type commercial buildings. The Chamber of Commerce occupies the firehouse. To the right stands the Cedar Key Historical Society Museum; on the opposite side of the street are prettily restored historic homes.

Continuing south on D Street, you reach the Dock, where activity heightens. A row of plain-wood, weathered buildings lines the waterfront from which the fishing pier extends. Old and new, they hold restaurants, motels, shops and galleries. To the north lies the marina. So-called Dock Street (there are no signs that say it) loops into A Street and passes the City Park with its small beach. Modern development lies to the east. If you cut across First Street to G Street, you can enjoy the waterfront drive along Goose Cove and take in a few more historic structures on Sixth and Seventh Streets. At Sixth and F, an Indian shell mound sits next to the Lions Club.

The Island Hotel dates to the 1860s.
(Chelle Koster Walton)

From H and Ninth Streets, you can get to the so-called Hudson Hill residential part of the island. Just follow the State Museum signs, which lead you along Gulf Boulevard to Hodges Avenue and Whitman Drive. This area is the island's most wooded. Homes of all varieties dwell among the natural vegetation. So does the town cemetery. Back on Gulf Boulevard, continue on to Palmetto Drive, which delivers you to the airstrip, Easy Street, and Uneasy Street.

Three of the Cedar Key islands are nearby and invite explorers and beachers. Access is limited to the beach. The closest is Atsena

Otie, which held the original town of Cedar Key. Remnants of its early settlements remain. On Seahorse Key, a lighthouse on the county's highest point of elevation pokes through the trees, remembering a settlement once stationed there. Snake Key has a nice beach. It once held a quarantine hospital. On Seahorse and Snake Keys, access is limited to the beach.

BACKFLASH

On Cedar Keys, Florida history moves in reverse. Once a thriving fishing and commercial port where pencils were manufactured from its namesake cedar trees, these islands now boast seclusion from the state's quickening pulse.

They are an island getaway in the true sense of the expression. Like many transplanted islanders, they've turned away from commercial success. They tasted the fast-paced world of booming business during their youth; then, having had enough, they reverted to a quiet, artsy haven with a salty flavor.

Amerindians first discovered the island, scientists suspect, around the year 200. Some believe renegade William Augustus Bowles built a watchtower for his "State of Muskogee" on Seahorse Key in 1801. Homesteaders began settling Way Key and Atsena Otie (then known as Depot Key) and plundering the islands' cedar resources in the 1830s. Depot Key, the site of a military hospital and depot in the Seminole Wars, was designated as a customs station. After a hurricane decimated the island's military installations, Depot Key was bought and homesteaded by Augustus Steele, who later built the first commercial and residential development known as Cedar Key. In 1845 it officially became a town. In 1858, the name was changed to City of Atseena (later spelled Atsena) Otie.

In 1855, Seahorse Key, used as an Amerindian detention station during the Seminole Wars, got a lighthouse as a result of all the shipping traffic. Legends grow thick as palmettos on Seahorse Key. They involve pirates' treasure, a headless horseman, and a drowned lass who turned into a white mule.

In the days when a train station put a town on the map, Way

Key, site of today's Cedar Key, was connected to the East Coast by Florida's first railroad. In 1862, it lost its rail connection in the destruction of the Civil War. Seahorse Key's doused lighthouse was used as a military prison for captured Confederates. The town on Way Key was incorporated as Cedar Key in 1869 — one of Florida's earliest official towns. As a major port and quarantine station, it built a yellow fever hospital on nearby Snake Key in 1880. Atsena Otie flourished as a lumber and fishing port, and developed as a factory site for Eberhard Faber, maker of pencils. Eagle pencils were manufactured on Way Key. When forest supplies became depleted, residents turned to the sea as their main source of income. Later, when developer Henry Plant wanted to bring his railroad to the town and its port, citizens refused to sell him their dock. His move to Tampa's deep port — along with other disasters natural and economic — swamped Cedar Key's manufacturing economy, and the community returned to a quiet fishing-driven society. In 20 years, the population dropped from 2,000 to 700.

In 1929, President Herbert Hoover designated Snake, Bird (Deadman's), and North Keys as a refuge for colonizing birds. That designation has grown to encompass 12 islands, including Seahorse. Since 1952, The University of Florida has leased the lighthouse on Seahorse, relighted after the Civil War but deactivated in 1905, as a marine and environment research center.

In 1950, a hurricane and fire dealt sound thwacks to Cedar Key's waterfront. The town survived to become a haven for weekenders and artists from the Gainesville area. Eventually word got out nationwide about Cedar Key's simple charms. In recent years, tourism has surpassed fishing as the number-one industry. Some fishermen have turned to clam farming, an experimental venture that started only a few years ago and continues today.

Historical Attractions

With dioramas and displays, **The Cedar Key State Museum** (170 Museum Dr.; 904-543-5350) documents island bygones, from its earliest inhabitants through its various phases of war, lumbering,

fiber manufacturing, shipbuilding, and fishing. Outdoors, the home
of an early settler awaits restoration, and a trail leads to the waterfront. The smaller, homier **Cedar Key Historical Society Museum**
(Second St. & Route 24; 904-543-5549) takes up residence in a
circa-1870 building. Through artifacts, photos and newspaper clip-
pings, it tells the story of Cedar Key past, throughout its various eras
of turtling, sponging, fishing, and pencil making. Pottery shards and
fossilized prehistoric finds delve deeper into the region's heritage.

THE NATURAL

Cedar Keys are vegetated by upland plants such as cabbage
palm and live oak. Some oaks, like the one in the yard of Cedar Key
B&B, are 500 years old or more.

Seahorse Key was formed by the drift of sand over the centuries, and today boasts a 52-foot-high ridge behind the beach,
Florida's highest coastal elevation. The island is an important nesting ground for pelicans, egrets, ibises, herons, and ospreys. The
entire refuge averages around 50,000 nesting birds a year. The
brown pelican is the icon of the islands. People care for the birds like
pets. Snakes, including cottonmouths and diamondback rattlers, are
plentiful in the out-islands. Between Cedar Key and the mainland,
salt marshes provide habitat for birds and marine creatures. At night
on the causeway, white-tailed deer are often caught in headlights.

Natural Attractions

Cedar Keys National Wildlife Refuge (Refuge Manager, Rte.
1, Box 1193C, Chiefland, FL 32626; 904-493-0238) encompasses
12 islands, each measuring from one to 165 acres. They have limited access; you can land only on the beach. On Seahorse Key, there's
a major seabird rookery, known for its brown pelican nests, a sand
beach, and a defunct 1850s lighthouse. In bird-nesting season
(March 1 through June 30), you are not allowed to set foot on the
island. Local naturalist Harriet Smith conducts **Naturalist Boat
Trips** (904-543-5395) into the marshes and backwaters of the keys.
Tours last one or two hours.

AQUA-ADVENTURE

Touring

You can dock or launch your boat from **Cedar Key Public Marina**. Extended stays require advance notice. Exploring wildlife on the uninhabited keys is the favorite pastime of boat tourists, especially nearby Atsena Otie Key (a privately owned island) and Snake and Seahorse Keys, part of the national refuge. Access is limited to the beach only. Seahorse Key is closed to the public March 1 through June 30 for bird nesting. Island Hopper (Marine Basin; 904-543-5904) offers scenic cruises to Seahorse Key a couple of times a day, usually once at sunset.

Fishing

The fishing way of life reigns. You can cast from the City Dock or charter one of any number of local guides at the Marine Basin. **Capt. Martin Sommers** (904-543-6331) escorts you to deep-water fish aboard the Gondola.

Boating, Sailing & Canoeing

Island Hopper (Marine Basin, 904-543-5904) rents boats reasonably by the hour, half day or day.

For other boating needs, check with **Norwood's Marina** (Rte. 24; 904-543-6148).

ISLAND ADVENTURE

Hiking

There's little nature hiking on Cedar Key, aside from a short path that takes you from the State Museum to waterside. But walking is the favored mode of transportation in downtown Cedar Key. Everything is within easy walking distance and there's little vehicular traffic to compete for road space.

Biking

For the same reason, biking works as well as walking. Many motels provide bikes. You can also rent at **Bayside Cottages** (Route 24; 904-543-5141).

Shelling & Beachcombing

The waters around the keys are quite shallow. At low tide, you can walk the shoals in the Gulf and Goose Cove and find lots of living shells. Atsena Otie offers good shelling on its beaches. The **Cedar Key State Museum** (170 Museum Dr.; 904-543-5350) keeps one of the most complete shell collections around, donated by former Cedar Key settler St. Clair Whitman.

CULTURE

The People

The islander profile changes here above the beachy barrier chain. The people are less transient, more settled in and personable. On Cedar Key, they descend from generations of fishermen and spongers. Some of the newer residents are artists, writers, or creators of another sort. Many islanders work in the hospitality trade. Because of Cedar Keys' distance from the mainland, you have the rare situation where most island workers are also island residents.

In general, Cedar Keyites — they number around 1,000 — are friendly people with a rural sense of community, honesty, and trust. Once, after eating dinner in the local Cook's Café, I found I didn't have enough cash with me to cover the bill. The café doesn't take credit cards. I asked the waitress what I could leave her while I drove the couple of blocks to my cottage to get the cash from my suitcase. She said, "Nothing; I trust you."

Islanders all know each other and are, I'm told, accepting of newcomers in business. They help each other when disaster or misfortune hits.

The people are concerned about the environment, but in an old-fashioned, maternal way. For example, they name and feed the pelicans. One of the town characters is the self-appointed keeper of pelicans, who fixes up injured birds.

Island Inspirations

The natural, uncommon beauty of Cedar Key has inspired creativity since its earliest days. Naturalist John Muir, founder of the Sierra Club, ended his famous 1,000-mile walk from Louisville, Kentucky, at Cedar Key, and wrote "Today I reached the sea and many gems of tiny islets called keys." Later, he published *A Thousand-Mile Walk to the Gulf* in which he describes his stay on the island while recovering from malaria.

John D. MacDonald used a Cedar Keyite named Hub Lawless as the victim in his *The Empty Copper Sea*, a Travis McGee mystery. Contemporary folk singer **Jimmy Buffett**, a frequent visitor in the 1980s, sings about the hero and Cedar Key in his song "Incommunicado."

A number of artists make their home on Cedar Key. Most famous and talented was the late **Claude Croney**, whose impressionistic earth-tone watercolors and oils rely on local themes. Watercolorist **Irv Brobeck** winters on Cedar Key. Resident **Lola Roppel** renders mood-evoking landscapes and portraits. Look for the dramatic photography of **Kevin Hipe**, the fine wood carving of **Gerald Lindstrom**, and the bright, happy paintings of **Mike Segal** as quality mementos of the islands.

Fairs & Festivals

Seafood and art define the culture of Cedar Key. Both themes are celebrated with festivity: **The Seafood Festival** occurs in October and the renowned **Cedar Key Sidewalk Arts Festival** in April.

Museums & Galleries

Cedar Key artists and artisans have made a name for themselves, and there's nowhere I enjoy shopping more than in the galleries and boutiques that sell their wares. My favorite is **Ibis Gallery** (On the Dock; 904-543-5060), which also exhibits the work of other artists from around the nation. Everything is one of a kind, from the glittery raku pottery to recycled rebar wall sculptures. Mike Segal's work is featured here.

Suwannee Triangle Gallery (On the Dock; 904-543-5744) is another that carries top-quality art, pottery, glassware, and jewelry. In the historic district, **Cedar Keyhole** (Second St.; 904-543-5801) is a co-op-run gallery with quality paintings upstairs, crafts downstairs.

Island Shopping

Island Gallery (On the Dock; 904-543-5834) carries a wide variety of gifts, from mundane shell souvenirs to nicely handcrafted jewelry. **Cedar Key Bookstore** (Second Street & C Street; 904-543-9660) has a great selection of regional and Florida books. It also sells kids books and recycles used books.

Architecture

The Historical Society publishes a booklet you can buy for $2: "Historic Old Cedar Key: A Walking Tour." It includes a map and a list of pre-1900 and other significant buildings in Cedar Key's historic district. Many of the commercial buildings on Second Street are listed. They have a benchmark two-story style with an upstairs balcony. The **Island Hotel** is a prime example. Built in 1859, it has withstood hurricanes with its oak-supported, seashell tabby-mortar walls.

Island homes span styles from vernacular Cracker (look along First Street's waterfront) to stylish Victorian (my favorite lives on Second Street, catty-corner from the Historical Society Museum). The Cedar Key B&B is another example of a wonderfully restored 1880 home.

On the Dock, buildings emulate the fish-house look portrayed by the 1959 **Thomas Guest House** in the Gulf, characterized by a weathered, unfinished wood veneer. Many of the newer homes in Hudson Hill's residential area borrow the look.

Music

The **Gordon Brothers Band** performs modern country at local clubs. It recently released its first album, *Sibling Rivalry*. At the other extreme, the music of the artist community seems to be New Age. You hear it and find tapes and CDs of it in all of the galleries.

Nightlife

Pelican's Roost (On the Dock; 904-543-5428) and the **Seabreeze Lounge** (On the Dock; 904-543-5738) host live entertainment, typically country or contemporary bands.

The Thomas Guest house typifies old fish-house style of architecture.
(Chelle Koster Walton)

TABLE HOPPING

Cedar Key is known for its seafood: grouper, mullet, blue crabs, soft-shell crab, stone crab, shrimp, and oysters. In recent years, clams and oysters have been farmed. Clams especially have become synonymous with the island, displacing oysters as the reigning culinary symbol. A source for clams-to-travel (and recipes), however unlikely, is the **Cedar Key Bookstore** (Second Street & C Street; 904-543-9660).

There are several seafood outlets in town — or just be around when the fishermen pull up their catches at the causeway bridge.

Also emblematic is hearts of palm salad. More dessert than salad, this has nothing to do with the brined product you buy in cans. The cabbage palm hearts are unprocessed, crunchy, sometimes bitter. The classic Cedar Key salad combines a couple of slices with iceberg lettuce, canned peaches and pineapples, dates, and either a scoop of peanut butter-based ice cream or peanut butter dressing. The peanut-butter ice cream dressing was invented by Bessie Gibbs, owner and operator of the Island Hotel in the late 1940s. Her recipe, altered by several island restaurants and cooks through the years, is reprinted below.

Evidently, Cedar Key inspires cookery as much as it does the other arts. On the shelves of the local bookstore I found several locally compiled cookbooks, each done by different women's groups: *A Taste of Cedar Key*, *Cedar Keys to Good Cooking* (featuring seafood), *The Flavor of Cedar Key*, and *We Save Our Favorite Recipes*. The one I like best for its coverage of local classics is Verona Watson's *Cedar Key Cookin'*. She's got another one called *Cooking Up Memories of Cedar Key*.

The **Brown Pelican** (On the Dock; 904-543-5428) is a long-standing island restaurant that serves standard island fare with two views from its second-story perch — one of the street, the other of the water and dock.

Downtown restaurants are less touristy. **Cook's Café** is a local favorite. **Island Hotel** (Second St.; 904-543-5111) and **Island Room** (at Cedar Cove; 904-543-6520) serve gourmet seafood. The latter pops a Champagne Sunday brunch.

Bessie Gibbs's Hearts of Palm Ice Cream Dressing

2 cup softened vanilla ice cream
4 tablespoons peanut butter
1-2 drops green food coloring

Combine ingredients prior to serving. Pour over a salad of torn iceberg lettuce and sliced hearts of palm. Sprinkle with chopped dates, pineapple chunks, and candied ginger.

ISLAND LANDINGS

Cedar Key does not suffer from lack of accommodations. Most are simple and inexpensive, though the newer breed of condos and time shares is changing that. Many of the traditional properties are family-run operations patterned after the personality of the owners.

The Island Hotel (P.O. Box 460, Cedar Key, FL 32625; 904-543-5111) is a good example. Witness its pot-belly stove, mosquito netting, paddle fans, and cozy bar with its historic wall murals depicting Old Cedar Key. **Cedar Key B&B** (P.O. Box 700, Cedar

Key, FL 32625; 904-543-9000) feels more homey, with a sunny breakfast room, rocking chair porch, and charming rooms — each with its own bath. The owners provide wading boots for shellers and bikes for cyclists. I've always liked **Faraway Inn** (P.O. Box 370, Third & G Streets, Cedar Key, FL 32625; 904-543-5330) because its unpretentious little cottages overlook the bay and sunset. The owners thoughtfully provide bikes, and porch swings face the sunset.

Many places accommodate boaters, including **Dockside Motel** (P.O. Box 55, Cedar Key, FL 32625; 904-543-5432) and the upscale **Cedar Cove Beach & Yacht Club** (P.O. Box 837, Cedar Key, FL 32625; 800-366-5312 or 904-543-5332).

TOURIST TRAPS

Fishermen and artists at heart, Cedar Keyites sometimes just aren't good at this tourism thing. Most often, the slowness of pace and the unsophistication of some restaurants and accommodations are endearing. Other times they can be bothersome. I was irked by treatment at Captain's Table (or should I say lack of treatment; I felt invisible) and by the town's habit of charging you for the flimsiest piece of information, such as a map of the town, the walking tour booklet, and a pamphlet that carried mostly advertising. It shows a "tourists will buy anything" mentality. Go to the Chamber and get comparable stuff for free, or least quality stuff for a price.

SOURCES AND RESOURCES

The Cedar Key Beacon (P.O. Box 532, Cedar Key, FL 32625; 904-543-5701) is a reliable weekly source of island news with entertaining columns and views from locals.

Cedar Key Chamber of Commerce (P.O. Box 610, Cedar Key, FL 32625; 904-543-5600). Visit Russel Brami, the executive director and a friendly, knowledgeable fellow. His office is on Second Street in the Fire Department building.

Florida's Nature Coast Salt Water Boating & Fishing Atlas by Free Lance Publications, $6.95, includes history and sights of the area. Several books record the island's history, folklore, and natural beauty, including *Cedar Key Legends* by Sally Tilestone and Dottie Comfort; *Of Chiefs and Generals: A History of the Cedar Keys to the End of the Second Seminole War* by local historian Charles C. Fishburne, Jr.; and *The Naturalist's Guide to Cedar Key, Florida* by Harriet Smith. Many of these are published in tract format, typeset by typewriter, and are available at the Historical Society Museum.

ISLAND PROFILE: QUITMAN HODGES

Whenever there's a question on a point of history in Cedar Key, Quitman Hodges has the last word.

A third-generation islander born on the island in 1915, he realizes his expertise by birth. Having fished in Cedar Key waters for 25 years, and served as city commissioner for 35 and mayor for ten, he has refined his birthright knowledge with hands-on experience.

Quitman's mother, who was also born on Cedar Key, worked in the Eagle pencil factory. His dad fished and "done a little of everything." During Quitman's 80 years, he lived off the island only five, when serving his country in Jacksonville for five years. Even then he managed to steal home at least once a month.

Quitman remembers when the railroad still ran to the island, and few cars were to be seen. "The biggest change I've seen on the island is from industrial to tourist," said the commissioner from his daily post at City Hall on Second Street. There he "hangs out and talks to people," holding court from his motorized cart, which wears the bumpersticker "Cedar Key. My City — I'm Part of It — I'm Proud of It."

Tourism take-over occurred gradually, as cedar lumber supplies dwindled and fishing was unseated as the number-one industry. Retired people would come and fall in love with the island and decide to move here. In the 1970s, Hudson's Hill began developing as a residential area. "I've seen it where there was only one house there past the school," said Quitman.

Retirees who settled on the island launched Cedar Key's reputation as a cure for sinus problems. "One old man came here, he was from Ohio or somewhere. The reason he fell in love with it was when he come across the bridge he had a bad case of sinus. When he came across the bridge it cleared up." Quitman tells stories of other newcomers like the Ohio man who claimed their sinus afflictions magically disappeared upon crossing the bridge to Cedar Key. "But there are a lot of people who live here still have sinus," he said with a shrug.

Other drastic changes to the island have come overnight — the hurricanes and storms Quitman and Cedar Key have survived together. He most vividly remembers Hurricane Easy of 1950.

"That was the worst storm. It came right in from out in the Gulf; there weren't no tide. It blowed for about six hours and then the eye came right over Cedar Key and stayed for two hours and 45 minutes. The sun came out and it was just about as calm as it is now. Then the winds came back and blowed at 185 miles per hour for another six hours. Every house in town was damaged to a certain extent.

"Now that storm of March, 1993, there was no wind but the tide came up to the porch here. You could run a boat down the street."

Quitman accepts all the change with a shrug and a "it's just one of those things." He said the city commission has tried to make laws to protect the island against rampant growth. "We've got some of them [laws]," he said, "but I don't know whether they work or not."

The one change that does get his blood pressure a'rising is the recent ban on net fishing. As a former mullet fisherman (he's been confined to a wheelchair since 1972), Quitman knows what effect the law will have on the island's commercial fishermen. He fears Cedar Key will lose that important segment of its population.

"It ain't gonna just hurt the island, it's gonna hurt the state of Florida," he opined with passion.

PINELLAS COAST

Spaniards named it first as they breached the shores of forested Mullet Key. They called it Punta Pinal, or point of pines. Later, tourism promoters christened it Holiday Isles. The fun-loving sobriquet stuck until recent years, when the image was modernized to Pinellas Suncoast, a name that reflects its near-constant state of solar warming.

The 28-mile-long beachfront of Pinellas County's barrier islands is known most readily for its highly developed resorts, which front the densely metropolitan area of St. Petersburg and Clearwater on their peninsula across the bay from big-city Tampa. For the most part, these islands deserve their commercialized image as a frivolous, borderline-tacky playground for snowbirds on the thaw. More than 3.8 million visitors each year make Pinellas County Florida West

Coast's most popular destination. The greatest percentage come from the Midwest, Europe, and Canada. From the southern tip of St. Pete Beach to the northern reaches of Clearwater Beach, high-rise condominiums rub shoulders with surf shops, 60s-era motels, and good-time bars along an apron of sifted-fine sand strewn with cabanas, volleyball nets, and beach rentals. At either end of this continuum of high-energy beaching, islands less spoiled remind visitors of how it was here before the concrete layers were applied.

The islands are close enough to the mainland to diffuse some of the traffic. This close proximity, however, subtracts the strong "island identity" maintained by other Gulf Coast islands for which distance and attitude separate them.

Anclote Key, a state wildlife preserve, marks the beginning of a chain of barrier islands that ends nearly 180 miles later at Cape Romano in Ten Thousand Islands.

Honeymoon and Caladesi Islands begin the squirm of islands as they head south. They announce the start of the chain with a whisper and an echo, an echo of days when birds and turtles outnumbered humans in these parts. Offshore the Scotch-spiked town of Dunedin, Honeymoon is anchored to the mainland. Caladesi, separated by hurricane force, requires a water crossing to visit. Both are maintained and operated by the state.

Below Caladesi, and practically connected to it at low tide, **Clearwater Beach** occupies its own island and part of another. As the transition between natural Caladesi and materialistic Sand Key, it holds a somewhat aloof stance slightly apart and above the crazed development that transformed its neighbors.

Sand Key's north end begins with pristine loveliness at a green county park, which immediately segues into high-rise resorts and condos. From Clearwater Beach, a litany of eye-blink communities line the emaciated island, some a little more prudish about development than others. Largest and loaded with the most character are Indian Rocks Beach and Madeira Beach. Down the length of the island and its diverse towns, you drive past cottages with lots of beach character, chain hotels with none, old-time fish houses, surf-wear supermarkets, paved beach parking lots, new upscale homes, rickety fishing piers, and marina shopping villages.

Next comes **Treasure Island,** a throwback to Pinellas's earliest days of tourism, with its neon-signed, funky resorts and mom-pop motels. Its Sunset Beach community holds on to island soul, tucked safely away from resort anonymity.

St. Pete Beach (recently officially shortened from its original name, St. Petersburg Beach) occupies **Long Key,** the most citified of the island group. Though it has its hold-backs against modernization, incorporated St. Pete Beach is more updated than Treasure Island. Blocks of residential area break the mold of resort-after-resort-after-resort monotony. At its southern end, the historic Don CeSar Resort acts like a bookmarker in the key's history book. Past it, the village of Pass-A-Grille feels like a fishing community of yore — laid-back and neighborly. Off its southern point, **Shell Key** makes a tossed-offshore destination favored by shellers and boaters.

The last group of islands settle into their own tempo, little affected by time and development. To get to the keys of Fort DeSoto County Park, you must first cross **Tierra Verde** on the beachless islands of Pine, Little Bird, and Pardee Keys, which have developed as a residential community with a marine heading.

Fort DeSoto's Keys seem like a different land compared to the beach scene of the upper islands. In this sanctuary — for birds and humans alike — camping, fishing, and exploring nature and the military history of Pinellas County are the favorite pastimes. Same goes for **Egmont Key,** a free-floater across the bay from Mullet Key, Fort DeSoto's main island. A favorite among weekend boaters, it grasps its past at the sites of a historic lighthouse and Spanish-American War fort ruins.

Terra Ceia probes deeper into Pinellas pasttimes with its Tocobago Amerindian mound centerpiece. The village that surrounds it is mired in its own timewarp, circa turn of the century.

From the Fort de Soto Pier, Egmont Key skyline.
(Chelle Koster Walton)

THE NITTY-GRITTY

Land Routes

Two international airports serve the Tampa Bay area, one in Tampa, the other in Clearwater. **Tampa International** (813-396-3690) receives more flights than **St. Petersburg/Clearwater International** (813-535-7600), which is principally for charters.

BATS: City Transportation System (813-367-3086) operates buses throughout St. Pete Beach.

Interstate 275, which feeds into Interstate 75 from the north and south, and Interstate 4 from the east (from Orlando), is the major thoroughfare of the St. Petersburg-Clearwater area. Highway 19 runs north-south on the east side of the Pinellas County Peninsula. Closer to the islands, Alternate Hwy. 19 takes you along the county's northern shores.

ANCLOTE KEY: You must take a boat to get to this state preserve island. There's no regular service. One company makes daily trips in summer. Check with charter or rental companies in the Tarpon Springs area for transportation. To get to Tarpon Springs' commercial/waterfront area, take Dodecanese Boulevard off Alternate Highway 19. From Highway 19, go west on Route 582, then north on Alternate 19 to Dodecanese Boulevard.

HONEYMOON ISLAND: From Alternate Highway 19, go west on Causeway Boulevard (Route 586). From Highway 19, follow Curlew Road (Route 712) west until it merges with Route 712.

CALADESI ISLAND: Caladesi Island is accessible by boat from Honeymoon Island, on Route 586 (Causeway Boulevard), or from downtown Clearwater, on Alternate Highway 19, at the Drew Street Dock. The ferry from Honeymoon Island (813-734-5263) departs hourly weekdays, semihourly weekends, and costs $4 for adults, $2.50 for children. Stays on the island are limited to four hours. From downtown Clearwater (813-442-7433), it costs $4.95 for adults and $3 for children.

CLEARWATER BEACH: From Alternate Highway 19 (Fort Harrison Avenue), head west on Memorial Causeway at the end of Cleveland Street (Route 60). Off Highway 19, Route 60 is called Gulf to Bay Boulevard.

Clearwater Yellow Cab (813-799-2222) provides transportation to and from the Tampa and St. Petersburg/Clearwater airports. **The Jolley Trolley** (813-445-1200) wheels around Clearwater Beach and to Clearwater downtown. Tours begin and end at the Clearwater Beach Memorial Civic Center, with pickups every 30 minutes.

SAND KEY: Clearwater Beach's Gulfview Boulevard crosses between Clearwater Beach and Sand Key. There's a 75-cent toll each way. Observe the enforced 25-mile speed limit on the bridge. On Sand Key, the road's name changes to Gulf Boulevard (Route 699). Four bridges cross from Sand Key to Highway 19. They are located (from north to south) in Belleair Shores at West Bay Drive (Route 686), in Indian Rocks Beach at Walsingham/Ulmerton Road (Route 688), in Indian Shores at Park Boulevard (Route 694), and in Madeira Beach at 150th Avenue, which intersects with Seminole

Catch of the day: sheepshead.
(Clearwater Area Convention & Visitors Bureau.)

Boulevard (Route 595) and Alternate Highway 19 on the mainland.

TREASURE ISLAND: Gulf Boulevard (Route 699) crosses John's Pass from Madeira Beach to Treasure Island. Central Avenue connects Highway 19 to Treasure Island at the Treasure Island Causeway on 107th Avenue.

LONG KEY: Cross Blind Pass from Treasure Island via Gulf Boulevard, which becomes Blind Pass Boulevard on Long Key. From Highway 19, take First Avenue South west to Pasadena Avenue and the St. Pete Beach Causeway; or take Pinellas County Bayway (50-cent toll) to the island's south end.

SHELL KEY: A shuttle boat between **Merry Pier** (801 Pass-A-Grille Way, Pass-A-Grille, 813-360-1348) and Shell Key makes three to four trips daily.

TIERRA VERDE: From Gulf Boulevard (Route 699) on St. Pete Beach, go east on Pinellas County Bayway (Route 682) (50-cent toll) and south on Pinellas Bayway (Route 679).

FORT DESOTO KEYS: Take Pinellas Bayway (Route 679) south through Tierra Verde to the entrance gate (35-cent entrance fee) to Fort DeSoto County Park.

EGMONT KEY: Charters out of St. Pete Beach make trips to the island.

TERRA CEIA: Heading south on Interstate 275 (Sunshine Skyway) off of Pinellas County Bayway (Route 682), take exit 2 to Highway 19 south after the toll booth. Follow the signs directing you west to Terra Ceia.

Island Life

This parade of islands begins around 27 degrees 30 minutes and ends at 28 degrees 20 minutes.

In the 1960s, St. Petersburg scored in the *Guinness Book of World Records* with the longest run of consecutive sunny days — 768 in all.

Water temperatures hit a low of 63 degrees around January, and peak out at 86 in August. Air temperatures range from 70 to 90 degrees throughout the year. For local weather forecasts, call 813-898-0019, ext. 4101.

Pinellas County's high season comes a bit later than it does for those islands to the south. Although it sees an early arrival of snowbirds around late October, the tourism action doesn't really kick in until spring break and Easter give families time to travel.

Despite its multidigited visitor figures, the islands of Pinellas seem less crowded in season than the smaller, less developed ones to the south. Perhaps this is because there's more beach to go around, or because the infrastructure has been better planned, reducing the traffic jams and restaurant lines.

You'll hear a lot about the green flash in these parts. It's a rare occurrence that involves all sorts of physics terms beyond my grasp. But6 it has something to do with the way the sun's light is refracted by ice crystals when it's setting. This causes a split-second explosion of green light on the horizon that you'll miss if you blink.

Skeptics may tell you that green flashes are merely a good excuse to sit on the beach at sunset, perhaps with a celebratory glass of champagne or rum punch. The drinking part of the sunset ritual, they further theorize, may be more responsible for green flash sightings than reality. That, and the staring blinkless into the sun. They, of course, have never seen a green flash. Few do. It requires a cloudless evening sky, tropic climes, patience and persistence. Binoculars or a small telescope can help, too.

Even if you never see one, you certainly can't regret the time you've spent trying in sunset's golden afterglow.

Sources & Resources

St. Petersburg/Clearwater Convention & Visitors Bureau, Florida Suncoast Dome, One Stadium Dr., Suite A, St. Petersburg, FL 33705-1706; 813-892-7892.

June Hurley Young's *Florida's Pinellas Peninsula* (Byron Kennedy Publishers, 1984) gives a historic overview of the islands and mainland with photos and text.

 ANCLOTE KEY

QUICK TOUR

A four-mile island of sand and tall pines three miles west of Tarpon Springs, Anclote Key is accessible only by boat and has no facilities. It comprises more than 180 acres. There's a lighthouse on the south end, which a local group is trying to restore. Campers can pitch a tent at the camping area, which is equipped with grills, tables, and pit toilets, but no drinking water. There are no formal trails on the island and visitors are cautioned to avoid damaging native vegetation.

BACKFLASH

Anclote Key got its name from the Spanish word for anchor or fair harbor. Legend places pirate Louis de Aury and his buried treasure on the island in the early days of European exploration.

In 1886, President Grover Cleveland commissioned the building of 101-foot Anclote Lighthouse fueled by kerosene. It was completed the next year and operated to guide local spongers from the nearby Greek community of Tarpon Springs, as well as other boaters, until 1933. Two families tended the lighthouse, and in the late 1890s they were appropriated a small cannon to protect themselves during the Spanish-American War.

Historical Attractions

Anclote Lighthouse, a kerosene lamp beacon, is a historic landmark in need of restoration. For information on contributing to the cause, write to Re-Light the Light, P.O. Box 188, Tarpon Springs, FL 34688-0188.

THE NATURAL

Anclote Key began forming about a thousand years ago from a limestone foundation, and continues to do so. Since 1957, the key's area has increased by 30 percent.

Rare bird sightings have been made on the key, including the red-cockaded woodpecker, bald eagle, and piping plover. Loggerhead sea turtles come in the summer.

Natural Attractions

Anclote Key State Preserve encompasses the entire island and its six types of habitat: marine sands, beach dune, maritime hammock, mesic flatwoods, tidal marsh and swamp. The four miles of sandy beach and shallow waters make the island a cherished stop for seclusion beachers.

AQUA-ADVENTURE

Touring

There is anchorage on Anclote's leeside, near Dutchman Key. Waters are shoal on all sides closer to shore.

Island Wind Tours (600 Dodecanese Blvd., Tarpon Springs; 813-934-0606) makes half-day trips to the island in summer. For private charter, try Karen Anne Yacht Tours (Tarpon Springs City Marina Tarpon Springs; 813-789-4361).

ISLAND ADVENTURE

Hiking

Jungle hiking, with no formal paths, is all that is available.

ISLAND LANDINGS

Primitive campers can tent on the key.

Sources & Resources

Anclote Key State Preserve, c/o Gulf Islands Geopark, #1 Causeway Blvd., Dunedin, FL 34698; 813-469-5942. **Tarpon Springs Chamber of Commerce**, 210 S. Pinellas Ave., Suite 120, Tarpon Springs, FL 34689-3697; 813-937-6109.

HONEYMOON & CALADESI ISLANDS

QUICK TOUR

At the entrance to Honeymoon Island State Recreation Area, you first see a housing development — an unfortunate eyesore that interrupts the otherwise unscathed skyline around these pristine beaches. After the entrance to the park ($3.25 fee) you drive past lonely spans of natural vegetation to the picnic-hiking area. Follow the one-way roads to the various parking lots for recreational areas. At the fourth and southernmost, Cafe Honeymoon sells snacks and beach supplies. This is the closest thing to a swimming beach, along a short stretch limited by currents and boat traffic.

A 15-minute ferry ride from Honeymoon's bay side takes you to Caladesi Island, one of Florida's loveliest possessions. You approach Caladesi Island on the bay side at a mangrove swamp habitat for birds. At the marina landing, you'll see picnic shelters, the park ranger's office, a food and beach supply concession, and restrooms. Behind these nature-compatible buildings, the boardwalk to the beach begins. Follow it past the playground-picnic area and nature trailhead over the dunes to the incredibly soft, plush sands of this beach gem. The beach stretches long in either direction (three miles in all), inviting solitary strolls. To learn about the island's natural makeup, return to the trailhead and follow the signs. The interior consists of a ridge thick with virgin pine and live oak.

BACKFLASH

Excavations in the 1900s unearthed proof of Amerindian presence during the pre-Spanish era on Caladesi, Honeymoon, and surrounding islands. Other artifacts proved Spanish explorers were here, followed by seafarers and fishermen. The only habitation structure was a homestead built by a University of Zurich biologist named Henry Scharrer in the late 1800s.

Honeymoon Island was originally called Sand Island, and later Hog Island, presumably for its animal population, since one historical account relates that in a 1918 hurricane, 300 hogs lost their lives (as did, tragically, three picnicking children).

In 1921, a hurricane separated Caladesi from Honeymoon Island, forming Hurricane Pass. Rum-runners allegedly used both islands as their hideaways. Honeymoon Island got its name change in the early 1940s, when it was promoted nationwide via television and *Life* magazine ads promising subtropical getaways for newlyweds. Developers built 50 thatched huts to lure romantics, which they did until World War II stole away the husbands. Subsequent developers envisioned mega-resorts, and a causeway went up in 1964. Luckily, before too much building took place, Florida woke up to the importance of barrier islands and took over Honeymoon.

It purchased Caladesi Island for a state park in 1968 for $2.9 million and opened it to the public in 1972. In 1985, another hurricane altered Caladesi geography by slicing two smaller islands from the main island.

THE NATURAL

Geologists believe Honeymoon Island to be a youngster on the calendar of earth years, perhaps only 7,000 years old. Six-hundred-acre Caladesi Island formed in 1921 when a storm created Hurricane Pass, separating the land from nearby Honeymoon Island. Another storm broke it into three pieces in 1985, and weather continually changes the geography of both Caladesi and Honeymoon islands. Caladesi Island State Park also encompasses five smaller islands — including Malone, Core, and Moonshine, given mostly to mangrove forests — for a total of 650 upland acres and more than 1,100 acres of mangroves and grass flats.

Honeymoon Island is known for its stands of virgin slash pines and their resident ospreys. Birds of all sorts make the park a popular spot for the binocular set. In the forests they find owls; along the marshes there are waterfowl; at the beach, shorebirds nest.

Cabbage palms fringe the beaches behind sea grapes, sea oats, sand other saltwater-tolerant species. The island grows more than 200 species of plants in all.

On the beach at Caladesi, and along its flank of dunes, seabirds, gopher tortoises, and an occasional rattlesnake nest. Its rarer flying species include the great blue heron, snowy egret, and double-crested cormorant. You'll also find raccoon, armadillo, and marsh rabbit tracks along sandy paths. A test burning program produces charred vegetation in an attempt to subvert out-of-control fires caused by lightning. Burning is an integral part of the natural process, and wildlife here not only adapt to it, but even require it for healthy survival.

On its bay side, Caladesi hosts a variety of birds in its mangrove forest. On its hammocks, twin pine grows. This is the northernmost point for many native tropical plants.

Natural Attractions

Osprey Trail begins at Honeymoon Island's picnic area mid-island and delves into mangrove swamps and forests of virgin slash pine, favored habitat for ospreys and owls. It connects with **Pelican Trail**, which skirts sea marsh, tidal pools, and coastal strand. Together, the trails cover 80 acres of prime birding territory.

In **Caladesi Island State Park**, the 3-mile trail ascends from beach scrub ecology to upland hammock pine growth. A self-guiding brochure is available.

AQUA-ADVENTURE

Touring

On Caladesi Island, a sheltered 99-slip marina lies directly cross-island from the beach. A limited number of boaters can dock overnight at the marina on a first-come basis, if they register before sundown.

Fishing

Fishermen prefer casting from Honeymoon causeway bridges.

Boating, Sailing & Canoeing

There are sailboats to rent from a concession on Causeway Boulevard.

ISLAND ADVENTURE

Hiking

Honeymoon Island's nature trails are easy and require a bit more than an hour to cover. On Caladesi Island, you can hike for an hour or so along a winding, serpentine path through scrub and sand in an environment that has seen little human habitation since prehistoric Amerindians. The trail is only three miles long, but don't be fooled. Paved with soft sand, it takes longer than you'd think, and can be hard on leg muscles. Wear supportive shoes.

Biking

Honeymoon Island's one-way roads give cyclists an easy, non-competitive route. Parking lots have bike racks.

Shelling & Beachcombing

On Caladesi, shellers find good specimens at low tide, but are forbidden to collect live shells. The same applies to Honeymoon Island. At its first parking lot area, a shell-cleaning station is provided.

CULTURE

Island Inspirations

The daughter of Caladesi's only homesteader wrote a book about her family's difficult, pioneering way of life: *Yesteryear I Lived in Paradise* by Myrtle Scharrer Betz. It is available locally in Dunedin shops and the library.

Architecture

The state has kept building compatible with nature in both parks. Honeymoon Island's is quite stylish, emulating New England–Florida style with rooftop cupolas and earth tones.

TABLE HOPPING

A concession stand sells sandwiches, snacks, and beverages on both islands. You can bring your own food and beverages, but no liquor, and use the picnic pavilions.

Sources & Resources

Caladesi Island State Park, #1 Causeway Blvd., Dunedin, FL 34698; 813-469-5918. **Honeymoon Island State Recreation Area,** c/o Gulf Islands Geopark, #1 Causeway Blvd., Dunedin, FL 34698; 813-469-5942.

CLEARWATER BEACH

QUICK TOUR

As you cross prettily landscaped Memorial Causeway (Route 60) from Clearwater to Clearwater Beach, Island Estates development lies to the north. Enter it via Island Way and turn left on Windward Passage to get to the Clearwater Marine Science Center.

Backtrack to the causeway. As you enter Clearwater Beach, you'll see a marina and shopping arcade on the left and a parking lot across the street on the right. The Clearwater Beach Chamber of Commerce is in the building across from the parking lot on Poinsettia Street. So is the Civic Center and library.

Turn right off Causeway Boulevard onto Mandalay Avenue to head north. This takes you into the island's quietest sections after passing the shopping district and a few resorts. Turn left on Rockaway Street to get to public beach parking. Return to Mandalay via Bay Esplanade. Mandalay continues into residential sections, with public beach accesses and small lodging properties down side roads to the west along El Dorado Avenue. Head back south on Mandalay, which turns into Coronado Drive (Route 255), with more shops and restaurants. A block to the east is Hamden Drive, which takes you into the motel district. To the west is Gulfview Boulevard along the main beaches and fishing pier. Gulfview and Coronado eventually merge (Route 245). Commercially developed Bayway Boulevard loops off and joins Gulfview just as it crosses the toll bridge to Sand Key.

BACKFLASH

The local Amerindians were the first to call the area Clear Water. Their word for it was Pocotopaug. Early settlers adopted the name for the intracoastal harbor, and later for the mainland settlement.

One of the island's first settlers was Prudence Chafer. She homesteaded six acres on the island's south end and developed a fish ranch. In 1896, Ernest Tate purchased the entire 200-acre island for

$250 and called it Tate Island. A few years later, he sold it for $450.

In 1916, a wooden bridge was built from mainland Clearwater to its barrier island. A sturdier model, the Memorial Causeway, replaced it in 1926.

Dunedin pioneer L. B. Skinner first developed the island, naming his subdivision Mandalay, in admiration of Rudyard Kipling's poem. Mandalay Road, the island's main thoroughfare, was still paved with sand in 1920. An extravagant beach pavilion was built in 1921, but then destroyed in the 1930s. In 1924, the community's name officially changed to Clearwater Beach. Building of the St. Petersburg/Clearwater airport began a new phase of tourism for the area beginning in the mid-'40s.

THE NATURAL

Clearwater Beach is not known for its teeming wildlife, save the pelicans and shorebirds on the beach.

Natural Attractions

The **Clearwater Marine Science Center Aquarium Museum** (249 Windward Passage, Clearwater Beach, 813-441-1790), located on the residential isle of Island Estates, conducts research. It also rescues and exhibits marine mammals and sea turtles. A touch tank, aquariums and other tanks hold local and exotic sea life, including mangroves, lionfish, seahorses, baby sharks, dolphins, Kemp's ridley sea turtles, and a 320-pound loggerhead named Mo.

AQUA-ADVENTURE

Touring

Clearwater Beach is a launching point for any number of day boating trips: especially to Caladesi Island, Tarpon Springs' Sponge Docks, and Sarasota. A popular excursion is dolphin-encounter cruises.

The **Clearwater Ferry Service** (Drew St. Dock, Clearwater; 813-442-7433) picks up at Sea Stone Resort, the north beach Recreation Center, and the City Beach Marina for trips to the mainland, Caladesi Island, and Tarpon Springs.

Most charter and marina activity occurs at the Clearwater Beach Marina (25 Causeway Blvd.). **The Show Queen** (813-461-3113) hosts narrated luncheon trips and dinner sunset cruises aboard a three-deck riverboat. Captain Memo's Pirate Cruise (813-446-2587) is a party excursion with a swashbuckling theme. It sets sail four times daily, including at sunset, and includes complimentary beer, wine, and beverages. Southern Romance (813-446-5503) does two-hour sailing trips four times daily.

Fishing

Pier 60 (Causeway Blvd. and Gulfview Blvd., 813-462-6466) has been recently renovated, with all the shops and facilities fisherfolk look for. There's a fee for fishing and one for walking beyond a certain point.

Snorkeling/Scuba

Rock ledges, drowned sinkholes, artificial reefs, and submerged vessels provide variety in local waters, where visibility can reach 60 feet. Most sites are well offshore. Near Clearwater, the Clearwater Reef is one of the area's largest and most popular artificial reef sites. Dunedin Reef and a steamer wreck provide other underwater opportunities in 20 to 30 feet of water.

Boating, Sailing & Canoeing

You can rent powerboats and sailboats from **Boating Zone** (Clearwater Beach Marina, 25 Causeway Blvd.; 813-446-5503).

ISLAND ADVENTURE

Biking

Biking around the south end commercial section can be dangerous. Stick to the north end. **Transportation Station** (645 Bayway Blvd.; 813-443-3188) has a full complement of bikes and equipment, from racers to tandems and child trailers.

Shelling & Beachcombing

The island's beaches are wide and carpeted with soft, thick sand. You may find a few shells at the waterline in low tide.

Tennis

If you're a tennis enthusiast, look for a resort with courts. There are facilities on the island, but you're required to purchase a temporary I.D. card for a minimum of three months, which is fairly costly if you're there for a short visit.

Other

Clearwater Beach is becoming known for its volleyball action, with permanent nets along the public beach and a forthcoming Pro **Beach Volleyball Hall of Fame** (40 Causeway Blvd.; 813-461-0011). In April, the island hosts the **Pro Beach Volleyball Hall of Fame Challenge** and the **Jose Cuervo Pro Volleyball Tournament**.

CULTURE

The People

Clearwater Beach is not an easy place to get to know islanders. For one thing, the island is often lumped in the same physical address as the mainland, so no strong island personality emerges. For another, I get the feeling most islanders work off island and most island workers live off-island.

Fairs & Festivals

October Jazz is the big happening of the year on Clearwater Beach. It's the largest free jazz festival in the southeastern U.S.

Island Shopping

The quality of shop merchandise improves as you head north on Mandalay Avenue. A shopping center called **Pelican Walk** (483 Mandalay Ave.) holds some interesting shops, and across the street there's more. Try **Hurricane Rita** (483 Mandalay Ave.; 813-441-2676) and **Wish You Were Here** (483 Mandalay Ave.; 813-449-8220) for tropical-themed gifts, objets d'art, and things for the home.

Music

Recently, the city initiated a Key West-type scene at sunset time on the Pier, with local musicians and performers. Called Sunset Buskerfest, it begins two hours before sunset.

Nightlife

Frenchy's Rockaway Grill & Bar (7 Rockaway St., 813-446-4844) on the beach hosts live musicians after sunset. **The Beach Bar** (454 Mandalay Ave.; 813-446-8866) features live contemporary music.

TABLE HOPPING

Compared to restaurants in Tampa and on islands to the south, Pinellas County restaurants stand out for their reasonable prices and their just-caught seafood.

Seafood & Sunsets at Julie's (351 S. Gulfview Blvd.; 813-441-2548) is, as its name advertises, a great place to watch sunset and eat seafood in a Key West sort of atmosphere. **Frenchy's Rockaway Grill** (7 Rockaway St., 813-446-4844) is a fun, islandy kind of place with colorfully painted fish-motif tables; seafood grilled, blackened, and jerk; and live music. Go for sunset on the beach.

ISLAND LANDINGS

Clearwater Beach, like its peers to the south, has no shortage of accommodations, both in numbers and types. All you have to do is decide whether you want bayside or gulfside, skyscraper or intimate, complete or barebones.

For an inexpensive option, **Clearwater Beach International Hostel** (at the Sands Motel, 606 Bay Esplanade Ave., Clearwater Beach, FL 34630; 813-443-1211) accepts hostel members and non-members with shared accommodations and adjoining bathrooms, kitchen and laundry facilities, linen rentals, free bike and canoe use, and games. There's no curfew. Private rooms are available.

Sea Stone Resort (445 Hamden Dr., Clearwater Beach, FL 34630, 813-441-1722) is a great place to pull up your boat and spend the night. Or your car, for that matter. From the street it appears, as do most of Pinellas's accommodations, packed in between more of its kind. But with a room or suite overlooking the marina and Intracoastal, you feel quite sheltered from bustledom.

Haddon House Inn (14 Idlewild St., Clearwater Beach, FL

34630-1556; 813-461-2914) has one- and two-bedroom apartments in a charming two-story house within crawling distance to the beach. Look for the bright toucan on the front.

TOURIST TRAPS

As is the case throughout the beaches of Pinellas County, the shops are the biggest traps of Clearwater Beach. Not that they're particularly overpriced, they're just, for a large part, selling junk.

Sources & Resources

Clearwater Beach Chamber of Commerce, 40 Causeway Blvd., Clearwater Beach, FL 34630; 813-461-0011.

A good source for what's happening culturally in the Clearwater area is *Event Magazine* (647 Cleveland St., Clearwater, FL 34615; 813-443-1500). For history on the area, check out *Yesterday's Clearwater* by Hampton Dunn (Seemann Publishing, 1973).

 SAND KEY

QUICK TOUR

The 12-mile-long curve of island suffers schizophrenia. With a new town every mile or so, it takes mood swings so severe the island is impossible to characterize, except to say that, like its fellow chain-gangsters, it is packed to the brim with structures.

The one exception lies at the island's northern welcome mat. A green mat it is, known as Sand Key Park. This 65-acre oasis amida forest of high-rises is the island's saving grace. It starts out, at its entrance, so very green and clean. The twisty, well-marked road takes you past picnic pavilions and playgrounds to the golden sands at its end. All is meticulously maintained. The beach is beautifully wide, with white sand and perfect swimming conditions.

South from there, the concrete jungle reaches its climax before mellowing out in the 2-mile-long community of Belleair Beach, where architecturally interesting condo developments give way to walled mansions. At 2.5-mile-long Belleair Shores, a causeway crosses to the mainland.

Down the road intervenes the true-to-island little town of Indian Rocks Beach, 3 miles long. Here, old-island personality takes over with a community that feels real and lived-in. Grocery stores and mini-marts are called by people's, not chain, names.

If you turn left on 16th Avenue and right on Bay Palm Boulevard, you'll reach the heart of the town — the art center, public library, city hall, city park, and, around the corner, the local historic museum. Old beach homes survive, restored, in this same neighborhood.

As you continue down Gulf Shore Boulevard south of Walsingham Road (the Indian Rocks Bridge Road; turn left here to visit the local Chamber of Commerce), humble motels and vacation cottages line the west shoulder, strip malls wall-to-wall with souvenir shops, seafood retailers, and restaurants the other. Between 15th and 27th Avenues and First and Eighth Avenues, about every block or so you'll see public beach accesses. At one juncture, around First Avenue, the island slims down so that the road runs bayside for a couple of blocks. Alongside the road, a historic marker tells about a time when a swing bridge connected this point to the mainland.

The next personality change comes in Indian Shores, where the road turns two-lane, making it feel less islandy, more race-track. Shortly after the Route 694 bridge to the mainland, you'll see a small sign on the right for Suncoast Seabird Sanctuary. Redington Shores Beach Public Parking lies to the south, followed closely by parking for the Redington Long Pier. Around about tiny North Redington Beach and Redington Beach, things upgrade again to that exclusive island personality. Still, there are a few old-time holdouts, such as Tides Theater & Ballroom and the Tides Resort next door, with their classic Florida neo-Mediterranean style.

To the south, accesses to Madeira Beach begin. The main public beach, Archibald Memorial Park, is sandwiched between developments. There are two more parking-lot accesses at the county park and at John's Pass. At 150th Avenue, Sand Key's fourth causeway goes ashore.

Less than 3 miles in length, Madeira Beach, sometimes called Mad Beach, is fishing oriented but in a highly commercial way. Fishing character and commercialism climax at John's Pass, where a salty-flavored shopping village has cropped up around the area's reputation for grouper-catching and boating.

Sanctuary's Ralph Heath and assistant.
(St. Petersburg/Clearwater Area Convention & Visitors Bureau)

BACKFLASH

Sand Key became its own island when in 1848 a hurricane covered Pinellas islands and flanking peninsula in a tidal surge, carving John's Pass between what is now Treasure Island and Madeira Beach. The pass was named for Juan Levique, an island turtle hunter, who with his colleague Joe Silva was the first to witness the new island profile upon returning from a selling trip to New Orleans. The gap was bridged by 1875 and shops heaped up around it. New bridges eventually replaced the original and the village was revitalized to look old but to be new.

Farther north, in Indian Rocks Beach, a swing bridge was opened in 1916 to the mainland to the island. It was used until 1958.

Historical Attractions

A collection of local historical memorabilia is found at **Indian Rocks Area Historical Museum** (1507 Bay Palm Blvd., Indian Rocks Beach; 813-595-2517), open only two days a week in an old and pretty house with blue shutters. **Holocaust Memorial Museum and Educational Center** (5001 113th St., Madeira Beach; 813-392-4678), the work of the local Jewish community, shares educational memorabilia, slides, and programs with the public.

THE NATURAL

Where the shoreline once extended into the Gulf, ledges remain, pocked with undercuts and beckoning the adventurous diver.

Natural Attractions

The highly respected **Suncoast Seabird Sanctuary** (18328 Gulf Blvd., Indian Shores; 813-391-6211) began as one man's concern over wildlife and has grown into the largest wild bird hospital in North America. It nurses more than 40 species — owls, hawks, sandhill cranes, pileated woodpeckers, wood storks, and lots of pelicans — in a zoological setting on the Gulf.

AQUA-ADVENTURE

Touring

Southern Sand Key is particularly marine oriented, with an unlimited number of rentals, charters, and tour boats to choose from, some of the latter offering entertainment. They cruise the waters of Boca Ciego Bay, Tampa Bay, or the Gulf. Some land you for a day or half day on Shell Key or Egmont Key.

Starlite Princess (Hamlin's Landing, 401 Second St. E., Indian Rocks Beach; 813-595-1212) is a Victorian-style paddleboat hosting dinner dance, luncheon, and sightseeing cruises. **FunKruz** (John's Pass Village, Madeira Beach; 800-688-7529 or 813-393-5110) is the premier casino cruise into the Gulf of Mexico.

Fishing

John's Pass is fishing headquarters. Charter fishermen claim some sort of record for tons of grouper brought to port here. Dozens of guides work out of the marina and the atmosphere reeks (figuratively speaking) with fish.

Hubbard's Marina (150 128th Ave., John's Pass Village, Madeira Beach; 800-755-0677 or 813-393-1947) will clean and cook your catch at its Friendly Fisherman Restaurant. Deepwater trips last from five hours to three days.

Locals claim the best onshore fishing is at the **Redington Long Pier** (17490 Gulf Blvd., Redington Shores; 813-391-9398). It extends more than 1,000 feet into the Gulf and offers a snack bar, bait and tackle, shelters, and restrooms. There are charges for both fishing and pedestrian use. No beach parking is allowed in the parking lot.

Snorkeling/Scuba

The wreck of the *Sheridan*, a 100-foot-long vessel in 80 feet of water, is one of the most popular artificial reef sites. The Blackthorn, a 110-foot Coast Guard cutter, is another. A proliferation of ledges provide cavelike conditions. Various other reefs and wrecks lie several miles from land, in water up to 45 feet deep.

Indian Rocks Tackle & Dive Center (1301 N. Gulf Blvd.; 813-595-3196) does Professional Assiciation of Diving Instructors (PADI) instruction and has complete diving services.

At the south end of the island, check with **Mad Beach Dive Center** (13237 Gulf Blvd., Madeira Beach; 813-398-6875).

Sailboarding & Surfing

The beach on the causeway from Belleair Beach to the mainland is a favorite of windsurfers.

Boating, Sailing & Canoeing

Clearwater Beach Sailing Center (1001 Gulf Blvd., Clearwater Beach; 813-462-6368) has launch ramps and instructors. **Suncoast Boat Rental** (545 150th Ave. Madeira Beach; 813-391-5266) rents fishing, ski, and runabout boats, 16 to 24 feet. Another source is **National Boat Rental** (17811 Gulf Blvd., Redington Shores; 813-397-5171).

Other

John's Pass Parasail (110 John's Pass Boardwalk, Madeira Beach; 813-391-7738).

ISLAND ADVENTURE

Biking

Bikers America (19709 Gulf Blvd., Indian Shores; 813-593-0665) delivers and picks up free. Bike paths are sporadic throughout the island.

Shelling & Beachcombing

Shell pickings are plentiful but small along Sand Key, best in the Madeira Beach area. You'll find mostly tiny bivalves, such as clams, kitten's paws, and scallops.

CULTURE

The People

Belleair Beach has a population of about 2,000, mostly year-rounders. The community is largely residential, with no public beach accesses and few vacation rentals. Canadians favor the destination as a winter vacation getaway.

Tiny Belleair Shores has a census of 60 and is strictly a residential area of single-family homes, many of them belonging to professionals who work in the larger mainland towns.

With 5,000 residents, Indian Rocks Beach is more densely populated and tourism driven. Indian Shores's permanent population of 1,400 swells to 5,000 in winter.

Redington Shores's 2,700 year-round population doubles with

snowbird arrivals. North Redington Beach holds a mixed bag of homes and people — about 1,100 in all. Resorts, restaurants, motels, and shops make up most of the town. Retirees and families compose Redington Beach's population of 1,600. The most upscale of Sand Key communities, it retires from tourism, with million-dollar homes and no public beach parking.

Madeira Beach grows from 4,200 to 10,000 people from summer to winter. Still a fishing village, its residents make their living at sea or at tourism-related enterprises.

Island Inspirations

Award-winning sci-fi author **Damon Knight** lived in Madeira Beach for many years. From Indian Rocks Beach, **Sharon Scalise** creates ornamental works and jewelry of clay, raku, metal, enamel, and glass.

Fairs & Festivals

John's Pass Seafood Festival Arts & Crafts Show (Madeira Beach, 813-397-1571) has grown to mammoth proportions in October. **John Levique Day** honors the Pass's namesake with piratical fun during Easter weekend.

Museums & Galleries

The Beach Art Center (1551 Bay Palm Blvd., Indian Rocks Beach; 813-596-4331) hosts classes and shows. **Madeira Beach Library Gallery** (200 Municipal Dr.; 813-391-2828) features shows by changing local artists. **Art Port** (In John's Pass Village, 110 129th Ave. E., Madeira Beach; 813-398-4539), ensconced in a sweet little Cracker cottage, displays originals by local artists in oil, watercolor, pottery and wood.

Island Shopping

Souvenirs, T-shirts, shells, and surf apparel is the stuff of shops up and down the island. **John's Pass Village and Boardwalk** (12901 Gulf Blvd., Madeira Beach; 813-391-7373) is a highly celebrated center for shopping, dining, and sea-bound entertainment. Begun along a waterside boardwalk, it has spread to little shops and another two-story arcade nearby.

Among John's Pass's buffet of gift shops, **A Different World** (12943 Gulf Blvd. E. #102, Madeira Beach; 813-393-4894) is different by virtue of its imported clothes, jewelry and gifts with a Caribbean beat. Besides gourmet coffees, you can buy unusual crafts by local artisans — particularly painted wood, whimsical items, clothes and note cards — at **East End Coffeehouse & Gifts** (At John's Pass, 12943 Gulf Blvd. E., #102, Madeira Beach; 813-393-4894). **Book Nook of Madeira** (15029 Madeira Way, Madeira Beach; 813-392-8541) carries books and tapes of classical music.

Architecture

Every type of modern architecture can be found on the island, from charming little cottages to ugly concrete towers to beautiful palatial homes. In North Redington Beach, the **Tides Hotel and Bath Club** puts on a classic Mediterranean face. It was built in 1936. In Madeira Beach, you'll find the greatest concentration of Cracker beach shack architecture.

Theater

At Tides Theater & Ballroom (16740 Gulf Blvd., N. Redington Beach, 813-393-1870), the **Seminole Players**, a community thespian group, performs musicals November through April, in a dinner theater format on some weekends.

Music

One of the area's hottest local bands hails from Indian Rocks Beach. The Bohemian Swingers plays a fusion of blues, folk, jazz, rock, Caribbean, and Latin styles.

Nightlife

Alley Cats Cafe Beachside (2721 Gulf Blvd., Indian Rocks Beach; 813-595-7877) often hosts The Bohemian Swingers and other contemporary bands. The lounge at **The Wine Cellar** (17307 Gulf Blvd., N. Redington Beach; 813-393-3491), reflecting the upscale neighborhood in which it resides, features live jazz, blues, and easy-listening tunes.

TABLE HOPPING

Needless to say, EAT FISH when you're on Sand Key. You can still taste the saltwater, it's so fresh. You'll find it prepared every which way, and often inexpensively.

Crabby Bill's (Gulf Blvd., Indian Rocks Beach; 813-595-4825) is a local legend that has expanded into a chain. The fare is pure fish house: fried oyster sandwiches, crab cakes, catfish, and key lime pie. Eat casually on long picnic tables amid sign-plastered walls.

Greenstreets Dockside Restaurant (20001 Gulf Blvd., Indian Shores; 813-593-2077) has boating slips, dockside dining, and a tiki bar with an all-around menu of sandwiches, seafood, meat, and pasta specialties.

For a quiet change of pace for lunch or dinner, try Cafe Med's (19325 Gulf Blvd., Indian Shores; 813-595-4488) brand of inventive southern French and Italian cuisine. There are three very pleasant indoor dining rooms, but the back porch, overlooking the Intracoastal Waterway and its privileged opposite shoreline, makes for a soothing experience among the hectic pace one often finds on the island in season. The owner tells me docking is soon in the offing.

The Lobster Pot Restaurant (17814 Gulf Blvd., Redington Shores; 813-391-8592), despite its appearances, is a good place for a special meal in a not-too-intimate atmosphere. Lobster every which way dominates. Next in the hierarchy comes grouper. This place is popular, so call ahead.

Friendly Fisherman Seafood Restaurant (150 John's Pass Boardwalk, Madeira Beach; 813-391-6025) is the epitome of island spirit, with its unsophisticated slump, view of bay waters, and fresher-than-fresh fish. There's docking nearby.

ISLAND LANDINGS

From a sky-high Hilton to a beach-bum cottage: There's no end to the possibilities. The two biggies near Sand Key Park are the **Sheraton Sand Key** (1160 Gulf Blvd., Clearwater Beach, FL 34630; 800-456-7263 or 813-595-1611) and **The Radisson Suites Resort** of

Sand Key (1201 Gulf Blvd., Clearwater Beach, FL 34630; 800-333-3333 or 813-596-1100).

For something more intimate, try the charming cottages at Villa St. Tropez (1713 N. Gulf Blvd., Indian Rocks Beach, FL 34635; 813-596-7133).

Sources & Resources

The Beach Bee (13002 Seminole Blvd., Largo, FL 34648; 813-586-5563) is a free distribution tabloid that covers Sand Key and mainland communities. Contact the **Gulf Beaches Chamber of Commerce** at 501 150th Ave., Madeira Beach, FL 33708; 800-944-1847 or 813-391-7373; or 105 5th Ave., Indian Rocks Beach, FL 34635; 800-944-1847 or 813-595-4575.

 TREASURE ISLAND

QUICK TOUR

Treasure Island, at only 3.5 miles long, may be small, but it is varied and packed full of playground amenities. Trickling down Gulf Boulevard (Route 699), you find John's Pass's more low-key counterpart around a marina at Kingfish Wharf — mostly water-sports and food facilities. The city maintains a scenic overlook at the end of Kingfish Drive.

Continuing down Gulf, you pass what seems an endless stream of motels, cottages, and high-rises scattered Monopoly board–like. Many of the businesses support the theory that Treasure Island got its name from pirate booty: a shop named Pirate's Cove, a motel named Buccaneer Resort, another named Swashbuckler Motel, and so on.

At 107th, the street exits to the mainland lined with souvenir strip malls. Finally, at a jerk in the road on Gulf, where most people go left on Blind Pass Road toward St. Pete Beach, you find island soul by veering right on West Gulf Boulevard. The community of Sunset Beach stretches along precious sands. First there are the beach bars. One of these holds special memories for me. Several years ago as we were enjoying a beer on the front porch, we observed a phenomenon I've never seen before or since: An unbroken parade of birds lined the horizon without end, the constant line occasionally rising and falling at the whims of air currents.

Aside from one monster tower and a couple of cellblocklike structures, the buildings of Sunset Beach have character; some are old, some new, some are just unusual. The public access beach is unspectacular; I prefer to park at one of the small beach bars with outdoor seating and take it from there. There are foot accesses at other points along the beach.

Around 77th Avenue, swing east (left) to Bayshore Drive. There's a metered parking lot near a half-mile boardwalk along the waterfront. You can fish from it or stroll along with a view of St. Pete Beach's northwest shore. Down other side streets, small, closely packed cottages exude old-island flavor. Return to Blind Pass via West Gulf or Harrell Avenue to get to the marina at the north end and St. Pete Beach.

BACKFLASH

Treasure hunters claim that a gold-laden Spanish galleon, circa 1700, lies beneath fill and dredge at Paradise Island, a residential community crossed by the Treasure Island Causeway en route to the mainland. Legend also tells of a man who found some of the ship's gold and hid it and himself on a nearby island, named Hermit Key.

In modern-day history, only a few dates define Treasure Island's past. It became an island of its own in 1848, when a hurricane ripped it from what is today's Sand Key. In 1955, Treasure Island incorporated into its own city. In 1986 it earned a place in the *Guinness Book of World Records* for having the World's Largest Sand Castle.

AQUA-ADVENTURE

Touring

Island Marine (11045 Gulf Blvd., 813-367-2131) does sightseeing, sunset, dinner, and sailing cruises.

Fishing

You can fish along the seawall at **Treasure Island Golf, Tennis & Recreation Center** (10315 Paradise Blvd., 813-360-6062).

Billfish, grouper, snapper, amberjack, cobia, kingfish, and shark are among the catches of local offshore fishing parties. **Island Marine** (11045 Gulf Blvd., 813-367-2131) does fishing charters and sells bait and tackle. At Kingfish Wharf, **John's Pass Seafood Co.** (Kingfish Marina; 813-360-6907) also has bait and fishing supplies. **Far Horizons** (At Captain Kosmakos Restaurant, 9610 Gulf Blvd.; 813-367-7252) makes half- to full-day trips in local and deep waters.

Snorkeling/Scuba

The Treasure Island Artificial Reef, a boat dive, attracts grouper and other fish. A barge wreck rests in 45 feet of water offshore. Call **Treasure Island Divers** (111 108th Ave.; 813-360-3483) for scuba and snorkeling charters and equipment.

Boating, Sailing & Canoeing

Ocean Adventures (John's Pass Marina, 12795 Kingfish Dr.; 800-363-1131 or 813-363-1131) rents Grady White boats and other watersports equipment. **Island Marine** (11045 Gulf Blvd.; 813-367-2131) rents boats and waverunners.

ISLAND ADVENTURE

Biking

Island Marine (11045 Gulf Blvd., 813-367-2131) rents bicycles.

Golfing

Treasure Island Golf, Tennis and Recreation Center (10315 Paradise Blvd., 813-360-6062) has nine holes open to the public.

Tennis

For a daily fee, visitors can play on the clay or asphalt courts at **Treasure Island Golf, Tennis and Recreation Center** (10315 Paradise Blvd., 813-360-6062).

Other

Treasure Island Golf, Tennis and Recreation Center (10315

Paradise Blvd., 813-360-6062) has basketball, shuffleboard courts, a sand volleyball court, a horseshoe pit, and a playground.

CULTURE

The People

Some 7,200 permanent residents call Treasure Island home. More than 100,000 visitors pass through Treasure Island each year.

Island Inspirations

Look for the work of **Sharon Pascarelli**, a resident who produces the brightness of Caribbean style using watercolors and simplistic subjects.

Fairs & Festivals

Ye Mystic Krewe of Neptune Beach Festival takes place in October. **Pirate Days** (813-360-0811, ext. 39) celebrates the island's swashbuckling heritage in conjunction with Fourth of July festivities; **Treasure Island Scottish Games** celebrates its Highlands heritage for three days in November.

Island Shopping

Books & Bagels on the Beach (119 108th Ave.; 813-367-8029) stocks exactly what it says. It buys and sells new and used books.

Architecture

Sunset Beach has the most interesting architecture: everything from charmingly historic to majestically modern to downright funky. Drive the sidestreets for the full flavor; they are tightly packed with character.

Music

During the season, the city hosts its **Twilight Concerts** series every Sunday afternoon at the Treasure Island Community Center (1 Park Place at 106th Ave.; 813-360-0811, ext. 39). Admission is free and the music comes from local bands performing in various genres.

Nightlife

Gators at John's Pass (12754 Kingfish Dr.; 813-367-8951) takes its theme to extremes with alligators and Gator team paraphernalia everywhere. It regularly hosts live entertainment. The **Dead Beats Club** (245 108th Ave.; 813-367-3400) hosts rock-and-roll artists Wednesday through Saturday nights. The stilted **Beach Nutts** (9600 W. Gulf Blvd.; 813-367-7427) has live music every night, with outdoor seating overlooking the beach. **Bedrox Night Club** (8000 W. Gulf Blvd.; 813-367-4114) is one of those unusual Sunset Beach structures. I think its roof looks like a mushroom, but the name implies a different motif. It's near the public beach access and features live contemporary music.

TABLE HOPPING

The reputation for seafood continues. At Kingfish Wharf, **John's Pass Seafood Co.** (12763 Kingfish Dr.; 813-367-8888) sells fresh products. Park or dock at **Captain Kosmakos Seafood and Steak House** (9610 Gulf Blvd.; 813-367-3743). The menu has something for everyone.

ISLAND LANDINGS

You'll find a few small properties with docking and/or launches on the bay. **Harbour Inn and Marina** (212 108th Ave., Treasure Island, FL 33706; 813-367-1191) has one-bedroom apartments and efficiencies with full kitchens and docking.

Sources & Resources

The Island Reporter (125 108th Ave., Treasure Island, FL 33706; 813-367-2646) is a little giveaway paper about the southern beaches. Its contents: from preacher's sermons to theater reviews. **The Treasure Island Chamber of Commerce** is located at 152 108th Ave., Treasure Island, FL 33706; 813-367-4529.

 LONG KEY

QUICK TOUR

As you approach 7.5-mile-long Long Key from the south end at Pinellas Bayway to the east, the stately Don CeSar Hotel gives you your first impression of the island: A magnificent historic impression, but an impression that's not, unfortunately, maintained throughout the island. As structural ambassador, The Don sits at the crossroads to island extremes. Turn left on Gulf Boulevard and you'll go under the resort's front entrance and make your way to the charming village of Pass-A-Grille.

Soon Gulf Boulevard becomes Pass-A-Grille Way and you'll see some interesting shops and galleries. Signs at 21st Avenue direct you to the beach on Gulf Way, to the right. Parking meters for the beach line one side of the street; homes, small inns, and motels the other. Between Ninth and Eighth Avenues, activity peaks around the Hurricane Restaurant, Pass-A-Grille Park, the Gulf Beaches Historical Museum, and the town's historic section. Eighth Avenue's old buildings hold some interesting shops and galleries.

At First Avenue, you'll loop back to the bay. Merry Pier focuses activity on this side, with its marina and fishing pier — flashbacks to Pass-A-Grille's early days. Hurley Park and the community center are the hub of a strongly knit community. Twentieth Avenue leads to the residential community Vina Del Mar Island, renamed from its original inelegant handle, Mud Key.

Pass-A-Grille Way returns you to The Don, the other side of which belongs to the more hectic pace of St. Pete Beach. Along Gulf Boulevard, you look at a kaleidoscope of development: huge resorts, modest homes, loud-looking surf shops, theme putt-putt golf, a built-to-look-ramshackle restaurant, a psychic reader placard in front of a sweet old house, family-run motels.

Public beaches lie between 44th and 50th Avenues. A left turn on 66th Avenue takes you to a less-mainstream part of St. Pete Beach favored by the locals. The beach is pretty much washed away, but the waterside bars and restaurants along Beach Plaza have strong island appeal. You have a view of Blind Pass and Treasure Island's south end. On Sunset Avenue, continue north to Corey Avenue. Head east and cross Gulf Boulevard to find the best shopping on Long Key.

(To bypass Gulf Boulevard traffic between 64th and 86th

Avenues, go east a block to Gulf Winds Drive and Boca Ciega Avenue.) At the St. Pete Beach causeway road (75th Avenue), the inter-island route jogs right, then left, to connect to Blind Pass Road. Pass churches, schools, and parks and you come to commercial development at the island's northern end.

BACKFLASH

The Timucuan Indians settled first on what was mapped in 1757 as Long Island. Four separate communities slowly emerged along the island, fed by fishermen and tourism: St. Pete Beach, Belle Vista Beach, Don CeSar Place, and Pass-A-Grille Beach. Pass-A-Grille, historians conjecture, got its name from French fishermen who paused there to clean and barbecue their catches, thus Pass aux Grilleurs.

As Tampa began to develop with the advent of Florida developer Henry Plant's railroad in 1883, the snowy beaches of St. Petersburg were discovered by day trippers and the boatline operators who brought them there. A bridge across Tampa Bay in 1924 made the beaches more accessible, and Long Key's population grew. The magnificent Don CeSar Hotel opened in 1928 to an era of flappers and excess. High-society folks the likes of F. Scott Fitzgerald, Clarence Darrow, Lou Gehrig, and Al Capone started the resort's reputation for catering to rich-and-famous clientele. Unfortunately, the Depression intervened and the pink palace sank into decline. It served as a convalescent center for World War II pilots and later a Veterans Administration regional office.

In 1957, the four towns incorporated into the city of St. Petersburg Beach, which was recently officially shortened to St. Pete Beach. By the 1970s, The Don reclaimed its status as a luxury resort when local preservationists gallantly undertook renovations. Restoration is ongoing. Today the hotel has regained the throne from which it was temporarily unseated as the dame of West Coast hotels.

Historical Attractions

Gulf Beaches Historical Museum (115 10th Ave., Pass-A-

Grille, 813-360-2491) is ensconced in a historic church near the beach. Through pictures and artifacts, it tells the story of settlement in these parts.

THE NATURAL

One of the most common natural sights, yet one we never tire of, is that of the bottlenose dolphin, which frequents the area. Many charters capitalize on the friendly resident's presence with dolphin-sighting cruises. Refuse to feed the dolphins if you take such a cruise. Like all wild creatures, they become dependent on people if hand-fed. Government efforts to prohibit the practice wax and wane.

AQUA-ADVENTURE

Touring

Lady Anderson Cruises (St. Pete Beach Causeway, 3400 Pasadena Ave. S., St. Petersburg; 813-367-7804;) conducts dinner-dance, luncheon-dolphin, and gospel music-dinner cruises. A **shuttle boat** between Merry Pier (801 Pass-A-Grille Way, Pass-A-Grille; 813-360-1348) and Shell Key makes three or four trips daily.

Fishing

A small seawalled patch of park on Sunset Way is designated **Fisherman's Park**, for angling into the pass. There's a public fishing dock at **Merry Pier** (8th Ave. and Pass-A-Grille Way), bayside in Pass-A-Grille, with restrooms, bait and tackle, and rod and reel rentals. It's also a good place from which to catch a fishing charter. The Captain Kidd (801 Pass-A-Grille Way; 813-360-6606) goes on deep-sea excursions.

Snorkeling/Scuba

Local dive sites include the St. Petersburg Beach Artificial Reef in less than 30 feet of water, and a deepwater wreck.

Boating, Sailing & Canoeing

Across from the Don CeSar Resort, there's a boat ramp with limited metered parking at West Maritana & Casa Blanca. Launching facilities are also available at **Blind Pass Marina** (9555

Blind Pass Rd.; 813-360-4281). You can rent a 14-foot fishing boat with an eight-horsepower motor at **Merry Pier** (801 Pass-A-Grille Way, Pass-A-Grille; 813-360-6606). Fishing license is included.

Sailboarding & Surfing

Totally Active Sports (7859 Blind Pass Rd.; 813-367-7059) offers lessons and equipment for windsurfers.

Other

Call 'em jet skis, waverunners, or personal watercraft — they're the hottest thing in watersports in the St. Pete Beach area. You can rent them from many places.

ISLAND ADVENTURE

Biking

Pass-A-Grille's quiet roads and one-way side streets are a nice place to cycle. **The Beach Cyclist** (7517 Blind Pass Rd.; 813-367-5001) has bike rentals available.

Golfing

You won't find any golf courses on the island, but miniature golf is everywhere, offering opportunities to brush up on your putting.

Tennis

Egan Park (Blind Pass Rd. and 93rd Ave.) has two lighted tennis courts and restrooms. The public can play at the courts at **St. John's Church** (82nd Ave.) except during school hours. They are lighted with pay meters. **Lazarillo Park** (W. De Bazan Ave. in the subdivision across from the Don CeSar) has four lighted courts. At **Vino Del Mar Park** (Isle Dr.) on the residential island off Pass-A-Grille there are two lighted courts and a playground. The tennis court at **Hurley Park** (15th Ave., Pass-A-Grille) has no lights.

Other

Eight shuffleboard courts are located at **Pass-A-Grille Park** (Eighth Ave.).

CULTURE

The People

The population of the island is 10,500, which more than doubles in season. It's comprised of a mix of young professionals and retirees. Pass-A-Grille has a reputation for artistic and community-minded folks.

Island Inspirations

F. Scott Fitzgerald and Zelda were frequent visitors to the historic Don CeSar Hotel back in its youth. Legend has it Fitzgerald revised *Tender Is the Night* during his visit. He described Pass-A-Grille beach: "Opalescent shells cupped the twilight on the beach and a stray dog's footprints in the wet sand staked out his claim to a free path round the ocean."

Much of the filming for the movie *Cocoon* was shot at the hotel and its vicinity.

Evander Preston is the foremost name in local artists. The Pass-A-Grille resident is known not only for his fine jewelry, but for

Don CeSar, palace of glories past and present.
(Chelle Koster Walton)

his eccentricities, long hair, eclectic collection, and kitchen wizardry. **Vincent Knauf** is a stained-glass artist who works from his island studio and gallery, the Vincent William Gallery. You'll find the work of local resident **Roberta Stark** in many galleries. She specializes in pastel-handpainted black-and-white photography.

Fairs & Festivals

Suntan Art Center Annual (813-864-1847) is a juried art show held every November. The holiday **Lighted Boat Parade** (813-363-9245) is a glittery event that begins at Merry Pier in Pass-A-Grille and ends at the St. Pete Beach Yacht Club.

Museums & Galleries

Vincent William Gallery (348 Corey Ave.; 813-363-1334) handles the work of many local artists and has an excellent display. Although **Jack Barrett** and **Jean Grastorf** are "mainland artists," their work struck me as having an impressive, islandy style. **Suntan Art Center** (3300 Pass-A-Grille Way, next to the Don CeSar Resort; 813-367-3818) has a teaching gallery for adults, with workshops, shows, and a gift shop featuring members' works. **Pass-A-Grille Art Colony** (107 Eighth Ave.; 813-367-5654) carries the work of local and national artists.

Island Shopping

My favorite places to shop on Long Key are in Pass-A-Grille and on Corey Avenue. **Moon Shadow** (338 Corey Ave.; 813-360-0559) sells angel-themed gifts, Mary Engelbreit things, and other whimsical items. **Corey Avenue 5 & 10** (300 Corey Ave.; 813-360-8503) is a classic — sign, merchandise, and all.

Dolphin Book Nook (Dolphin Village Shopping Center, 4667 Gulf Blvd.; 813-360-0186) is a source for foreign newspapers as well as used and mainstream books. **Nancy Markoe Gallery** (3112 Pass-A-Grille Way; 813-360-0729) carries American-made crafts, including unique pottery and jewelry, wood items, and weaving. **Evander Preston Contemporary Jewelry** (106 8th Ave., Pass-A-Grille; 813-367-7894) is the studio and gallery of a local character. You can also look at his private collection of art, including works by

John Lennon and a 1986 Harley Davidson. His studio is located within one of the historic buildings in downtown Pass-A-Grille, the heart of the art community.

Architecture

The Don CeSar Hotel rises as the best example of classic beach architecture, reflecting Florida's neo-Mediterranean period of the 1920s, with nuances of the Moorish style made popular in Tampa by Henry Plant's grand hotel. A few homes in Pass-A-Grille use the Mediterranean style; others, especially in the Historic District, are Crackerish with clapboard or painted shake siding and a lived-in look.

Theater

Beach Theatre (315 Corey Ave.; 813-360-6697) shows offbeat movies.

Music

Hurricane Restaurant (9th Ave. & Gulf Way; 813-360-9558) gives Pass-A-Grille beach a reputation among jazz aficionados.

Nightlife

Bali Hai (At the St. Petersburg Hilton Inn, 5250 Gulf Blvd.; 813-360-1811) is a revolving rooftop lounge featuring live music and great sunsets. **Crackers Bar and Grille** (at Silas Dent's Restaurant, 5501 Gulf Blvd.; 813-360-6961) hosts live contemporary and reggae bands. **At Harp and Thistle Pub** (650 Corey Ave.; 813-360-4104) you can listen to Irish folk music while you sip an Irish beer.

TABLE HOPPING

For many years, local restaurants reflected the tastes of the island's largely Midwestern tourism clientele. **The Pelican Diner** (7501 Gulf Blvd.; 813-363-9873) still addresses the common appetite for comfort foods. You can't miss its classic diner-car architecture right where Gulf Boulevard merges with Blind Pass Road.

Elsewhere, grouper and shrimp are standard fare. The old fish houses traditionally fix them fried or steamed. More daring restaurants have expanded to grilled, char-grilled, blackened, and jerk methods borrowed from Florida's neighbors. **Ybor Gold**, made next door in a Tampa microbrewery, is a recently released local beer.

At Blind Pass, you can dock and dine at **Blind Pass Grille** (9555 Blind Pass Rd.; 813-363-1800), a pleasant waterfront place with lots of windows looking onto the marina. Lunch and dinner feature creative use of local seafood, plus meat selections. One of the most perennially popular places for seafood in Pinellas County is **Leverock's Seafood House** (10 Corey Ave.; 813-367-4588). There are seven in the area. The one near the St. Pete Beach causeway has free docking available.

Silas Dent's (5501 Gulf Blvd.; 813-360-6961) has the flavor of old island times, based on the legendary lifestyles of the hermit of Cabbage Key. The outside looks like an old island shack with a sand sculpture of Silas himself. It serves Florida-style cuisine, from alligator to lobster. **The Maritana Grille** (at the Don CeSar, 3400 Gulf Blvd.; 813-360-1881) does new Florida cuisine refreshingly well — no bizarre experiments, just solid creativity using local products. The atmosphere is localized with aquariums and exotic plant motifs. On the bayfront with docking, **Wharf Seafood Restaurant** (2001 Pass-A-Grille Way; 813-367-9469) is a local's kind of place with a fish-house exterior, more polished wood interior. Fish, shrimp, crab cakes, and crab claws dominate the menu.

Hurricane Restaurant's (9th Ave. and Gulf Way, Pass-A-Grille; 813-360-9558) menu tells the history of Pass-A-Grille, of which it is a part. Its reputation is hooked on grouper, which was out of supply when I last visited. The three-story Victorian building contains the original restaurant on the ground floor, a trendier tropical venue on the second, and a rooftop deck above. Be prepared for staff rudeness.

For a sampling of Pass-A-Grille's seafood-intensive restaurant cuisine, step in on **Taste of Pass-A-Grille** (813-360-9558) in September. Fish Broil & Carnival (813-893-2630) began in 1930 when mullet fishermen donated their catches to benefit teachers during the Depression. Continued by a local elementary school, it features char-grilled mullet and is held in October.

ISLAND LANDINGS

The variety of lodging options is endless on the island, ranging from unassuming family-run motels to skyward chain hotels, intimate guest cottages, and bayside fishing havens.

The half-century-old **Don CeSar Resort** (3400 Gulf Blvd., St. Pete Beach, FL 33706; 800-282-1116 or 813-360-1881) is the doyenne of beach resorts. Recently modernized with an underwater pool sound system, a new Florida restaurant and other trappings of the 1990s, it remembers the 1920s and such illuminati as F. Scott Fitzgerald and Lou Gehrig. Today, commingling with ghosts of the famous are guests from the modern rock-star world and government upper echelons, including Rod Stewart and Bill Clinton.

For something with fewer visions of grandeur, try the **Inn on the Beach** (1401 Gulf Way, St. Pete Beach, FL 33706, 813-360-8844) in Pass-A-Grille — cozy, clean, comfortable, and nicely appointed. Most of its 12 rooms let you see the beach. For dock-and-sleep alternatives, look to the island's bayside. Many, such as the **Islander Motel** (4321 Gulf Blvd., St. Pete Beach, FL 33706; 813-367-1387), have boat slips and fishing piers. **Long Key Beach Resort** (3828 Gulf Blvd., St. Pete Beach, FL 33706; 813-360-1748) has both Gulf and bay waterfronts.

Sources & Resources

St. Pete Beach Area Chamber of Commerce, 6990 Gulf Blvd., St. Pete Beach, FL 33706; 813-360-6957.

TIERRA VERDE

QUICK TOUR

Principally developed for residential uses, Tierra Verde offers little in the way of sightseeing. To get there on Pinellas Bayway, you first cross Isla del Sol, another upscale, mostly condominium island community with some shopping. The town of Tierra Verde occupies the islands of Pine, Little Bird, Pardee, and Cunningham Keys. Marine oriented, its core consists of the yacht harbor off Pine Key Cutoff. By land, it's on Madonna Boulevard, where the Tierra Verde Resort, its marina, and restaurants are located. More restaurants and stores line Pinellas Bayway (Route 679) in strip malls.

AQUA-ADVENTURE

Touring

Sailing cruises to Shell Key and for dolphin watching with **Destiny Yacht Charters** (Tierra Verde Marina, 100 Pinellas Bayway, 813-430-7245) depart for half days and sunset.

Fishing

On the way to or from Tierra Verde, toss a line from the **Skyway Fishing Pier**. It parallels the spectacular new suspension bridge, and was created from the remains of the old bridge, which was destroyed when a sea-going vessel crashed into it several years ago.

Boating, Sailing & Canoeing

You can launch your boat from the **Tierra Verde Marine Center** (100 Pinellas Bayway; 813-867-0255). It also rents slips to transient boaters. **Tierra Verde Boat Rentals** (Tierra Verde Marine Center, 100 Pinellas Bayway; 813-867-0077) rents bowriders and center and dual consoles by the hour, half day, and full day.

ISLAND ADVENTURE

Tennis

The four tennis courts at **Tierre Verde Resort** (200 Madonna Blvd.) are open to the public.

CULTURE

The People

Many of them part-time residents, the people of Tierre Verde have seawater in their veins and are partial to the yachting way of life. Many are retired.

Theater

The Tierra Verde Resort hosts Tierre Verde Dinner Theatre (200 Madonna Blvd.; 813-867-0257).

Nightlife

Cocomo's (at Tierra Verde Resort, 200 Madonna Blvd.; 813-867-8710) features live entertainment on weekends.

TABLE HOPPING

At **Good Times** (1130 Pinellas Bayway; 813-867-0774), continental cuisine has a German/Slavic bearing. For example, try Bohemian sauerbraten with lingonberries. Desserts smack of Old World richness: apple strudel and Black Forest cake, for example. The emphasis is on fresh seafood at **Billy's Ft. DeSoto Joe's Wharf** (at Tierra Verde Resort & Marina, 200 Madonna Blvd.; 813-867-8710), served in a marina-side atmosphere. It has docking facilities and seating inside or out, overlooking the marina.

ISLAND LANDINGS

Tierra Verde Yacht & Tennis Resort (200 Madonna Blvd., Tierra Verde, FL 33715; 800-934-0549 or 813-867-8611) is marina oriented, but with all-around amenities: lighted Har-Tru tennis courts, a huge swimming pool, jacuzzi, restaurants, bars, and comfortable accommodations complete with kitchenettes and balcony or patio.

Sources & Resources

The Tierra Verde News (150 2C Pinellas Bayway, #209, Tierra Verde, FL 33715; 813-573-0005) contains mostly canned features advising seniors.

 FORT DESOTO PARK

QUICK TOUR

Five among the area's most pristine keys make up this county park. You approach from the north via Tierra Verde on the Pinellas

Bayway (Route 679). Pay tolls both at the approach to Tierra Verde and the park (85 cents total).

Crossing Bunces Pass from Tierra Verde, you come first to Madelaine Key, where you'll find the park's boat ramp. The road continues through St. Jean Key. To the west, St. Christopher Key holds a squeaky clean campground of 235 sites, most of which front bay or canal waters. Mullet Key is the largest of the five. It forms a wishbone with one leg perpendicular to St. Jean Key. If you head east, you'll find East Beach, the park's more secluded sands facing Tampa Bay. Nearby lies Bonne Fortune key, open only to park employees.

To the west on Mullet Key, a 500-foot fishing pier stretches into the bay. The park's activities are centered at the elbow of the wishbone. Climb back into Spanish-American War days at the remains of Fort DeSoto. No hostile shot ever emitted from this hedge against possible invasion from Cuba. From the fort, you can see Egmont Key, where a supporting fort once stood, and Bradenton's Anna Maria Island. There's a gift shop and snack bar adjacent. The nearby 1,000-foot-long pier extends into the Gulf and is popular with pelicans and fishermen alike. A natural, sea oats-fringed beach edges this recreation area.

To get to North Beach, continue north up the wishbone's other leg. The lagoon beach is calmer and more popular than East Beach. It takes some hiking to get to the Gulf beach on the other side of the lagoon. Arrowhead Picnic Area lies on the waterfront to the east and offers an inland nature trail.

BACKFLASH

Mullet Key, the largest of Fort DeSoto Park's five keys, is considered the birthplace of modern civilization along Pinellas County's coastline. Ironically, today it is one of the least developed of its islands. Here, in 1513, historians claim Ponce de León landed and was later shot down by an Amerindian arrow. That the park's namesake, Hernando de Soto, later explored the key is a claim better documented. He and his *conquistadore* cohorts gave the county its name, Punta Pinal, meaning "point of pines."

Fort de Soto's nonhostile cannons.
(Chelle Koster Walton)

The Spanish did not linger long, discouraged by the local Tocobaga tribe. Marauding pirates on the lam later frequented the remote islands. War brought the key its earliest permanent settlers. In 1848, Robert E. Lee recommended Mullet Key as a military post site. The Union Navy set up a blockade based on the island to gain control of Tampa Bay. Later, during the Spanish-American War of 1898, construction on Fort DeSoto began, but was not completed until after the war. The fort became obsolete before its cannons could be fired. Post buildings around the fort, completed in 1906, included a hospital, a stable, a mess hall, and a kitchen. One hundred twenty-five troops were stationed at the fort. Their worst enemy, according to reports, was the hordes of mosquitoes also stationed there. During the same time, a local health board established a quarantine sanitarium on the island.

After World War II, Pinellas County bought back Mullet Key. In 1963, Fort DeSoto Park opened.

Historical Attractions

Fort DeSoto (813-866-2484) takes center stage and credit for the park's naming. Part of the fortifications are preserved, mostly the gun and ammunition rooms. Twelve-inch mortar cannons — the only ones of their type remaining in North America — stand below fort walls, ready to be guided by remote communication to their Gulf target. Two other cannons come from Egmont Key. Forty-five steps take you up to the fort's battery embankment, where the view of the now peaceful scene is the best part of the tour.

THE NATURAL

Fort DeSoto Park is designated an animal and bird sanctuary, boasting more than 150 bird species, the most exotic of them being the mangrove cuckoo, red-bellied woodpecker, and black-crowned night-heron. Thieving squirrels and raccoons are plentiful in the camping area.

AQUA-ADVENTURE

Fishing

The fishing is fine off Mullet Key's two piers: The 1,000-foot **Gulf Pier** and 500-foot **Bay Pier**. Both are equipped with bait, tackle, and snack bars. Call 813-864-3345 or 813-864-9937.

Boating, Sailing & Canoeing

A boat ramp with vehicle and boat trailer parking and a picnic ground with barbecue grills is located near the park's entrance on Madelaine Key. Between the two piers, sailboaters can launch their boats.

ISLAND ADVENTURE

Hiking

The hike around the fort, and up and down its steps, provides good exercise and historic discovery opportunity. A one-mile inter-pretative nature trail takes you through scrub and mangrove terrain at the Arrowhead Picnic Area near North Beach.

Biking

Bicycle riding is popular along the park's ten miles of wide paths, and in the campground.

Shelling & Beachcombing

The best shell finds lie on the Gulf front of North Beach. Common shells include pear whelks, king's crown, lettered olive, apple murex, fighting conch, scallops, kitten's paws, and cockles.

CULTURE

Island Shopping

A gift shop at the fort sells souvenirs.

ISLAND LANDINGS

We prefer the campground here over most state park facilities in the area. It's clean and planted with hibiscus at each site, most of which have a water view. It's popular with locals from St. Petersburg and Tampa.

Sources & Resources

Fort DeSoto Park, Box 3, Tierra Verde, FL 33715, 813-866-2662.

 EGMONT KEY & SHELL KEY

QUICK TOUR

Egmont Key, a less than two-mile-long island containing 398 acres, is a national wildlife preserve where you can explore history as well as nature. The ruins of Fort Dade occupy the northwest end of the island, tumbling into the water where there once was beach. A pier at the northern end is known as the coal dock. The key's nature trails lead to gopher tortoise nests and a historic lighthouse.

Shell Key is a narrow strip of island with mostly sand, shells and birds to see.

BACKFLASH

Egmont Key was believed to have been a pit stop for Spanish *conquistadores* as early as Ponce de León in 1513. Once labeled Castor Key, it was, says legend, the home of pirate Henry Castor and his ill-gotten treasure in the 1700s.

Egmont Key's recorded history began in the 1830s as the town of Tampa began expanding into an important shipping port. Situated at the mouth of Tampa Bay, surrounded by tricky sandbars, Egmont was a natural location for a lighthouse. In 1848, by Tampa-citizen petition, it became the first West Coast lighthouse between St. Marks in the Panhandle and Key West.

That first lighthouse lasted less than a year, damaged severely by a hurricane that forced flood levels to six feet over the top of the tiny key. The lighthouse keeper, who with his family rode out the storm in a small boat tethered to a cabbage palm, promptly resigned. A new, hurricane-resistant lighthouse was built in 1858, after two more bouts with tropical fury. It still stands at the north-eastern point of the key.

Between then and now, Egmont served its share of war duty. First came the last of the Seminole skirmishes. Egmont's role was as holding camp for Amerindians to be deported to Arkansas after the wars had ended. One proud warrior named Tiger Tail created the key's second legend when he took his life with a cupful of water laced with powdered glass to protest having to leave Florida.

In Civil War days, Egmont Key went from gray to blue as the Union Navy wrenched control of its lighthouse from the Confederates. Problem was, the Confederates had shrewdly removed the lens from the lighthouse, rendering it useless to their enemy. For the remainder of the war, Egmont served as refuge for runaway slaves and Union sympathizers. Confederate prisoners were also held on the island. It served as the local headquarters for the Union Navy, which shelled Tampa Bay military installations from its strategic location.

The Spanish-American War of 1898 put Egmont more direct-ly in the line of fire when Fort Dade was built to protect the mouth of the bay from Spanish invasion. A sister fort was built across the way at Mullet Key. With Egmont's fort came a small city of more than 70 buildings and 300 residents. Nary a shot was fired in anger from the fort, which was deactivated in 1923. The now-peaceful island town hosted military operations throughout the Spanish-American War and World Wars I and II. Today all that remains of the city is the lighthouse, the lightkeeper's cottage, and a Coast Guard pilot lookout. Maintained as a National Wildlife Refuge since 1974, its only other residents are birds, turtles, and snakes. In 1978, the island was placed on the National Register of Historic Places.

Historical Attractions

Egmont Key Lighthouse still functions on the island and can be visited from the outside. **Fort Dade ruins** are in a sad state of dis-repair, damaged by storms, beach erosion, and disfiguration by vis-itors.

THE NATURAL

As far as wildlife, Egmont Key is best known for its popula-tion of gopher tortoises, found inland on its south end. Birdlife is also abundant; many types of seabirds nest here. Rattlesnakes, which share nesting holes with the tortoises, are fairly prevalent amongst the inland scrub. Nesting birds favor Shell Key, most notably the threatened blackwing skimmer.

AQUA-ADVENTURE

Touring

Tours and charters out of both the St. Pete Beach and Bradenton areas visit Egmont and Shell Keys. Private boaters nor-mally anchor off the west shore of Egmont, where waters are fairly deep, to spend the day. A shuttle to Shell Key departs from **Merry Pier** (801 Pass-A-Grille Way, Pass-A-Grille; 813-360-1348) three times daily and makes three return trips also.

Snorkeling/Scuba

Medium visibility, submerged fort ruins, and coral formations off the northwest coast make for fine underwater sights and marine life.

Boating, Sailing & Canoeing

Boat slips are located on the bayside near the lighthouse, but permission to dock is required from the on-site Pilots Association.

ISLAND ADVENTURE

Hiking

Paths cross Egmont Key, some of them still brick-paved as reminders of the city that once grew there. One leads from the fort to the lighthouse, others wander.

Shelling & Beachcombing

Less populated than Pinellas's bridged beaches, Egmont and Shell Keys offer the area's best shelling.

CULTURE

The People

Approximately three people occupy Egmont Key, to operate the lighthouse and maintain a Federal Aviation Administration radio beacon to guide air traffic into local airports. Reportedly, the Coast Guard personnel keep themselves from going stir-crazy with island recreational pursuits and diversions within their keepers' cottage, such as a computer, pool table, and stereo.

Sources & Resources

Egmont Key National Wildlife Refuge, Refuge Manager, 9721 Executive Dr., Suite 1H, St. Petersburg, FL 33702.

 TERRA CEIA ISLAND

QUICK TOUR

Located ten miles north of Bradenton, west off Route 19, this is not an easy place to find. It's almost as if the locals want to keep the historic gem a secret. Who can blame them?

Historic homes line Bayshore Drive. On Center Street, a 1903 Post Office is still in service, along with an 1870 Methodist Church. The island's centerpiece is Madira Bickel Indian Mound at mid-island. A flat-topped temple or ceremonial mound of yore, it measures 100 by 170 feet at the base and 20 feet high. A 10-foot-wide ramp, built by the Indians, leads up the west side.

BACKFLASH

Ancient Amerindians built the island's first structure — a 20-foot-high mound of sand, shell and debris — perhaps one of the state's earliest compost piles. Archaeologists believe it to have been part of a 10-acre village called Ucita. In a plaza near the mound, the Amerindians held games and ceremonies. A small burial mound flanking the big mound has been removed.

The site was occupied through three periods of Amerindian culture dating back to the time of Christ. It is named for Mrs. Madira Bickel, who purchased and donated the site to the state in 1948 in an effort to preserve it.

Historical Attractions

Madira Bickel Indian Mound is the state's first archaeological site, a 20-foot-high mound built by Amerindians who settled the area about 2,000 years ago.

Sources & Resources

Madira Bickel Mound State Archaeological Site c/o Gamble Plantation, 3708 Patten Ave., Ellenton, FL 33532; 813-722-1017.

A view of the gulf from the shade of a chickee hut.
(Chelle Koster Walton)

S A R A S O T A / M A N A T E E   C O A S T

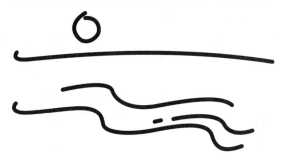

Two counties give their names to this stretch of developed coastline. The barrier islands of Sarasota and Manatee counties front the cities of — north to south — Bradenton, Sarasota, Venice, and Englewood, plus a number of small suburban-type communities in between. Altogether, the islands encompass more than 50 miles of Gulf beach within easy distance from the mainland. Most of them, by proximity to culturally rich Sarasota, identify strongly with the upscale, artsy personality of the mainland.

The islands themselves, with a couple of exceptions, are fairly citified. Taking it from the top, there's **Anna Maria Island** with its three family-oriented resort communities of Anna Maria, Holmes Beach, and Bradenton Beach.

Down the road, **Longboat Key** languishes in privileged splendor. The south end, which resides in more sophisticated Sarasota County, holds deluxe destination resorts, dressed-for-dollars shopping centers, and landscaping with never a leaf out of place. In contrast, Manatee County's north end has grown interestingly varied, like a coconut palm tree reaching for the sky. The bottom, older layers look a bit wind-whipped and rough around the edges, carrying memories of the island's first fishing village: humble homes, a flock of neighborhood peacocks, ramshackle fish houses. The graceful middle layer shapes the island with the upscale character of fine but eccentric restaurants and a proud community art gallery. Sprouting new chain hotels allow the family clientele of Anna Maria in and beachgoers a chance to sample Longboat sands without buying a room for the night.

The spirit of south-end Longboat Key siphons into neighboring Lido Key and its world-famous companion, **St. Armands Key**. This clump of islands in the interconnected archipelago starts out feeling quite natural, with a few eco-attractions at its northernmost doorstep. By the time you reach the celebrated shopping district of St. Armands Circle, you've become thoroughly entrenched in the flip side of island life — pricey exclusivity. Dizzying loops of designer shops, art galleries, and antique stores spin around the park's vegetation, distinguished by the memories of Sarasota circus days, when John Ringling brought to town great art with the Greatest Show on Earth.

Siesta Key, though not connected to this parade of showy islands, can be reached via two bridges from the mainland. The island, through its separateness, has developed a sassy personality. Artsy, yet still exclusive — but in a more down-to-earth fashion than Longboat. Along with its beautiful south-end homes, you'll find tacky souvenir shops and the world's whitest beach — somewhere under all those tanning bodies.

Casey Key, too, remains separate and aloof, but in a gracious manner. Its winding, difficult roads thread between beautiful homes that, unlike those of Longboat, defer to nature's own landscaping talents. At the south end, a resort persona surfaces at Nokomis Beach, where fishing holds sway and accommodations remain unpretentious.

Casey's southernmost point all but kisses the island of Venice, a slice of land cut sharply from mainland Venice by a razor-thin Intracoastal Waterway. Venice Beach and Brohard Park to the south stake their reputation on shark teeth, an abundant find on their salt-and-pepper sands. Architectural memories of the area's 1920s neo-Mediterranean phase earn the town its Italian nomenclature.

Manasota Key takes up where Venice's southernmost Casperson Beach leaves off. Despite the lack of a pass between the two, a wide gap in personality exists; Manasota's is more comparable to Casey Key. Less than a mile along, public beach accesses interrupt the tone of hidden exclusivity along this skinny stretch of island, until you reach the county line where Sarasota meets Charlotte. Here, like Nokomis Beach, Englewood Beach flairs pedestrian and resort-happy, with mom-pop motels and a public beach popular with the high-school crowd.

THE NITTY-GRITTY

Land Routes

Sarasota-Bradenton International Airport in Manatee County provides easy access to the barrier island chain via Anna Maria Island's south bridge. Head north from the airport on Highway 41 to Cortez Road, or head south into Sarasota and take the John Ringling Causeway (Route 780) across to Bird Key and then St. Armands.

East of Highway 41, Interstate 75 parallels the islands of the Sarasota-Manatee coast. Highway 70 cuts across the state above Lake Okeechobee to connect the East Coast to Bradenton, and to Sarasota via Route 72.

For ground transportation from the airport to the islands, call **Airport Shuttle Service** (941-355-9645), **Diplomat Taxi** (941-355-5155), or **West Coast Executive Sedans** (941-359-8600).

ANNA MARIA ISLAND: From I-75, take exit 42 east to the island's north bridge. From the airport via Highway 41, Route 684 (Cortez Road) to the south bridge is most expedient. Both bridges connect to Gulf Drive (Route 789), the island's major thoroughfare.

LONGBOAT KEY: Not directly connected to the mainland, Longboat is reached by bridge from its northern and southern neighbors on Route 789 (Gulf of Mexico Drive).

CITY ISLAND, ST. ARMANDS KEY, LIDO KEY: Route 789 continues south into the lower islands. The John Ringling Causeway (Route 780) branches off of Highway 41 from the mainland and skips along Coon Key and Bird Key to reach this clump of islands. From I-75, take exit 39 (Route 780/Fruitville Road).

SIESTA KEY: To get to Siesta Key from 41, head west on Siesta Drive or Stickney Point Road (Route 72); from the interstate, take exit 38 (Route 616/Bee Ridge Road) or 37 (Route 72/Clark Road, which becomes Stickney Point Road east of 41).

Siesta Key Trolley (941-346-3115) makes a dozen or so stops around the island and charges adults only a buck. Reboardings are free with an advertiser's receipt.

CASEY KEY: Blackburn Point Road connects 41 to Casey Key south of Osprey. Albee Road, south of Laurel, also takes you from 41 to the island.

VENICE BEACH: Take Venice Avenue to get to Venice Beach from Highway 41, then Harbor Drive to reach Casperson Beach. Exit 35 or 34 off I-75 will get you to Venice Avenue.

MANASOTA KEY: To drive to Manasota Beach and Englewood Beach, take Englewood Road (Route 776) south off 41 to Manasota Beach Road or Beach Road, respectively.

Englewood Taxi (941-475-1111) does airport pickups in Tampa, Sarasota, and Fort Myers.

Water Route

The Intracoastal Waterway slips between the mainland and the islands from Anna Maria to Englewood Beach, with channels well marked along the way and several passes for access to the Gulf. See individual island water touring for more information on navigating local waters.

Island Life

The length of Sarasota/Bradenton's keys runs from 27 degrees 30 minutes to 26 degrees 45 minutes north.

The average temperature in the Bradenton area is 75 degrees; the average annual rainfall, 55 inches (most of it in the summer months). In the winter, temperatures average around 62 degrees; in summer, around 81. At the area's southern extremes, on Manasota Key, the average annual temperature is 75 degrees, with a range from 69 in January to 84 in July. Gulf temperatures range from an average of 64 degrees to 86.

Seasonal weather and tourist patterns are much the same as around St. Pete Beach and on the Lee Island coast, except that the Sarasota area tends to get more rain (and fewer bugs) than its southern neighbors. For weather updates, call 941-351-1655 or 941-953-2900. Siesta Key and Anna Maria Island notice the greatest influx of visitors during the season. In general, the Sarasota beaches receive less publicity than the islands to the north and south, especially Casey and Manasota Keys.

Siesta Key has the worst traffic problems. Avoid getting on and leaving the island at typical rush-hour times, when islanders are traveling to and from work. Try to leave before 3 p.m., when day-trippers begin their beach exodus.

Sources & Resources

Sarasota Arts Review (P.O. Box 2252, Sarasota, FL 34230; 941-364-5825) is an excellent alternative, ten-issues-per-year tabloid that covers cultural and lifestyle trends and events throughout Sarasota, its islands, and nearby communities. **Sarasota Visitors & Convention Bureau** 655 N. Tamiami Trail, Sarasota 34236; 800-522-9799 or 941-957-1877.

 ANNA MARIA ISLAND

QUICK TOUR

Anna Maria is a roomy island, wider than its southern counterparts, measuring 7.5 miles long and comprising three separate communities. From the north, you reach the island via Route 64 (Manatee Avenue) at the in-between town of Holmes Beach. The road connects with Gulf Drive (Route 789), which abuts Manatee County Public Beach, then zigzags north. Tolerate the big city feel for a few blocks, then keep left where the road splits off at Marina Drive. Now you're on your way past the resorts, low-rise condominiums and mom-pop motels that line the beach, interspersed with restaurants humble and boastful, and a souvenir shop or two. Holmes Beach is the most upscale of the island communities.

Continue on to Anna Maria, where the island widens and the road goes inward. Take a right on Pine Avenue, which takes you to the town's most scenic section along Tampa Bay. Stop in at the Anna Maria Island Museum and have a chuckle at the "City Jail." The City Pier is the centerpiece here, with nearby seafood restaurants and a city beach park for other things to do. At the north end of Bay Boulevard, round the island along North Shore Drive and return Gulf side via Los Cedros Drive to Willow Avenue. Now you've seen some of the older residential character of the island. Head south again on Gulf and return on Marina Drive to see the business end of Anna Maria and Holmes. Key Royale Drive, along the way, crosses onto a separate island comprising a residential canal development.

Back again on Gulf Drive, take East Bay Drive until it reconnects with Gulf Drive on the south side of Manatee Avenue. Right before Bradenton Beach, Cortez Road (Route 684) connects with the mainland. The city pier is a short hop south of the bridge. Along this narrow bottleneck lies funky beach homes on one side of the road, beautiful, recently renourished sand on the other. Coquina Beach is a popular stretch that rounds the south end, gulf to bay.

BACKFLASH

Many conflicting stories guess at how Anna Maria got its name. Pick your favorite. One says Ponce de León named the island after the queen of Charles II, his benefactor. Another attributes the original Spanish name, Ana-Maria-Cay, as a blessing to Christ's mother, Mary, and grandmother, Ann. Other theories have to do with explorers and settlers and their mothers, wives, and sisters-in-law.

The first Anna Maria Island settlers of record were George Emerson Bean and family in 1893. Indian and Spanish settlements predated Bean up to the late 1880s. Bean developed the then-called Anna Maria Key in the early 1900s. Tourists arrived by boat to the Anna Maria City Pier in those days. The island remained a free floater until 1921, when a bridge was built from Cortez. In the 1950s, a new bridge replaced it, and the old bridge became the Bradenton Beach fishing pier. Another bridge spanned Tampa Bay at Perico Island mid-island. In 1993, controversy centered around replacing the Manatee bridge with a 65-foot-high structure. It never happened — yet, anyway.

Passage Key off Anna Maria Island once held a spring-fed lake and a fishing village. In 1921, a tidal wave wiped it off the chart, but it has recently reappeared.

Historical Attractions

Once an old ice house, **The Anna Maria Island Museum** (402 Pine Ave., Anna Maria; 941-778-0492) contains circa-1920 photographs, maps, records, and memorabilia, along with shell collections and historic videos.

THE NATURAL

Loggerhead turtles, oblivious to the development, come to lay their eggs where they were born, before the condos took over. The Anna Maria Island Turtle Watch group keeps an eye on the products of maternal instinct, and relocates those endangered by foot traffic. Any number of rare birds can be spotted in the vicinity, especially on Passage Key: roseate spoonbills, Louisiana herons, yellow-crowned night herons, blackwing skimmers, and wood storks. Peacocks wander freely around Holmes Beach.

As beaches will, those of Anna Maria Island wear away with tidal action. All the island communities except Anna Maria restored theirs in 1993. Part of the project placed artificial reefs offshore, using chunks of concrete from the old Sunshine Skyway Bridge to St. Petersburg.

Natural Attractions

Passage Key is a protected bird sanctuary north of the island. You can't come aboard, but bring your binoculars and head out by boat.

AQUA-ADVENTURE

Touring

The Intracoastal Waterway, though tricky and fraught with drawbridges in these parts, allows passage to all the local islands. Egmont Key is a popular destination to the north, with a lighthouse, fort remains, and a shelly beach. Nearby Passage Key, which comes and goes with the shifting of sands, once held a freshwater lake. It still serves as a protected home to the local bird population. Landings are prohibited.

The Anna Maria Yacht Basin (941-778-7171) at the island's northern end lies west of ICW channel markers 63 and 64. There's a restaurant next door and others down the way at marker 62. **Miss Cortez Fleet** (12507 Cortez Rd. W., Cortez; 941-794-1223), a long-respected operator on the mainland side of the Cortez bridge, offers a variety of cruise tours in local waters.

Fishing

The Intracoastal Waterway and converging rivers support snook, flounder, redfish, and trout. Deepwater fishermen catch tarpon and black-tipped shark. Furthermore, Gulf waters along this stretch of coastline are known as Jewfish Country. The huge fish is attracted in great numbers to the area's many wrecks and ledges.

Two piers in Anna Maria extend into the waters of Tampa Bay: The historic 700-foot **City Pier** (Bayshore Park), with a restaurant and bait concession, and **Rod and Reel Pier** (875 North Shore Dr.; 941-778-1885), part of a resort complex. The latter charges admission. The **Bradenton Beach City Pier** (200 Bridge St.; 941-778-3845) juts into intracoastal waters, has a restaurant, and sells bait.

Anna Maria Pier.
(Jack Elka)

You can go deep-sea fishing at Miss Cortez (12507 Cortez Rd. W., Cortez; 941-794-1223) on four-, six-, or nine-hour trips.

Snorkeling/Scuba

A sunken sugar barge and a close-to-shore ledge provide beach dives at Bradenton Beach. Other wrecks and ledges lie 10 to 19 miles from shore.

Sailboarding & Surfing

Surfing World (11904 Cortez Rd. W., Cortez; 941-34215) carries all the latest surfing and windsurfing gear, with rentals and lessons.

Boating, Sailing & Canoeing

Boat ramps are located at **Kingfish Ramp** in Holmes Beach at the end of the bridge and bayside at **Coquina Beach**. Rent powerboats at **Bradenton Beach Marina** (402 Church Ave.; 941-778-2288). **Bradenton Beach Sailboat Rentals** (1325 Gulf Dr.; 941-778-4969) offers free sailing lessons, as well as jet-ski rentals and fishing charters.

ISLAND ADVENTURE

Biking

Rent bikes at **Get in Line** (5604 Marina Dr., Holmes Beach, 941-778-4853).

Shelling & Beachcombing

Sanddollars and cockles are the popular find on Anna Maria's Bayfront Beach.

Tennis

Anna Maria Youth Center (Magnolia Ave., Anna Maria) has two lighted courts; **Holmes Beach Courts** (near City Hall, Holmes Beach) has three.

CULTURE

The People

Anna Maria's population of around 1,740 is composed largely of retirees. Holmes Beach, population 4,800, and Bradenton Beach, 1,650, tend to be more family oriented. Holmes Beach is largest and fastest growing. Tourism provides most of the jobs for working-class residents, though a portion commute to mainland employment.

Island Inspirations

Sarasota's islands have attracted more than their share of artistic fame. On Anna Maria, **Wyatt Blassingame** wrote in the late 1940s. His novel *Live from the Devil* was based on the cattle trade that made the Sarasota area profitable early in the 1900s. It is believed that Joseph Arnold Hayes wrote his *The Desperate Hours*, a novel later to become a popular play and movie, from Anna Maria Island. Two other of his novels, *The Ways of Darkness* and *Missing and Presumed Dead*, were set in Florida.

Several local art associations organize those who find inspiration on Anna Maria and environs, and provide an outlet for their talents. On the island, there's the **Anna Maria Island Artist Guild** (5414 Marina Dr., Holmes Beach; 941-778-6694).

Fairs & Festivals

Manatee Heritage Week fills the last full week in March with county-wide historical and crafts events. In December, the **Anna Maria Festival of Fine Arts** hosts local and visiting artisans at Holmes Beach City Hall.

Museums & Galleries

Artist Guild Gallery of Anna Maria Island (5415 Marina Dr., Holmes Beach; 941-778-6694) exhibits local works.

Island Shopping

Beach and surf shops make up the greater part of what you find in Anna Maria's shopping district. In Holmes Beach, there are major shopping centers with chain discount stores.

Theater

The Island Players perform at **The Island Playhouse** (Gulf Dr. and Pine Ave.; 941-778-5755) in Anna Maria.

Nightlife

Some clubs with live entertainment: **Cafe Robar** (204 Pine Ave., Anna Marie; 941-778-6969), **The Anchorage** (101 Bay Blvd. S., Anna Maria; 941-778-9611), **Harbor House Patio** (200 Gulf Dr. N., Bradenton Beach; 941-778-4822), **Key West Willy's** (107 Gulf Dr. S., Bradenton Beach; 941-778-7272), and **Pete Reynard's Lounge** (5325 Marina Dr., Holmes Beach; 941-778-2233).

To get in on true islander events, check out the **Anna Maria Island Community Center** (407 Magnolia Ave.; 941-778-2908), which schedules everything from tap dance and latchkey TLC for kids to chess and writing classes for adults.

TABLE HOPPING

To find the best of Anna Maria restaurant character, head to the island's north end, where casual seafood restaurants look onto the water and serve the fishing and boating clientele.

One of the oldest here is called **Rotten Ralph's** (902 S. Bay Blvd., Anna Maria; 941-778-3953). It squats homily at the yacht basin with an old Florida look and menu. Specialties include steamer pots and British fish and chips.

ISLAND LANDINGS

There's something for everyone on Anna Maria Island, from mobile home rentals, to elegant condos, to quaint B&Bs. The range in prices is just as wide.

Duncan House B&B (1703 Gulf Dr., Bradenton Beach, FL 34217; 941-778-6858), scrunched between a breakfast joint and some mobile homes, across the street from the beach, is an oasis of whimsy in hyperpastel shades of purple, pink, and blue, with carved balustrades and scalloped edging. Built in the 1800s, this home was moved from downtown Bradenton in 1946 to its present locale and turned into a charming two-room-and-two-apartment facility.

Harrington House B&B (5626 Gulf Dr., Holmes Beach, FL 34217; 941-778-5444) is considerably dressier, and right on the beach, one of Florida's few B&Bs to enjoy a seaside stance. The circa-1925 building of local coquina rock, pecky cypress, and Mediterranean flourishes has been refurbished with "casual elegance." Room size varies from spacious with a king-sized bed to comfortably cozy. Each room has its own bath, refrigerator, TV, and antique furniture.

A few resorts on Bradenton Beach offer boat docking, among them **Catalina Beach Resort** (1325 Gulf Dr. N., Bradenton Beach, FL 34217; 941-778-6611).

Sources & Resources

The Island Sun (5344 Gulf Dr., Holmes Beach, FL 34217; 941-778-6675). Weekly. **Anna Marie Island Chamber of Commerce** P.O. Box 1892, Holmes Beach, FL 34218; 941-778-1541.

 LONGBOAT KEY

QUICK TOUR

This emaciated 11-mile-long island (only a half-mile across at some points, 2.5 miles at its widest) provides little opportunity to stray from its main thoroughfare, Gulf of Mexico Drive. Approaching the island from the north, you'll see a beach the locals refer to as "Beer Can Beach," named, I believe, for a previous reputation as a party spot. Maps show it as Greer Island, a peninsula reachable by boat or car (via North Shore Boulevard). Off toward the mainland lies Jewfish Key, accessible only by boat. On Gulf of Mexico Drive, there's a public beach access to the south, below L'Auberge du Bon Vivant restaurant. On the left side of Gulf Drive, watch for Broadway. This takes you into the old part of town, now called The Village, once known as Long Beach. Older homes, wandering peacocks, and an island attitude mark the character of the neighborhood, though new homes are going up. There are a couple of good waterfront restaurants and taverns here. From this vantage, you can spy the Sister Keys, saved by Longboat Keyers from development a few years back.

On the main road again, you'll pass mile after mile of beautifully landscaped homes, resorts, restaurants, and shopping centers.

BACKFLASH

Like the annals of Anna Maria, Longboat Key chronicles offer a couple of options on how the island got its name. It was first called Palm Island, labeled by an English cartographer who landed with an exploration team in 1775. They named the northern cut between it and Anna Maria Island Longboat Pass, after the type of craft necessary to navigate it. This evolved into the name Long Beach for the island's first community, established in 1895. Eventually Longboat Key took over as the island's nomenclature. This seems to be the most authentic naming version, though variations claim Hernando de Soto's party actually landed first on Longboat Key, in longboats.

As today, Longboat Key was a tourist destination back in the days of prehistory. Historians call it a picnic and recreational area for Timucuan and Calusa Amerindians, because the only traces they have found of early peoples are middens — early landfill dumps. They surmise that mosquitoes drove the day trippers home as the sun lowered in the sky.

Juan Anasco, de Soto's scout, was the first to land on Longboat Key, after the party went ashore at what is now DeSoto Park on the Manatee River in Bradenton. Later, legend likes to place pirate Jean LaFitte in these parts, crediting the name of Lefitt's Island, north of Longboat Key, to the wily swashbuckler.

The first permanent settlers came to Longboat Key in the late 1890s to fish, farm, and escape yellow fever on the mainland. Farming prospered at the south end until a high tide flooded the entire island in 1921. That same year the island was split into two counties.

That's when John Ringling brought his act out to the island and headed Longboat Key down the road of tourism. The wealthy circus mogul envisioned Longboat Key, then just another wild island in his Sarasota-area kingdom, as a luxury golf resort. He built the course and began his Ritz-Carleton [sic] in 1926. Sixty days away from completion, work stalled on the resort. For years, the hotel's skeleton haunted Longboat's white sands as a reminder of the Depression years, which finally robbed Ringling of the assets to fulfill his dream. In the 1960s, Arvida Corporation bought out Ringling's Longboat holdings, which comprised about half of the island. The rusting remains of his hotel were finally torn down to be replaced by the Resort at Longboat Key Club.

On the north end, progress, like the pace of life on Longboat today, moved slowly. Thomas Mann, Civil War veteran, was one of the first settlers in the village of Long Beach. He homesteaded 144 acres in the late 1880s. In 1911, he sold property to Rufus Jordan, who built the Longbeach Hotel and subdivided the village.

Longboat Key incorporated in 1956 and in 1962 a bridge built between Anna Maria Island and Longboat opened the doors to full-scale settlement and development, but with a commitment to low density and tastefulness. In years to come, the wealthy would claim the island with a fierce sense of propriety. Still today they ward off commercialism with a vengeance.

THE   NATURAL

Scientists believe that 2,500 years ago, the Gulf of Mexico was six to eight feet lower than it is now. Longboat Key and Lido Key were connected until 1845, when a fierce hurricane cut New Pass, which was named by Sarasota pioneer John Whitaker. Today, Longboat's elevation ranges from three to 18 feet.

Natural Attractions

Greer Island Beach is a good birding spot.

AQUA-ADVENTURE

Touring

For captained charters, bareboat adventures, and party cruises, contact **Spindrift Yacht Services** (410 Gulf of Mexico Dr.; 941-383-7781).

Fishing

The bridge at Longboat Key's northern end, spanning Longboat Pass toward Anna Maria Island, is a hot fishing spot. **Capt. Bob Smith** (941-366-2159) takes small deep-sea bay and backwater charters from the south end of Longboat Key.

Boating, Sailing & Canoeing

Cannon's Marina (6400 Gulf of Mexico Dr.; 800-437-8865 or 941-383-1311) rents out top-quality fishing boats, skiffs, and pontoons.

ISLAND   ADVENTURE

Biking

Highway 789, or Gulf of Mexico Drive, bisects the skinny island right up the center. Eleven miles of bike path run parallel with the road and take riders along the manicured resorts and luxury housing developments for which the island is famous. Beware of vehicular traffic at driveways, especially during tourist season. Feeder roads expand the possibilities for cyclists, especially in the vicinity of The Village.

Golfing

Longboat Key has its share of good courses, but they're all private.

Tennis

Several touring professionals are based on Longboat Key, thanks to the fine reputation of the Colony Beach & Tennis Resort.

Other

With no public recreation areas, Longboat Key has only a privately owned **Recreation Center** (4020 Gulf of Mexico Dr.; 941-383-3136) to offer those willing to purchase memberships. It has tennis courts, aerobic classes, and soccer and baseball fields.

CULTURE

The People

About 9,000 folks inhabit Longboat Key year-round. In winter, that grows to around 18,000.

As one islander described it to me, Longboat Key people can best be divided into two groups: the working class and the upper class or, as I call them, "The Pub people" (for the crowd that hangs out at one local lair) and "L'Auberge people" (wealthy sophisticates).

A recent illustration of the protectiveness of this latter group came when the idea of a trolley was introduced to the island. Longtime winter residents particularly protested that the vehicle carried advertising on the outside, claiming this was a breach of law forbidding billboards and such. The protesters went so far as to suggest tolls at Longboat bridges and to stand along trolley routes making obscene gestures at the trolley. Folks at the other end of the social scale made their own tongue-in-cheek statement by stopping cars with bumper stickers. Last I heard, the conflict continued.

Island Inspirations

The island sees its share of celebrities. **Don Johnson** visits, as did the late **Audrey Hepburn**. Cartoonists **Dik Browne** (Hagar the Horrible) and **Jim Davis** (Garfield) have homes there.

Fairs & Festivals

Longboat Key Art Center Festival convenes the second Saturday in March. **Islandfest** is a celebration of food, arts, and crafts the first Sunday in May. At **St. Jude's Festival** in November, area restaurants set up food booths.

Museums & Galleries

The Longboat Key Art Center (6860 Longboat Dr. S.; 941-383-2345) displays the work of local and other artists to purchase, and holds classes in pottery, metalwork, and a variety of other media. Shows change monthly.

Architecture

At first appearance, Longboat Key is one long string of modern palaces and upscale developments (although, surprisingly enough, there is actually a trailer park on Gulf of Mexico Drive!). Get off the main road and you'll find more time-honored character, especially in The Village, where Northeast styles have been translated into tropical temperament.

Nightlife

Not much happens on the after-hours beat in Longboat Key. Head thee to St. Armands Key for action and live music.

TABLE HOPPING

Some of the area's finest and priciest restaurants are found on Longboat Key. Out of these, you'll find award-winning continental and experimental cuisine, and some snootiness. At the other extreme lie The Village's two great landmark restaurants, known for their waterfront view and casual island attitudes.

Mar-Vista Dockside Restaurant & Pub (The Village, 760 Broadway St.; 941-383-2391) is more commonly known as just The Pub. Slightly askance in stance, and nautically kitsch inside, it serves fish-house fare with a flair: oysters Longboat for an appetizer (topped with crabmeat, horseradish, and hazelnut dressing); grilled grouper reuben, Cajun-fried oysters, and blackened catfish sandwich for lunch; garlic-fried shrimp. Docking available.

Moore's Stone Crab Restaurant (The Village, 800 Broadway St.; 941-383-1748) recalls old Florida with cafeteria-style openness and plain good eats. Fresh fish of the day, whether it includes grouper, mullet, freshwater catfish, or Spanish mackerel, comes broiled, fried, or almondine. With hush puppies, of course. Docking available.

When the occasion calls for super-splurge, try **Euphemia Haye** (5540 Gulf of Mexico Dr.; 941-383-3633), a unique restaurant in all ways. The menu treats local products to global foodways with stunning results. The restaurant is charming, intimate, and somewhat Bavarian in feel.

ISLAND LANDINGS

Two mega destination resorts set the tone for Longboat Key vacationing. They represent the elite side of island life, but endanger visitors who like to get into a more local, island, nautically oriented way of life.

Several small properties offer boat docking, including **Field's Buccaneer Inn** (595 Dream Island Rd.; 941-383-1101). Up in time-stilled Long Beach, **Rolling Waves Cottages** (6351 Gulf of Mexico Dr.; 941-383-1323) accommodates with the appropriate attitude.

Sources & Resources

You'll find the **Longboat Key Chamber of Commerce** (5360 Gulf of Mexico Dr., Longboat Key, FL 34228; 941-383-2466) in The Centre of Shops complex.

 LIDO KEY/ST. ARMANDS

QUICK TOUR

Lido Key is like a mango. Nibble around the edges, and you'll savor a natural sweetness. You can't help but bite deeper and deeper into it. Get to the center and it's an entangled mass you wish you'd avoided. Some people, many in fact, come to Lido Key just to get entangled in the commercialism and traffic of St. Armands Circle. If that's what you're looking for, just go straight to the heart of the island.

Those interested in Lido Key's natural gifts should take a sharp left turn after the bridge from Longboat Key. Here, on City Island, a few sights deal with the fragile flora and fauna of the barrier islands. Most highly regarded and popular is Mote Marine Laboratory, known for its 135,000-gallon aquarium full of sharks, grouper, and other local species. Before you get there, you'll see signs for Sarasota Bay Walk, an opportunity for a quiet, self-guided walk along bay, estuarine, lagoon, and uplands habitats. Nearby, Pelican Man's Bird Sanctuary offers refuge and TLC to injured pelicans and other birds. You can tour for free.

Returning to John Ringling Parkway, you'll arrive at St. Armands Circle. You can park in the ramp at Madison and Adams drives if you wish to walk around, have a bite, and shop. Check out the park's center, where plaques honor bygone circus folks and classic statuary gives you a taste of Ringling's artistic verve.

The three other spokes in the St. Armands wheel radiate out toward the beach and residential areas. The west arm off of Ringling Parkway leads to the beaches on John Ringling Boulevard. To the south, Boulevard of the Presidents jogs into Benjamin Franklin Road, which leads to South Lido Beach. This area encusps the island's lower extremes within 130 acres on three different waterfronts. It's as popular for hiking, picnicking, and sports as for beaching. John Ringling Boulevard to the east delivers you to the mainland, first skipping across Bird Key, an old, prestigious residential development guarded by gates.

BACKFLASH

Historians have placed people — Paleoindians migrated from Asia — on the islands of Sarasota as early as 8200 B.C. They were followed by a parade of Ice Age fishermen, Timucuans, Calusas, and Tocobagas. As eons passed, islanders became more sophisticated in architectural arts. And in martial arts. By the time Europeans arrived, the natives had somehow received word from their Caribbean counterparts. They were ready for the *conquistadores*. Eventually, nonetheless, native numbers were decimated by disease and the land left to intrepid immigrants from the south and north.

Once called Sarasota Key, Lido Key came into existence after cosmetic augmentation and a change of identity. Dredge fill from New Pass got applied to the key's north end, and voila! Lido. As part of the Ringling Isles development in the 1920s, Lido benefited from a causeway built from the mainland to Bird Key, then to Lido. Legend has it Ringling won the islands of Bird Key, Otter Key, Wolf Key, and St. Armands Key in a poker game. Tales of the circus master's influence on the area's development grow taller with each telling. They involve also elephants that built bridges, dwarfs who built fortunes, and an eccentric who built himself an Italian palazzo.

As part of his development, John Ringling planned a magnificent shopping arena so his wife Mabel wouldn't have to travel to Palm Beach to spend. Today, St. Armands Circle, with its nearly 150 business outlets, easily outrivals its East Coast counterpart.

St. Armands Circle got its name from one of Lido Key's earliest homesteaders, Frenchman Charles St. Amand. Only someone spelled his name wrong, and so it has been passed down through the years.

Natural Attractions

Sarasota Bay Walk (1550 Ken Thompson Pkwy., City Island, next to Mote Marine; 941-361-6133) leads you around a boardwalk and shell paths, past mangroves, old fishing boats bobbing on the bay, egrets, and illustrated signs detailing nature's wonders.

Mote Marine Laboratory and Aquarium (1600 Ken Thompson Pkwy., City Island; 800-691-6683 or 941-388-2451) is known around the world for its research on sharks and environmental pollutants. Its original visitors center educates the public on projects and marine life. A 135,000-gallon shark tank is the centerpiece of the attraction, kept stocked with sharks and fish typical of the area: grouper, snook, jewfish, pompano, and snapper. Twenty-two smaller aquariums and touch tanks hold more than 200 varieties of common and unusual species: starfish, seahorses, skates, and scorpion fish. In 1994, the facility added a new visitors center, where you can watch via closed-circuit TV the goings-on inside two 55,000-gallon tanks of rehabilitating injured or ill dolphins, whales, and manatees.

Pelican Man's Bird Sanctuary (1550 Ken Thompson Pkwy., City Island, next to Mote Marine; 941-955-2266) is the result of Dale Shields's love of avian life. A refuge for injured pelicans and other birds, it's a must for bird lovers. Don't expect exotic birds, just rehabilitating local varieties: wild turkeys, little blue herons, ibises, barred owls, and, of course, pelicans.

Hundred-plus-acre **South Lido Beach** (South end of Benjamin Franklin Dr.) features a wide sugar beach that wraps around Gulf to bay, plus a canoeist-friendly bayou. Australian pines shade and carpet picnic areas.

AQUA-ADVENTURE
Fishing

On and around Lido Key, anglers congregate on City Island at the north end, casting into New Pass and the bay. The **New Pass Bridge** itself yields good catches. **Tony Saprito Fishing Pier** (Hart's Landing, Ringling Causeway Park on way to St. Armands Key) accommodates fishermen with a bait store across the road. From **South Lido Beach,** you can fish the fertile waters of Big Sarasota Pass.

ISLAND ADVENTURE
Hiking

At **South Lido Beach,** trails take you through woodsy parts into the swampland of Brushy Bayou.

Biking

The Longboat Key bike path crosses the New Pass Bridge and continues for a while through Lido Key's northern residential section.

Other

Go to **Flamingo Coast Rollerblade** (478 John Ringling Blvd., 941-388-1889) for your wheels.

Museums & Galleries

St. Armands Circle has its share of the galleries that have made Sarasota famous. Some of the oldest, most respected include **Four Winds Gallery** (17 Fillmore Dr.; 941-388-2510), specializing in Southwest Native American art, and **Oehlschlaeger Galleries** (28 S. Blvd. of the Arts; 941-388-3312), showcasing American, European, and South American artists.

Island Shopping

St. Armands Circle is a prizewinning shoppers arena. Amateurs beware. The clothing stores flutter high price tags; gift shops carry merchandise for the person with everything (and their friends with big bank accounts). There are a few affordable options, and some regular chain stores as well.

Kingsley's Book Emporium (24 N. Blvd. of the Presidents; 941-388-5045) is the premier bookstore in the area. Indicative of the expendable income that comes to St. Armands Key is **Big Kids Toys** (24 S. Blvd. of Presidents; 941-388-3555), stocked with quirky gifts such as juke boxes, unusual games, and an antique-looking gas pump.

Nightlife

St. Armands Circle is one of the great hubs of Sarasota nightlife. In its clubs and restaurants, you can hear live local rock bands or national artists in an intimate setting. **The Patio** (411 St. Armands Circle at the Columbia Restaurant; 941-388-3987) is a popular dancing spot for the must-be-seen. **Cha Cha Coconuts** (417 St. Armands Circle; 941-388-3300) has live entertainment nightly.

TABLE HOPPING

"Chic" is the word for St. Armands dining. The Florida string of Spanish-cuisine **Columbia** (411 St. Armands Circle; 941-388-3987) restaurants has a storefront on "The Circle." Another called **Hemingway's** (325 John Ringling Blvd.; 941-388-3948) emulates

St. Armands Circle.
(Jack Elka)

the popular upscale Key West air. **Cafe L'Europe** (431 St. Armands Circle; 941-388-4415) is a bastion of fine classic French fare with a warm red-brick setting.

At the City Island end, **Old Salty Dog** (at Gulfwind Marine; 941-388-4311), a spin-off of its Siesta Key counterpart, offers casual atmosphere and docking.

ISLAND LANDINGS

The island's most popular hangout is the **Holiday Inn** (233 Benjamin Franklin Dr.; 941-388-3941). Favored by getawayers, **Half Moon Beach Club** (2050 Ben Franklin Dr., Sarasota, FL 34236; 800-358-3245 or 388-3694) is expensive but unique. European style underlies neo-art-deco architecture.

Sources & Resources

The Arthur Vining Davis Library (1600 City Island Park; 941-388-4441) at Mote Marine Laboratory, the research center for lab scientists, is open for public reference.

 SIESTA KEY

QUICK TOUR

Let's approach Siesta Key from the north bridge on Siesta Drive. A cyclone-shaped island, Siesta measures a little over seven miles long. Its fattest part, about 1.5 miles wide, lies at the north end where most of the commercial enterprises cluster. The island tapers to a quarter-mile width at its southern point.

Following Higel Avenue from the north-end bridge, take Ocean Boulevard when you reach a Y in the road. This is the heart of the key, the Siesta Village shopping district. It meets up with Beach Road which takes you along the famed porcelain-white sands of Siesta Beach. Condominiums and beach houses line the way. Beach Road turns into Midnight Pass Road, along which the resort row continues, fronted now by Crescent Beach. As Midnight Pass

Road goes deeper south, the resorts and homes become more exclusive. Near the end, Blind Pass Road skirts Turtle Beach Park.

Heading back north up Midnight Pass Road, you'll come to a catch of traffic at the Stickney Point bridge. You can exit to the mainland here, or continue up to the leg of Midnight Pass you missed and leave the island the same way you came on. This is a mostly residential area.

BACKFLASH

Siesta Key was a late bloomer. Only fishermen and a few homesteaders took interest in the remote island in early centuries. The most prosperous settler was Louis Roberts, who moved to Siesta from Key West and married the daughter of a Sarasota homesteader. As their family grew, so did their home. In 1906, they turned it into the Roberts Hotel. Later, Roberts and developer Harry L. Higel joined with winter visitor E. M. Arbogast to form the Siesta Land Company. They platted the village of Siesta and waited for the investors.

Roberts renamed his hotel Siesta Hotel, after the name adopted for the key's north end. In 1916, Higel was elected mayor of incorporated Siesta, which eventually came to include all of the island. After the first bridge was built in 1917, the island's population shot up and Siesta Key entered its modern era of tourism and resort development. Artists and writers were some of the first attracted to the remote wilderness, among them novelist John D. MacDonald, who set many of his works around a Florida barrier island cadre.

Later years turned the island exclusive, while young artists continued to congregate around the older, developed parts of town.

THE NATURAL

Like the other islands in the chain it links, Siesta Key began forming millions of years ago as the remains of sea creatures began to accumulate and form a long ridge that slowly rose from the water. From the other side, rivers and streams deposited matter at the elevation in the sea's bottom, and before long (say 10 million years) keys began to surface.

Today, most of the island measures under five feet above sea level. Its most astonishing natural feature is the whiteness and fineness of its sand. Like the beaches of Florida's Panhandle, the sand comes from hard quartz rock that's been pulverized over centuries. Geologists believe it drifted down from the Panhandle to accumulate here. They're not sure why this is the only gulf coast beach to have benefited from such a welcome drifter; perhaps, they conjecture, it's due to the beach's crescent shape.

Natural Attractions

Neville Wildlife Preserve occupies Bird Key in Little Sarasota Bay. You can watch the native life with binoculars. **Heron Lagoon,** which divides the island at its lower extreme, is a quiet bird sanctuary favored by canoeists. It once constituted the pass between Siesta and Casey Key to the south, before a hurricane created Midnight Pass.

AQUA-ADVENTURE

Touring

The local Intracoastal Waterway allows plenty of access points to Siesta Key between channel markers 47 and 62 in Little Sarasota Bay. Don't try cutting from Gulf to bay through Midnight Pass. It's closed for the time being. The Intracoastal Waterway between Sarasota and her islands affords enough opportunities for waterfront dining and backwater sightseeing between Casey Key to the south and Anna Maria Island to the north.

Inquire about rentals at **Mr. CB's** (1249 Stickney Point Rd.; 941-349-4400), **Siesta Key Boat Rental** (Siesta Key Marina, 1265 Old Stickney Point Rd.; 941-346-8880), and **All Watersports** (1504 Sitckney Poinmt Rd.; 941-921-2754).

Fishing

Good catches are recorded at **Siesta Bridge and Bay Island** (on the island side of the bridge). Take North Shell Road off Higel Avenue to a spot, with some parking, on Sarasota Big Pass. At

Stickney Point, you can fish bay waters from the bridge or seawall. There's bait, tackle, and parking nearby. Point of Rocks (Point of Rocks Rd.), south of Crescent Beach, has lots of limestone rock and coral, which attract both fish and divers (be careful). There's limited parking at Access #12 near Siesta Breakers resort.

The lagoon that cuts into **Turtle Beach** has a pier and seawall where fishing is good and a playground keeps kids busy. If you're willing to walk a half-mile, hike from Turtle Beach to **Old Midnight Pass,** where catches are plentiful on Gulf and bay.

Fishing charters are available from **Mr. CB's** (1249 Stickney Point Rd.; 941-349-4400).

Snorkeling/Scuba

Point of Rocks, south of Crescent Beach at the island's central zone, has an unusual formation of rocks, underwater caves, and coral that make good underwater sightseeing. The rocks are protected by county ordinance and may not be removed. **Mr. CB's** (1249 Stickney Point Rd.; 941-349-4400) rents snorkel equipment.

Boating, Sailing & Canoeing

Mr. CB's (1249 Stickney Point Rd.; 941-349-4400) rents runabouts and pontoons. **Sweetwater Kayaks** (5263 Ocean Blvd., Sarasota; 941-346-1179) rents kayaks with instruction, and offers dolphin-sighting and sunset tours.

Other

Siesta Key Parasail takes off from the beach. Contact at 1265 Old Stickney Point Rd., 941-346-5052, and All Watersports (1504 Sitckney Point Rd., 941-921-2754) offer parasailing.

ISLAND ADVENTURE

Biking

Cyclists and joggers take to the path that starts at Siesta's north bridge and ends at Turtle Beach, about 12 miles later. You can rent bikes from **Mr. CB's** (1249 Stickney Point Rd.; 941-349-4400) and **Fun Rentals of Siesta Key** (6551 Midnight Pass Rd., 941-346-1797).

Shelling & Beachcombing

Best at **Turtle Beach,** which is known for its cockles and sand dollars. The sands at Siesta Public Beach are uncommonly free of shells.

Tennis

Siesta Public Beach (on Midnight Pass Rd. at Beach Way Dr.) has four tennis courts open to the public.

CULTURE

The People

From a population of 300 in 1940, Siesta has increased its year-round size to more than 12,000. Another 6,000 part-time residents live there, and the island receives some 358,000 visitors per year.

Siesta's population still tends toward the artistic, especially in the vicinity of Siesta Village. But, as on many of Florida's more popular islands, rising costs caused by a proliferation of soaring high-end condominiums and mansions are changing the social complexion of Siesta Key. Millionaires' Row, along southern Midnight Pass Road, sets a new standard for upscale island living. Still, a Bohemian tenor persists, fed by the art school, galleries, and lively arts scene of Sarasota proper.

Island Inspirations

Siesta Key has historically attracted creative types. One of its most well-known citizens of yore was prolific writer **John D. MacDonald.** While living in Sarasota, he wrote more than 70 novels and over 500 short stories. MacDonald is best known for his Travis McGee detective novels, most of them set in Florida. One of his most famous novels, *Condominium,* was later adapted to television and is set on Siesta Key during a hurricane. MacDonald died in 1986. Pulitzer Prize–winning author **MacKinlay Kantor** settled on the island in the past (his novel *The Noise of their Wings* takes place in Florida). Abstractionist **Syd Solomon** and Pulitzer Prize–winning cartoonist **Mike Peters** live there today. Playwright **Lillian Hellman** spent two winters on the island.

Fairs & Festivals

April brings two events to the island. **Siesta Fiesta** is a two-day community celebration and art show. A **Sandsculpture Contest** is held later in the month. **Siesta Key Sandfest**, capitalizing on the island's superlative sands, is held in November.

Museums & Galleries

Hang It Up Gallery is small and Siesta-style, showing the work of a few local artists as well as national ones.

Island Shopping

Sea Chantey (5150 Ocean Blvd., 941-349-6171) makes an exception among Siesta Key's usual tacky gift shops with a carefully selected collection of imports and other island-appropriate gifts and apparel.

Architecture

Little remains of historic architecture on Siesta Key. You'll find some on the back streets, such as the clapboard beach cottages along Point of Rocks Circle. **Cresent House B&B** (459 Beach Road, 941-346-0857) occupies a 1920s home. The **Siesta Key Fish Market** (221 Garden Lane, 941-346-2602) is located in an old but still active fishing village.

Nightlife

The island hotspot, especially for the young, is the **Beach Club** (5151 Ocean Blvd., 941-349-6311), where you may hear local or national bands playing rock, reggae, or jazz. Jazz is the main course at **Fandango's** (5148 Ocean Blvd; 941-346-1711), a funky Mediterranean restaurant.

TABLE HOPPING

Midnight Pass Pub (8865 Midnight Pass Rd.; 941-349-2280), around ICW marker 48, offers casual family fare and has docking for patrons. A little trickier to reach, **Ophelia's on the Bay** (9105 Midnight Pass Rd.; 941-349-2212) excels in creative cuisine in an old-Florida-style setting. **The Summerhouse** (6101 Midnight Pass Road, 941-349-1100) is a romantic, upscale restaurant with a lounge.

ISLAND LANDINGS

Siesta Key is a bustling resort packed with places of every stripe to stay, save franchise hotels. Most of the places boast their own character, whether it's old-time Florida resort, charming B&B, or posh club.

Its two B&Bs, **The Wildflower Inn** (5218 Ocean Blvd., Sarasota, FL 34242, 941-346-1566) and **Crescent House** (459 Beach Road, Sarasota, FL 34242, 941-346-0857), provide alternatives to the beach resort scene. So does **Banana Bay Club** (8254 Midnight Pass Rd., Sarasota, FL 34242, 941-346-0113), which is typically Siesta Key only in that it is small and unique. Instead of a beach, it faces a quiet bird-infested lagoon.

TOURISTS TRAPS

The shops on Siesta Key tend toward tacky Florida souvenirs, with a few exceptions.

Sources & Resources

Siesta Key/Sarasota Pelican Press (230 Avenida Madera, Sarasota 34242; 941-349-4949) gives good local coverage of issues and lifestyles. **Siesta Key Chamber of Commerce** (5263 Ocean Blvd., Sarasota, FL 34242; 941-349-3800)

 CASEY KEY

QUICK TOUR

From the north, you cross onto the eight-mile-long island via an archaic swing-span bridge that residents fought to preserve. It puts you in the proper mood — and speed: the sign dictates 10 M.P.H. The snaky Casey Key road twists you from Gulf front to bay front and back and forth a few more times. This, combined with the head-swiveling that the beautiful homes inevitably cause, can give you whiplash. Vegetation is fairly natural and the sea views are divine. Even in season, traffic is light — a good thing, because the road, free of center lines, is not meant for squeezing past anything larger than a VW.

The island's personality takes a sudden swerve as you approach the south end and the fishing resorts of Nokomis Beach. The scene is a throwback to Florida islands' earliest development. The accommodations are borderline funky, the beach facilities at Albee Road less than modern (Nokomis Beach is the county's oldest public beach). Continue to the island's southern end, where the architecture looks newer and residential. More beach facilities line the west side until you reach the park at the end, made fisherman-friendly by a jetty that parallels the one across the pass on Venice Beach. Return to Albee Road to leave the island.

BACKFLASH

Casey Key was named for Seminole War captain John Casey. While serving in the Sarasota area to quell Amerindian attacks, he assisted with the original coastal survey in the late 1840s. In the process, he lent his name to a pass in southern Little Sarasota Bay. On a later map, Casey's contributions were further honored when the name of an island called Chaise's Key became Casey Key.

Longtime a retreat for the casually wealthy, residents have striven to keep their island — particularly the north end — a secret, and to keep development noncommercial.

THE NATURAL

In the 1950s, the island was known for its quail population. Residents used to stop to let the birds cross the road.

A portion of the island from Midnight Pass to the south bridge has been designated as a conservation district by the state legislature. The land at the north end is clotted by Australian pines and 100-year-old oaks.

AQUA-ADVENTURE

Touring

Marinas at both bridges provide fuel, docking, and food for boaters along the Intracoastal. They are **Blackburn Point Marina** (941-966-3735) and **Casey Key Marina** (941-966-1730) at the north end and **Gulf Harbor Marina** (941-488-7734) at the south bridge.

Fishing

The **Nokomis Beach Jetty** (south end Casey Key Rd., Nokomis Beach.) is a man-made rock projection into the Gulf, with beach and picnic area, perfect for casting into the pass.

Boating, Sailing & Canoeing

Don & Mike's Boat Rental (520 Blackburn Point Rd. at Casey Key Marina, Osprey; 800-550-2007 or 941-966-4000) has a variety of rental boats, including ski boats, jet skis, waverunners, pontoons, sailboats, and sailboards. Sailing and water skiing instruction is available.

CULTURE

The People

The portfolios and resumes of many old-time Casey Key islanders are every bit as sterling as you'd find on Palm Beach. The difference? This ilk of corporate magnates prefers beach attire to ball attire when attending social functions. Today the complexion of the 250 homeowners is looking more yuppie. All still hold tenaciously to fragments of life as it once was: quiet, undeveloped, natural, casual.

Island Inspirations

The most famous of Casey Key's exclusive, gifted residents was artist **Jimmy Ernst**, son of Dada art movement founder Max Ernst. Jimmy Ernst extracted much inspiration for his abstract-surrealistic paintings from the landscape of Casey Key and the Florida Everglades. Jimmy and his wife Dallas built a winter home and studio on the island after their first visit in 1978. They had come from East Hampton, New York, to visit friends and escape winter. From there, the story begins to sound like every other tale of northern transplantation: They came, they loved, they stayed.

"I said, 'Jimmy, this is not Florida. I don't see a condominium.' There was a lot of jungle then. We still have good mangroves here that haven't been chopped up," Mrs. Ernst told me a few years ago. She and her husband loved boating, fishing, and coastal living and always lived near the water. Ernst died in 1984, shortly after finishing *A Not-So-Still Life*, the autobiography he wrote from his Casey Key studio.

Novelist **John D. MacDonald** moved first to Casey Key before settling on Siesta Key, where he furthered a prolific career. Children's writer and publisher **Joseph E. Lippincott** also called Casey Key home for many years. His *The Wahoo Bobcat* and *The Phantom Deer* arose out of Florida experience. Richard Jessup, best known for *The Cincinnati Kid*, is also counted among Casey's former famous, as are writers **Babs Deal** and late husband **Borden Deal**.

Architecture

Casey Key residents are not exactly pension-pinched. Yet for the most part, original homes were modest concrete block, one-level structures. Plans were, among the island's early wealth, to keep it that way. If it strays toward pretentiousness these days, blame it on the Simpsons and Lippincotts. As the story goes, the two old-island families agreed to keep to island style. Then the Simpsons broke out and put a second story on their cinder-block cottage.

Today, the new breed is tearing down the more humble abodes in favor of grandeur. Laws that in 1982 limited building to one- and two-acre lots have driven up land values, making simple housing look more and more out of place. At the south end, past the flurry of honky-tonk motels and beach houses, you will find more modern, showy building going on, even an Art Deco house (a style I find island-incompatible).

TABLE HOPPING

The island's restaurants are located along the Intracoastal Waterway at its two bridges. They cater to boaters and fishermen with fresh seafood and casual style.

Urbanek's (110 Circuit Rd., Nokomis; 941-488-2941) is across the south bridge from Casey Key, on the Intracoastal at Marker 10. It's got docking, an old oyster bar atmosphere, and outdoors waterside seating. The food is a bit bland, and the service less than swift. It remains popular with boaters nonetheless. Unusual for a fish house this old: it has no fried food!

ISLAND LANDINGS

Among Nokomis Beach's clutter of south-end small resorts, **Sea Grape Motel** (106 Casey Key Rd. Nokomis, FL 34275; 941-484-0071) addresses Nokomis Beach's fishing reputation with prime location on the Gulf-accessible back bay, directly across the street from the beach. Six boat docks and five units, with kitchens, accommodate guests and their vessels. Nothing elaborate, but clean, comfortable and — most importantly — close to the fish.

 VENICE

QUICK TOUR

Highway 41 splits when it gets to Venice. Take the business end of it to cross the Intracoastal Waterway onto the island, which holds the town of Venice proper. At the base of the bridge, you can stop at the Chamber of Commerce for information and a sample of shark's teeth. Follow 41 to West Venice Avenue, turn right, and the atmosphere immediately changes from highway anonymity to the quiet character of Venice's main street. It's one of the prettiest downtowns you'll see. Continue down West Venice's palm-lined boulevard. To your right, a street over, you'll see the historic Venice Centre Mall on Tampa Avenue. As you pass beautiful Mediterranean-style homes, you are heading right smack into Venice Municipal Beach. Turn right on The Esplanade, which delivers you to Venice's resort district. Tarpon Center Drive picks up the waterfront route to the south jetties, rocky ribs jutting into the pass between Venice and Casey Key. Fishermen favor this beach and recreational area.

Now you must backtrack to West Venice and take a right on Harbor Drive into the residential layer of island life. You come to Brohard Park, marked by the landmark Venice Pier, a center of beach activity. Harbor Drive edges more remote Casperson Beach until it dead ends at the skinniest stretch of the island.

Back at the island's top-heavy bulge, Nokomis Avenue parallels Harbor Drive. Turn right on Shore Road to get there and head back north to town center, where you'll usually find something happening at the Venice Area Art League, Venice Community Center, or Venice Public Library. Nokomis Avenue returns you full circle, along a side street of stores, galleries, and restaurants, to West Venice Avenue.

BACKFLASH

Identity crisis would seem to be the theme of Venice's history. The first Venice was established in 1888 around a post office where Nokomis now sits. In 1911, when the railroad was extended south from Bradenton, it ran past the original town of Venice and out into the middle of nowhere. That's where today's Venice grew up, around that misplaced train station. The settlement was first known as Horse and Chaise, named by seamen describing a landmark clump of trees. The Knight clan from Georgia settled there in 1868. Frank Higel (who also developed Siesta Key) changed the name to Venice, reminded of the Italian city by the area's many bayous and creeks, and undoubtedly looking for a luring marketing ploy.

In 1925, the Brotherhood of Locomotive Engineers chose the community as its retirement center, bought up 77,000 acres, and contracted for a model city to be built in North Italian guise. The city benefited with neo-Mediterranean architecture, which has become its trademark, and a boost to the economy. Additional financial security came when first the Kentucky Military Institute moved its winter headquarters to town in 1932, and later Ringling Brothers, Barnum & Bailey Circus moved operations from Sarasota to Venice in 1960.

The Venice of today still suffers identity crisis as it hides in the shadow of Sarasota and its better-known reputation for beachy resorts and high-brow culture.

Island purists perhaps would dismiss Venice from the list, because its separating canal did not have a natural birth but was created by developmental manipulation. It calls itself an island, however, and has for many years — so many years it's adopted an attitude much more indicative of an island than an ordinary beach town.

Venice remains one of the state's most underrated coastal areas, with mainly its fame for prehistoric shark-tooth fossils to take a bite out of the tourism market.

Historical Attractions

The old **Kentucky Military Institute** (226 Tampa Ave. W., Venice) is today occupied by Tampa Centre Mall. The spit-and-polish building is listed on the National Register of Historic Buildings.

THE NATURAL

Perhaps the most unusual feature of Venice shorelines is caused by ancient offshore graveyards. Unlike any other gulf coast beaches, Venice's tan sands are cluttered with bits of asphaltlike pebbles and fossilized bone and shark's teeth. Evidently a nearby reef historically attracted fish and their toothy predators. Besides marine mammals, fossils from ancient camels, bison, tapirs, and other prehistoric fauna are found on the beach.

Natural Attractions

Casperson Beach (South Harbor Dr.) occupies 9,150 feet of Gulf frontage that stretches from south of the developed pier area to strands reachable only by foot. The road ends way before the beach does at the south end, making for a relatively undisturbed hideout for birds, turtles, and humans.

AQUA-ADVENTURE

Touring

The Intracoastal Waterway sucks in its sides at this narrow cut. Venice Inlet allows passage into the waters of Dona Bay, Roberts Bay, and intracoastal waters to the north and south. **Crows Nest Marina** (941-484-9551) and **Fisherman's Wharf Marina** (941-484-9246) service boaters in these backwaters. **Bay Lady** (Fisherman's Wharf, 505 N. Tamiami Tr.; 941-485-6366) conducts two-hour narrated nature cruises in Venice's bays, intracoastal waters, and bird sanctuaries.

Fishing

Best fishing spots are the **South Jetties** (Tarpon Center Dr.), which jut into the pass toward Casey Key, and the famed 750-foot long **Venice Fishing Pier** (South Harbor Dr.), with its bait and tackle, restaurant, and bar. There's a small fee to enter the actual pier.

Blue Seas (Fisherman's Wharf, 505 Tamiami Tr.; 941-484-5788) takes party boat fishing excursions into deep water.

Snorkeling/Scuba

Avid fossil-finders search underwater for shark's teeth and other finds, but the water is not very clear — three to four feet at best. The greatest caches are found in water around 18 feet deep. Venice is also known for its marine-life-rich ledges in an area between one and five miles from the jetties at the north end.

ISLAND ADVENTURE

Hiking

Take a hike on Casperson Beach. It's remote and connects to Manasota Key, about 1.5 miles from Casperson's southernmost parking lot.

Biking

Venice is making plans for a linear park bike and pedestrian path that would edge both sides of the Intracoastal Waterway and would encourage appreciation of the city's historical and environmental assets.

Shelling & Beachcombing

Venice Beach's claim to fame is its abundance of shark's teeth mingled with the Gulf front's black pebbly sands. Serious and casual collectors alike bring their "Florida snow shovels" (locally sold screen-scoop shovels) to sift the sands for prehistoric fossils and, more commonly, recent sheddings. They're easy to find, ranging in color from gray to black, in size from one-eighth inch to three inches. Guide materials from the local chamber and other businesses help you identify the toothy creatures whose dentures you own.

Golfing
The municipal **Venice Golf & Country Club** (250 Venice Golf & Country Club; 941-492-9600) skirts the Intracoastal Waterway.

CULTURE

Island Inspirations
Neighboring Sarasota's artistic influence bleeds into this community, whose name begs for culture. Among its inspired was **Walter Farley**, author of *The Black Stallion*.
Venice Area Art League sponsors cultural events, exhibits, and classes. **Venice Art Center** (390 S. Nokomis Ave.; 941-485-7136) allows interaction between artists and art lovers.

Fairs & Festivals
The big event every August is **Sharks Tooth & Seafood Festival**, marked by natural exhibits and seafood chowing. **Venice Sun Fiesta** is another community party that takes place in October.

Museums & Galleries
Triana (Venice Center Mall, 222 W. Tampa Ave.; 941-485-8582) features original handcrafted and handpainted ceramic art made by Spanish artisans.

Architecture
No other Florida west coast island claims such an affinity to architectural style as Venice. Introduced by Massachusetts city planner John Nolen, Venice's neo-Mediterranean hallmark style survives in buildings contracted by the Brotherhood of Locomotive Engineers, back when it chose Venice as a retirement center, and in modern buildings that echo the stepped parapets and cool stucco style of the earlier era.

The town's best examples of historic Mediterranean style include the **Venice Centre Mall**, which was originally the San Marco Hotel until the Kentucky Military Institute took over in the 1930s. **Hotel Venice**, built in the 1920s and today occupied by a nursing home, is listed on the National Register of Historic Places. A drive along **West Venice Avenue** reveals first shops in the prevalent style

Venice Center Mall.
(Carol Tornatore)

and then, as you continue west to the beach, magnificent Italianate homes adorned by exotic date palms. On Harbor Drive the homes are a bit more modest and the historic ones farther between. **Banyan House Bed & Breakfast** is one of the town's oldest.

Recently, the old **Triangle Inn** was rescued from demise by concerned citizens and moved to Riviera Street, near the library. It also survives from the 1920s. Its tower, arcaded loggia, and unusual features make it stand out from other period structures.

Theater

Venice Little Theatre (140 W. Tampa Ave.; 941-488-1115) claims to be one of the most successful nonprofit community theaters in the U.S. It runs its season during the winter months in a modern Mediterranean-style building.

Music

The Venice Opera Guild holds monthly meetings and concerts September through May at Emmanuel Lutheran Church (800 S. Tamiami Tr.; 941-493-0612). **The Venice Symphony** (941-488-1010) performs January through April at the high school auditorium. In season, local musicians play every Wednesday, outdoors at the gazebo on Tampa Avenue, as part of the Brown Bag Lunch Concert Series. Band names tell you something about the tone of the tunes: Riverboat Jazz Band, Joe Bruno's Dixieland Hot Dogs, Ray Siebenmark and Sophisticated Swing, and Dr. Gene and the Swing Machine.

Nightlife

Crow's Nest (1968 Tarpon Center Dr.; 941-484-9551) features live jazz musicians and singers on a changing calendar.

TABLE HOPPING

The Crow's Nest Marina Restaurant (1968 Tarpon Center Dr. on the South Jetty; 941-484-9551) has docking and a great second-story yacht marina view. Tall windows look down upon spiring masts; birgies (yacht signal flags) and navy blue trim decorate soaring ceilings. The lunch and dinner menus rely heavily on seafood.

The most popular place in town, especially for visitors, is **Sharky's** (1500 S. Harbor Dr.; 941-488-1456) on the Venice Fishing Pier at Brohard Park. Named to associate with Venice Beach's reputation for shark-tooth collecting, Sharky's enviable pier-top location brings a frenzy of diners to its busy and buzzing dining rooms. It's a great place for sunset and atmosphere; the seafood menu is only so-so. Sunday brunch features a make-your-own Bloody (or Virgin) Mary bar.

ISLAND LANDINGS

Venice Beach is not known for its great resorts. For most character, you might want to check out condos, or check in at **The Banyan House B&B** (519 S. Harbor Dr., Venice, FL 34285; 941-484-1385). Behind its historic home sits the town's first community swimming pool. Classic statuary, fountains, flowery vegetation, a courtyard, a hot tub, and a red-tile-roofed Iberian home share the property. Four rooms, each with a private bath, exert their individual personality.

If you don't make it to the beach to sift for shark's teeth, stop at the **Venice Area Chamber of Commerce** (257 Tamiami Trail N., Venice, FL 34285; 941-488-2236) for a sample. It's tucked underneath the bridge that crosses to the island from mainland Venice. Read Janet Snyder Matthews's *Venice: Journey from Horse and Chaise* (Pine Level Press, 1989) for local history.

 MANASOTA KEY

QUICK TOUR

Technically speaking, Manasota Key is a continuation of Venice Beach. But to get from one to the other by land, you'd never know it. You approach Manasota Key in a roundabout fashion from Venice's southernmost point. The Manasota Bridge crosses the Intracoastal Waterway to land square at Manasota Beach. From there southward on the seven-mile-long island is a straight shot. Manasota Key Road (Route 776) passes mostly homes — massive mansions, spaced well apart, some set back out of sight from the road. There are also a few low-key resorts at its northern end. This is the part of the island people think of when they say Manasota Key.

A few miles down-island you encounter another beach access known as Blind Pass or Middle Beach, naturally vegetated and less crowded than Manasota Beach. The lovely, quiet, woodsy drive continues 'neath a canopy of trees and with glimpses of the bay, until you cross the Sarasota County line into Charlotte County and Englewood Beach. The road is called Beach Road from that point.

The resorts and restaurants continually thicken as you reach Chadwick Park public beach, a beehive of beach-happy activity. South of it, Gulf Boulevard leads to humbler homes, small resorts, new condo beach clubs, fishing motels, and the lovely and pristine Port Charlotte State Recreational Area beach at the end. Route 776 (Beach Road) returns to the mainland at Englewood via a bridge across Lemon Bay.

BACKFLASH

As archaeological excavations on Manasota Key indicate,

humans lived on the island centuries ago, perhaps as far back as 600 B.C. — sometime between then and 1400 A.D., in any case. Back before history was written, the key kept the dead — at least 100 men, women, and children — of an early civilization in a north end graveyard.

In more recent times, the island was a haven for nudists. When resorts first arrived to Manasota Key, circa 1930, they catered to the then-trendy brand of tourist who preferred enjoying sand and sea au naturel. Early nudist resorts were the Hermitage and the Palm Ridge Club, located about mid-island. The fad faded by the end of the decade. The Hermitage closed and the Palm Ridge Club donned attire. Nonetheless, they ushered in the island's coming era of tourism which was slow to take hold, discouraged by wealthy and powerful landowners.

The Manasota Beach Club opened in 1960 on 25 acres at the site of the former Hermitage.

THE NATURAL

The Manasota Key's Conservation Act designates the entire Sarasota County portion of the island as a wildlife sanctuary. Lots must be one acre or more to build. People were environmentally conscious here before it was fashionable to be so. One group met a couple of times a year to plant sea oats on the beach. Resident vigilance about keeping lights off during loggerhead turtle nesting season (artificial light confuses the creatures' natural instincts) has brought back populations to a census of more than 1,000 nests.

Lemon Bay, a pristine estuarine and mangrove environment, is designated as an Aquatic Preserve and Outstanding Florida Water. A fertile seagrass environment, the bay attracts the herbivorous manatee in winter and spring. These lovable 1,300-pound blimps, with skin like burlap and a face only an environmentalist could love, are endangered. The ancient, gentle sea mammals consume up to 100 pounds of seaweed daily. They make no enemies and have only one stumbling block to survival: homo sapiens. Their lumbersome girth makes them a prime target for boaters speeding through their habitat. Warning signs designate popular manatee areas. Instead of zipping through these waters and further threatening the seriously endangered manatee population, boaters can better benefit by trying to spot the reclusive creatures as they surface for air. Watch channels during low tides, when the manatees take to deeper water. Concentric circles, known as "manatee footprints," signal surfacing animals. They usually travel in a line and appear as drifting coconuts or fronds.

If you spot an injured sea cow, please report it to the Manatee Hot Line at 800-342-1821.

Natural Attractions

Fourteen-acre **Manasota Beach** (8570 Manasota Key Rd.) is well developed with picnicking and shower facilities. Sixty-three-acre **Blind Pass Beach** (6725 Manasota Key Rd.) is less busy and developed. Both parks are naturally vegetated and without structural eyesores. To get a glimpse of what the island might have looked like before settlement, take to the sand roads behind the Blind Pass parking lot.

Port Charlotte State Recreation Area has few parking spaces and no other facilities. What it has is prehistoric landscape and a beach that goes on and on to Stump Pass.

AQUA-ADVENTURE

Touring

Boaters love to do restaurant hops in this part of the watery world, and opportunities are plentiful between Englewood Beach and Gasparilla Island. At Manasota's north end, county-maintained docks and a ramp on the Intracoastal are a short walk away from **Manasota Beach.** Stump Pass, at Manasota's southern end, lets boaters in from the Gulf. Here, the Intracoastal merges with wide Lemon Bay. Marinas are on the mainland side of the bay, in the city of Englewood.

Ko Ko Kai Charter Boat Service (5040 N. Beach Rd.; 941-474-2141), at the low-rise condominium resort by the same name (located at the Sarasota-Charlotte county line) takes you island hopping to Gasparilla, Palm, Cayo Costa, Cabbage Key, North Captiva, and Captiva islands.

Fishing

Prime fishing spots are in Lemon Bay and at Stump Pass. Fishing is a major preoccupation in these parts, and services are plentiful. Tarpon is king, but mackerel, snapper, grouper, and sheepshead also make worthy trophies. Most charter captains practice catch and release.

Charter Boat Center (Beach Rd., next to Barnacle Bill's; 941-475-9476) takes you deep-sea fishing.

Boating, Sailing & Canoeing

Weston's Resort (985 Gulf Blvd.; 941-474-3431) rents boats and motors. Or try at **The Beach Place** (1863 Gulf Blvd.; 800-314-4838 or 941-474-1022). It's headquarters for boat and beach gear rentals.

Snorkeling/Scuba

Local waters, with their deep-seated pirate legends, hold a number of wrecks and reefs worth exploring in 45 to 60 feet. A local former dive operator said they got out of the business because visitors were expecting Keys clarity and were unused to diving below 20 feet. A beach dive from the south end of Manasota Beach takes you to an area known as The Rocks. Snorkelers search for sharks teeth inshore. Waters are clearest in summer.

Sailboarding & Surfing

Windsurfers favor the waters of Lemon Bay. **Bikes & Boards** (1249 Beach Rd., Englewood; 941-474-2019) rents, sells, and services surfboards, sailboards, skimboards, and bodyboards.

ISLAND ADVENTURE

Biking

About four miles of Route 776 (Beach Road) is shouldered with a bike lane, which begins in Englewood Beach and ends at the Sarasota County line. You can rent bikes at **The Beach Place** (1863

Gulf Blvd., Englewood Beach; 941-474-1022).

Shelling & Beachcombing

Shelling is good on all of Manasota's beaches, particularly Port Charlotte Park, where there's less competition from other shellers. Manasota Key gets shark-tooth wash-up, but not to the extent of Venice beaches.

CULTURE

The People

Just as Manasota is divided into two counties, so are its people split into two types. Islanders on the north end are private for the most part, their homes set back from the road, their lives guarded by a sort of casual snobbery and suspicion of strangers who happen into their space.

South-end people are slap-you-on-the-back kind of folks. Down to earth. Friendly. They depend on tourism and fishing. I once commented to a local — at the height of tourist season — how nice the visitors were. I'd just come up from Sanibel where everyone was remarking how arrogant and crabby vacationers were becoming. The Englewood islander replied, "That's because it's so expensive there. We get regular people here." Furthermore, the clientele around Englewood Beach is younger, including families and spring breakers.

Nightlife

Beaches (2095 N. Beach Rd., Englewood Beach; 941-473-9229) and **New Captain's Club** (1855 Gulf Blvd., Englewood Beach; 941-475-8611) are the island hot spots. Captain's Club has an outdoor tiki bar with live music, and docking.

TABLE HOPPING

The restaurants of Manasota Key's south end are beachy and casual. **Barnacle Bill's** (1975 Beach Rd., 941-474-9703) serves gargantuan sandwiches and homemade soup and pies in a relaxed picnic-table dining room. **New Captain's Club** (1855 Gulf Blvd.; 941-475-8611) is a bit dressier, occupying a building of some historic value and offering creative seafood dishes. Both have boat slips.

ISLAND LANDINGS

Lodging is plentiful, but for the most part low-key, unpretentious and truly islandy — from its old shakes-sided cottages to its marina-side condos.

One of the island's most unique resorts is the classic **Manasota Beach Club** (7660 Manasota Key Rd., Englewood, FL 34223; 941-474-2614). This family-run, 25-acre complex feels like a summer camp, except that it closes in the summer. During the winter, you stay in a cabinlike room in wooded, beachy surroundings and eat in the dining room. It's somewhat exclusive (the club doesn't advertise) but the focus is on nature and resting — aside from the tennis courts, pool, bocci ball, shuffleboard, basketball, horseshoes, croquet, bicycling, sailing, windsurfing, and charter fishing available.

Several resorts have docking and boat ramps, including **Weston's Fish 'n Fun Resort** (985 Gulf Blvd., Englewood, FL 34223; 941-474-3431), which has apartments on the beach or back bay, tennis, pools, slips, a boat ramp, rentals, and a fishing pier.

Sources & Resources

Englewood Today (Unit 32, Box 8, 2828 McCall Rd. S., Englewood, FL 34224; 941-473-9711) does a fine job of covering island events, fishing, and natural phenomena. *Images Magazine* (P.O. Box 1406, Englewood, FL 34295-1406; 941-474-4351) covers history and culture for the islands of Manasota Key, Venice, Gasparilla, and vicinity. **Englewood Area Chamber of Commerce,** 601 S. Indiana Ave., Englewood, FL 34224; 941-474-5511. For historical background, read *Manasota Key: Some Reminiscences* by Walter Van B. Roberts, or the two local accounts by Jo Cortes.

LEE ISLAND COAST

Under the local tourist board's heading of Lee Island Coast gathers the family of islands in Lee County, from Boca Grande's Gasparilla Island south to Bonita Beach's Little Hickory Island. I have also included Gasparilla's neighbors, which — with part of Gasparilla itself — lie in next-door Charlotte County. But let's not get technical. These islands don't lend themselves to it.

As in any family, Lee islands have diverse personalities as well as stand-out characters. The southernmost islands are the boisterous family show-offs. **Estero Island**, home of rowdy Fort Myers Beach, throws parties with loud music and is looked upon as the terminal adolescent who refuses to grow up. **Little Hickory Island**, upon which the town of Bonita Beach lives, often imitates Estero's tendency toward overdevelopment, but remains less hectic by dint of association with the islands that separate the two. **Lover's Key, Black Island, Big Hickory Island,** and **Mound Key** shy away from crowds, preferring birds and trees to human companionship. This litany of islands is strung together by a loop of road that plugs in to the mainland at beginning and end.

Sanibel Island, north of Estero, is the brother who made good. Its name is spoken in all the right traveling circles as an upscale resort town with just the right proportion of environmental awareness. Little sister Captiva Island is the quirky, artsy one in the family, the one people like to take advantage of. Connected to the mainland solely by Sanibel's causeway, it manages to hide from big brother's limelight. Across a narrow pass, **North Captiva** chose to break away from family ties. Separated at a young age by a hurricane, it is reachable only by boat.

Hidden in Sanibel and Captiva's shadow, **Pine Island** is the reclusive old uncle who'd rather toss a bait net than tan on the beach. Long, skinny **Cayo Costa** is the family's nature freak. It wears pristine sands, natural jungle, and no makeup. It likes to go off by itself and camp by the sea.

Some of the family feels **Useppa Island** is too snooty. It sits out there by itself on a shell mound throne feeling high and mighty and allowing only exclusive club members to board. Not like good old **Cabbage Key,** which welcomes boaters of any and all ilk to climb up into its currency-wallpapered inn.

Gasparilla Island is one of those hard-to-define characters. Sometimes it spends thousands of dollars just to go fishing; other moments it settles in at a local bar for a good whiskey and some fishing lies.

Its neighbors, **Little Gasparilla, Palm,** and **Don Pedro** islands, keep their wealth a secret. Legendary **Cayo Pelau** reputedly buries its treasure.

Exploration of the Lee Island Coast begins with this exclusive, northernmost group and descends down the map and the social ladder to the Everyman islands around Estero.

THE NITTY-GRITTY

Land Routes

Southwest International Airport in Fort Myers gets you closest to most of the Lee islands. If you're headed to Gasparilla Island, you have the option of arriving in Sarasota's airport, though flights there are fewer and less frequent.

Interstate 75 is the major transportation corridor down the west coast. Highway 41, also known as Tamiami Trail, runs parallel and closer to the Gulf. I-75 is faster; 41 less antiseptic in its permission to drive through the middle of towns and local lives.

GASPARILLA ISLAND: Out of Sarasota, follow Highway 41 south to Port Charlotte. Turn right on Route 771 and follow it to the island.

From Fort Myers, hop on Interstate 75 headed north and take exit 32. Jog northward on Highway 41 to get to Route 771. Route 776 off of 771 will get you to the Cape Haze and Grove City areas, where you can find transport to Little Gasparilla, Palm, and Don Pedro islands.

Boca Grande Taxi & Limo (941-964-0455 or 800-771-7533) provides 24-hour connections to all Florida airports. For more grandiose arrivals and departures, call **Gasparilla Island Limousine** (941-964-0263 or 800-771-7655) or **Boca Grande Seaplane** (941-964-0234).

PINE ISLAND AND OUT ISLANDS: Pine Island is the departure point for water taxis and charters to Useppa, Cayo Costa, Cabbage Key, and North Captiva islands. To get to Pine Island, take Route 78 (Pine Island Road) off I-75 or Highway 41 west to Pine Island and Route 767 (Stringfellow Road). To get to Pineland Marina, go right on Stringfellow, then left on Pineland Road and follow it to Waterfront Road. Call 941-283-1113 for schedules and rates.

Pine Island Taxi and Limousine Service (941-283-7777) provides 24-hour service anywhere. Private charter service from airports in Sarasota and Fort Myers can be arranged for guests to Useppa Island through the Useppa Island Club. On-island, club vehicles and electric golf carts help with luggage and goods (bring your own supplies). No personal cars are allowed.

Light-aircraft owners can use North Captiva's 2,300-foot grass airstrip. Golf carts can be rented on the island.

Cabbage Key operations are based in Bokeelia on north Pine Island, but transportation from Captiva Island, Boca Grande, and Punta Gorda (on the mainland) can also be arranged. For reservations and information on transportation call 941-283-2278.

SANIBEL AND CAPTIVA ISLANDS: From Southwest International Airport or I-75's exit 21, head west on Daniels Parkway. Turn left on Six Mile Cypress Parkway, which turns into Gladiolus Drive after Highway 41 (Cleveland Avenue). (Turn on Gladiolus Drive if arriving via Highway 41.) Take Gladiolus to Summerlin Road (Route 867) and go left to Sanibel Island. To cross the Sanibel Causeway, it costs $3 for most vehicles without stickers.

To continue to Captiva, go right on Periwinkle Way once you reach Sanibel, then right on Tarpon Bay Road and left on Sanibel-Captiva Road. For transport to the upper islands, go to 'Tween Waters Inn and Marina (941-472-5161) or Jensen's Twin Palms Resort and Marina (941-472-5800), both on Captiva Road.

Sanibel Island Taxi (941-472-4160) and **Sanibel/Captiva Airport Shuttle** (800-566-0007 or 941-472-007) make airport pickups and delivery for Sanibel and Captiva visitors. A trolley provides public transportation on Sanibel and Captiva. Call 941-472-6374 for a schedule.

ESTERO AND LITTLE HICKORY ISLANDS: From Fort Myers's Southwest International Airport or exit 21 on I-75, follow Daniels Parkway west to Summerlin Road (Route 867). Go left and follow Summerlin until you reach San Carlos Boulevard; go left to San Carlos and Estero islands. Turn left on Estero Boulevard (Route 865) and follow it to Lover's Key.

Reach the Bonita Beach area by continuing south on Route 865. Or take I-75 to exit 18 (south of the airport) and head west on Bonita Beach Road until you get to Little Hickory Island. The local

Chamber of Commerce touts Bonita Springs as Gateway to the Gulf because its exit off the interstate gets you closest to the beach.

Fort Myers has a trolley that shuttles people to the mainland and to the beaches. Call 941-275-TRAM (8726).

Water Routes

Though no one land route interconnects this loosely strung strand of islands, the Intracoastal Waterway (ICW) provides a protected water route from Ten Thousand Islands to north of St. Petersburg.

Island Life

The Lee Island Coast extends north at a latitude of 26.8 to a southern extreme of 26.5 at Bonita Beach.

High season falls in winter, beginning with Thanksgiving week. After that, traffic drops dramatically until a day or two before Christmas, the islands' busiest time of year. To the chagrin of holiday visitors, rain and cold weather are not uncommon over the yuletide season. December high temperatures average around 75 degrees with lows in the wee 50s.

Depending upon Easter's calendar placement, visitor counts remain fairly steady after Christmas, with peaks during spring break and Easter week. Weather is dependably warm and sunny late February through April (averaging about 80-degree highs), with cool-enough evenings (lows around 60). Summers rival the Caribbean for humid heat. Air conditioning and a swimming pool are tantamount to survival. Island temperatures average a high of 90 degrees May through mid-September, with little relief after sunset. No-see-ums and mosquitoes are the bane of the summer visitor, although the resort islands do exert some control. Relative humidity throughout the year averages around 70 percent, topping out in summer. Most of the area's 53 inches of annual precipitation falls in summer months, usually late afternoon in polite deference to summer activity. Visitors during the September-November shoulder season find cooler days (around 83-degree highs), fewer bugs, thinner crowds, and more congenial islanders. Gulf temperatures range from an average of 65 to 87 degrees. Call 941-335-8111 for current weather reports.

Sources & Resources

Chart Art Boater's Destination Guide (1616 W. Cape Coral Pkwy., Suite 222, Cape Coral, FL 33914; send $22.95) is an invaluable chart guide to water-accessible facilities in Lee and Charlotte Counties. "Reefs in Motion," a video pinpointing and depicting natural and man-made reefs between Naples and Gasparilla Island, can be purchased from JAWS (Just Add Water). Call 941-472-2576. It's geared for both the fisherman and the diver.

 GASPARILLA ISLAND

QUICK TOUR

Route 771 brings you to Gasparilla Island from Placida on the mainland and carries you through the heart of Boca Grande. Pay $3.20 at the blessedly nonautomated toll to cross the state's only privately owned causeway. Proceed through the newer island developments on your left. Notice the street signs on your right. When you get around 29th Street, know that you are passing the winter homes of high society. You won't see many of these homes; they hide behind flamboyant shrubbery and stucco walls down dead-end lanes leading to the Gulf front.

At 10th Street, a pink stucco facade will grab your attention, and it merits it. Admire the beautiful and slightly eccentric architecture of the Johann Fust Community Library.

Head into "downtown" Boca Grande, if there is such a thing, along Park Avenue, after the four-way stop. The Railroad Plaza and other shops and restaurants assemble between Fifth and First streets. Go left on Third and left again either on Palm or Tarpon Avenue to delve into the island's so-called "Whitewash Alley" neighborhood, where many of the old-time fishermen live. You'll run out of street at the graciously refined Gasparilla Inn. Go right and follow the twisting road to the neighborhood of Boca's attitude-revealing Dam-If-I-No, Dam-If-I-Care, and Dam-If-I-Will streets.

Boat charters and rentals out of the marinas in this area permit exploration of the area's unbridged islands.

Return to downtown along Harbour Drive. Take a religious pilgrimage down Fourth Street to Gilchrist Avenue and onto Banyan Street. Within this four-block area, you will pass the island's four lovely, historical churches. Our Lady of Mercy Mission Catholic Church dazzles with its royal-palm escort on Park Avenue. Walk on in; the door is usually open. You don't have to be Catholic to worship the Iberian inspiration here. It's repeated at the community center, housed in a restored old schoolhouse, down the block on First Street.

Take the peaceful, almost ethereal ride 'neath the banyan tree canopy that lends its name to the oft-photographed crossroad to Gilchrist Avenue. Then head to the beach along Gilchrist, which becomes Gulf Boulevard and runs side-by-side with the beach. At island's end, you can see the historic lighthouse, the remains of an old phosphate dock, and the colorful old dock-workers' neighborhood.

BACKFLASH

Underlying the low-slung isles of lower Charlotte Harbor persists a deep-seated tradition of buried treasure. This tradition stems from the popular legend of José Gaspar, or Gasparilla, whom romanticists like to believe bestowed his and other names to many of the local islands.

High Town was the name of the village that José supposedly established on Gasparilla Island in the late 1600s. Here Gasparilla, a lover of epic proportions, entertained the most beautiful and refined of his captured women. He created a palmetto palace in imitation of the grandeur he had left behind when he forsook Spain for adventure on the high seas.

In modern times, the village on Gasparilla Island is known as Boca Grande, and the pirates have been replaced by the millionaires and power brokers of the modern world.

Today, in the mind's thesaurus, Gasparilla Island cross-references to the mighty silver tarpon and to the historic village of Boca Grande. Long before tarpon brought to Boca Grande hordes of sportsmen wielding 50-pound test line, however, a different fish meant the spawning of a different village. Mullet and Gasparilla village spelled the humble beginnings of an island grown grand.

Settlement of the island's northern bay shores dates back to Peacon's Fish Ranch and prerefrigeration. In the late 1880s, fishermen from Key West and Bermuda migrated to the island to harvest the great population of mullet that ran in roe season, working mid-August to mid-January at the ranch. Before the arrival of the railroad, Peacon's Ranch operated a salt fishery which supplied Cuba with an alternative to the salt cod it imported from New England.

The Charlotte Harbor & Northern Railway came to Gasparilla Island in 1906 to transship phosphate from inland mines to Boca Grande, the nearest natural deepwater port, perched on Boca Grande Pass between Gasparilla Island and Cayo Costa to the south. A lighthouse, military quarantine cottage, and pilot bunkhouse were all that occupied that end of the island — the southernmost tip — when the railroad was built.

With the building of the railroad and the success of a recent fresh-fish operation in Punta Gorda, a new era stormed Gasparilla. Ice replaced salt. Refrigerated train cars replaced Cuban "smack" boats. Gasparilla village absorbed Peacon's Ranch to become a settlement of fishermen, which died of abandonment and eviction by 1945.

The town of Boca Grande grew overnight by 1920, from a collection of houses for railroad employees to a buzzing town. Activity centered around the new Gasparilla Inn as it began to attract wealthy winter residents and tarpon fishermen.

Names such as DuPont, Crowninshield, Astor, Eastman, and J. P. Morgan splashed the pages of the inn's guest book. Many of the "old money" families built homes on the island. Some continued to

Tarpon boat off Boca Grande.
(Lee County Visitor & Convention Bureau)

rent cottages at the inn during "social season," December through April. These "beachfronters," as they were known, played an important role in the community. They built a school and a library and used their money and influence to halt development.

Despite a recent accelerated rate of growth, Gasparilla Island continues to cling to its fishing roots. Today the emphasis lies on tarpon, that silver king of all sport catches.

Gasparilla's entourage of islands claim similarly lusty and fishy legacies. In the José Gaspar scheme of things, one tiny island steps above its physical proportions to hold grand allure. Cayo Pelau is the name of the mangrove island where the haughty pirate established Low Town for his less-refined crew. The island today is rife with legends of buried sea chests, murder, and inhospitable spirits. One hears, from time to time, of plans to develop the sandy outpost, three miles off Gasparilla shores. But mysteriously, the best intentions get stymied.

Little Gasparilla Island attracts a fish-crazed breed of mainland escapees who flee to second homes like moray eels to coral caves. It is separated from Gasparilla by a narrow pass. Passage to the mainland is by ferry out of Placida or by boat. Don Pedro and Palm Islands, to the north, were once separate but are now connected to Little Gasparilla due to the sifting sands of time and tide. Bridges once connected these islands to the mainland. In 1964, the Intracoastal Waterway was dredged and the bridges removed. Don Pedro undergoes preparation as a state park. Palm holds an exclusive, deluxe resort for reclusive vacationers.

A boating chart will reveal a half-dozen or so miscellaneous keys in the Gasparilla vicinity, with names such as Devilfish, Sandfly, Hoagen, Loomis, and some unidentified. Boca Grande Isle lies a stone's throw off the island's Gasparilla Sound shore. Another island, separated from the main island by Boca Grande Bayou, holds the Gasparilla Inn's golf course.

Historical Attractions

You can explore one vintage beachfronter home, that of John

Amory. It is now known as the **Johann Fust Community Library** (10th Street and Gasparilla Road; 941-964-2488) and is typical Boca in its atypicality and no-holds-barred eccentricity. With its pink paint job, hand-carved cypress doors, coquina walls, and restful reading garden, it ranks as one of the world's most congenial libraries. It was built in 1949 and also houses the shell collection of Henry Francis DuPont.

The **Boca Grande Lighthouse** at Gasparilla Island State Recreation Area celebrated its centennial in 1990. In 1986, it was renovated in Old Florida style and put back into service after 20 years of abandonment. It is the most photographed and painted landmark on the island. The lighthouse is open for tours the last Saturday of each month and by prior arrangement for groups. Call 941-964-0375.

The old **Railroad Depot** on Park Avenue stood as the focal point in the community back in the days when visitors, residents, and supplies arrived on the 11:45 train. Begun in 1909, it is staidly built of brick, hardwood and boxcar tongue-and-groove, with expressive flourishes. It was restored during a massive project in the 1970s to serve as a shopping arcade in keeping with the town's character.

The **Theater Mall** (321 Park Ave.) occupies an old wood structure built in 1928 as home to The San Marcos Movie House.

THE NATURAL

Unspoiled beaches and barrier island ecology typify this area's nature reserves. It is known mostly for its fish, especially the beautiful silver tarpon, which migrates through the deep Boca Grande Pass during the early summer months. Birdlife also abounds throughout the islands. This is a good spot for spotting flocks of white pelicans as they travel through. Unlike their brown cousins, who live in these parts year-round, white pelicans flock together and feed cooperatively in island shallows.

Typical semi-tropical vegetation forests Gasparilla and surrounding islands. Boca Grande is known for its one street lined with

banyan trees, planted in 1941. These trees get their unique character from gnarled limbs and aerial roots that lend them a bearded
appearance.

Natural Attractions

The long stretch of beach along **Gasparilla Island State
Recreation Area** lies at the island's southernmost extreme, around
the site of the old, restored Boca Grande lighthouse. It encompasses
135 acres. The wide beach overlooks the deepwater pass separating
it from Cayo Costa. Unfortunately, the view of oil tanks tends to
intrude upon the otherwise reality-shucking ambience. You can also
see the remains of the old phosphate docks. Many fishermen tie up
at the dock to try and nab what the structure attracts.

The Public Beach stretches to the north where you see covered
picnic tables, fireplaces, and restrooms. The beach is narrow here
and typically coarse with an abundance of shells. It's a great spot for
family picnicking.

Just recently completed, the development at **Don Pedro Island
State Recreation Area** minimally accommodates visitors, who must
arrive by boat. Facilities include restrooms, a large picnic pavilion,
boat dock, fresh running water, picnic tables, grills, and dune
walkovers. Secluded beaching is the attraction at this 129-acre free-
floater.

AQUA-ADVENTURE

Touring

Boaters typically approach Gasparilla along the Intracoastal
Waterway and enter into Boca Grande Bayou to dock, around
Channel Marker 2. Day trips to Don Pedro Island, Cayo Costa and
other natural areas constitute the greatest pleasure for sea adventur-
ers on Gasparilla. Lunch on Cabbage Key is another popular activity. Inquire about charters at **Millers Marina** (Harbor Drive; 941-
964-2283).

Fishing

Fishing is mainly what Gasparilla Island is about. Tarpon season runs from April through July, culminating in The World's Richest Tarpon Tournament with its hefty entry fee and up to $100,000 purse. Eight other tarpon tournaments also take place. During the four-month season, the 40- to 70-foot-deep waters of Boca Grande Pass boil with the feisty activity of rolling tarpon. Fishing boats are gunwales to gunwales and it takes a skilled guide to simultaneously maneuver through the idling traffic and choreograph the catch. The effort results in Hemingwayesque battles and prize tarpon of up to 100 pounds and more, which are usually freed to live out their 60 years' life expectancy.

Guides and charters are as plentiful as fish. Ask at the Chamber of Commerce or one of the marinas for references. Or contact the **Boca Grande Fishing Guides Association** at P.O. Box 676, Boca Grande, FL 33921; 941-964-2266. Be prepared to pay in the four figures for a tournament set-up.

The bridge that the train once used to cross to the island now serves as a public fishing pier. Enter it from the parking lot near Courtyard Plaza at the island's north end.

Boating, Sailing & Canoeing

Whidden's Marina (First and Harbor streets; 941-964-2878) rents powerboats.

Other

Para-Scapes (at Millers Marina, 222 Harbor St.; 941-964-0877) operates parasailing charters.

ISLAND ADVENTURE

Biking

Pedal the route along which railroads once carried phosphate from the mainland to Boca Grande's deepwater port. Seven miles of pathway travel Gasparilla Island from tip to tip along Railroad Avenue and Gulf Boulevard. Bike rentals are available at **Bike N' Beach** (333 Park Ave.; 941-964-0711) or for boaters at **Millers Marina** (Harbor Drive; 941-964-2283).

Shelling & Beachcombing

South Beach provides the best cache of wash-up on Gasparilla Island, including fossilized shark's teeth. Look for shiny, dark (the darker the tooth, the older it is), triangular pieces from one-eighth inch up to three inches. Cayo Pelau carries legends of buried pirate's treasure and is thereby a great destination for the dedicated seeker of beach treasures. But beware! Tales of wrenched backs and muddled-up boat motors have perpetuated legends of pirate spirits.

CULTURE

The People

It would be easy to divide Gasparilla's population of 700 into the haves and have-nots, but that doesn't quite tell the story. Sure, millionaires live in coexistence with oldtime fishermen; mansions sit in juxtaposition to meanly leaning Cracker houses sans telephones. Yet these two extremes of island economy cohere in their desire to keep overdevelopment from crossing the causeway.

A middle class does separate the two polarities, consisting of the charter fish guides, shop owners, and other service personnel. All in all, the feeling on Gasparilla Island tends more toward camaraderie than snobbery. Folks are not overly hospitable to visitors. You get a feeling you are being tolerated by a community where everyone knows one another and has shared the kind of good times inspired by working hard to cater to tourists.

On the out-islands, around 45 families have year-round homes.

Island Inspirations

Betty Barndollar describes Gasparilla in the book *A Very Special Place*, which is illustrated with the watercolors of her late husband Jack Barndollar. The **Boca Grande Art Alliance** (941-964-0177) promotes local artists and their work. Meetings, workshops, art shows, and children's programs come under the alliance's jurisdiction. Local art concentrates largely on island historical scenes and nature.

Architecture

The neo-Mediterranean influence of Florida's 1920s era exerts itself on Gasparilla island's public buildings and some of its mansions. Characteristics include stucco siding, archways, bell towers and red barrel-tile roofs.

Along **Whitewash Alley** slumps some prime examples of Cracker vernacular architecture, recognizable by its open verandas, squareness, clapboard siding, and tin roof, preferably rusting and curling up on the corners like a stubborn cowlick.

Museums & Galleries

Galleries that carry local artists' work include **Smart Studio & Art Gallery** (383 Park Ave.; 941-964-0519), **The Serendipity Gallery** (Old Theatre Mall; 941-964-2166), and **Cabbage Court Gallery** (333 Park Ave.; 941-964-0501).

Nightlife

At nightfall, especially on weekends, you are bound to run into partying types easing the tensions of the work day. One of their favorite spots is **Lighthouse Hole** (Harbor Drive; 941-964-0511) at Miller's Marina. A newcomer is **South Beach Bar 'n Grille** (777 Gulf Blvd.; 941-964-0765). It features live weekend music and volleyball tournaments in season.

TABLE HOPPING

Boca Grande serves the freshest grouper there is. One of the most-loved Florida food fishes, grouper generally avails itself to diners year-round. Slightly sweet and clean-tasting, it works for innumerable preparations. Fried grouper sandwich, nonetheless, is the unadulterated grouper experience, if your LDL count can take it. Of course, tartar sauce must accompany. The grouper grows large and filets are usually meaty thick, unless the cook has sliced it thin for even cooking. In any case, be wary if you get charged for grouper and you get a thin dry filet.

Lighthouse Hole (Harbor Dr., 941-964-0511) serves grouper the way it should be, and in a marina atmosphere with a collection of baseball hats hanging from the ceiling. Off the screen porch, the view of katrillion-dollar yachts dazzles.

To get to **Rum Bay** (Palm Island Resort; 941-697-0566), come by private boat to Marker 9A in Lemon Bay, or reserve a launch lift from the mainland, south of Englewood. Fall-off-the-bone baby back ribs are the drawing card. Burgers, salads, chicken wings, fish, and steaks round out the menu.

Island Landings

If spending the night, a room at the **Gasparilla Inn** (Palm Ave.; 941-964-2201) would be the quintessential Boca experience. But don't try during the social season, December through April, when potential lodgers are often turned away even though rooms may be available — all to protect the interests of the duPonts, Vanderbilts, and their ilk.

Uncle Henry's Marina Resort Motel (941-964-2300) has docking, a pool, and luxury accommodations. **Palm Island Resort** (7092 Placida Rd., Cape Haze, FL 33946; US 800-824-5412, FL 800-282-6142 or 941-697-4800) monopolizes Palm Island and satisfies spendy, recluse whims. Reach it via Harbour Island Resort on the mainland, which offers boat docking.

Palm Island.
(Palm Island Resort)

Sources & Resources

Two weeklies serve the island: *Boca Beacon* (P.O. Box 313, Boca Grande, FL 33921; 941-964-2995) and *Gasparilla Gazette* (375 Park Ave., Boca Grande, FL 33921; 941-964-2728). The **Boca Grande Chamber of Commerce** can be contacted at P.O. Box 704, Boca Grande, FL 33921; 941-964-0568. It is situated in Courtyard Plaza at the island's north end. A fertile source of first-hand island history is librarian Pansy Cost at the **Community Library** (10th Street and Gasparilla Road; 941-964-2488).

 CABBAGE KEY

QUICK TOUR

No other way but quickly exists for exploring this hump of an island at Intracoastal Channel Marker 60. A Calusa Amerindian shell mound accounts for its 37-foot height. You arrive by boat, no other way, to the docks on the island's east side. Cabbage Key Inn faces the docks and crowns the gently sloping mound. Ducks greet your arrival and beg cracked corn, available from the dockmaster. Inside, the restaurant and bar are known for their George Washington wallpaper. Boaters, tour cruisers, celebrities, and visitors from around the world pitstop here for lunch, leaving behind their autographed bills.

A short nature trail around the 100-acre island identifies native vegetation and provides a stretch of digestion.

BACKFLASH

Alan and Grace Rinehart, son and daughter-in-law of mystery novelist Mary Roberts Rinehart, bought the island of Cabbage Key for $2,500 in 1928. With Mom's help, they erected a $125,000 home of Florida pine and cypress upon a shell mound poking 37 feet above sea level.

In 1944, an artist bought the island, turning it into an artists' haven that evolved into the inn, restaurant, and bar it is today. Rob and Phyllis Wells, two North Carolina escapees, purchased it all in 1974 and still manage the outpost of island hostelry.

THE NATURAL

Cabbage Key is a mangrove island, one formed by the busy roots of those "walking trees," rather than by shifting sands. Thick red mangroves still fringe the islands, except where they were once cleared for dockage. (Today it is illegal to cut down mangroves.)

Inland, a jungle of natural and exotic vegetation entangles: Cabbage palms (which give the island its name), poincianas, ixoras, periwinkles, and 350-year-old Cuban laurels. Butterflies, imported mallard ducks, ospreys, herons, and an occasional bald eagle thrive in this unscathed environment.

AQUA-ADVENTURE

Touring

Channel Marker 60 in the Intracoastal Waterway marks the spot for Cabbage Key. Boaters find easy dockage on the lee side in front of the Cabbage Key Inn. A dockmaster is on duty to help.

ISLAND ADVENTURE

Hiking

A short, easy nature trail leads you through Cabbage Key's pristine innards.

CULTURE

The People

Cabbage Key's population consists of restaurant and inn staff, a special breed of folks who can live in a confined area and not go stir-crazy. Au contraire, they do nothing but rave about the seclusion and way of life. Of course, they get all the off-island input they need from the hordes of people who cross their welcome mat daily. Four private homes, one belonging to the owners, inhabit the island. Workers reside in inn rooms.

Architecture

The Cabbage Key Inn, the isle's crowning architectural achieve-

Cabbage Key Inn.
(Lee County Visitor & Convention Bureau)

ment, was built around 1930 of native Florida pine and cypress. (Florida heart pine, which hardens like steel shortly after being cut, is known for its termite resistance.) Quite impressive upon its shell-midden perch, its $125,000 price tag reflected the difficulties of building on unbridged islands, not any measure of glamour or luxury. Sprinkled around the island's perimeter, unpretentious cottages fit the decor of this throwback to old-island lifestyles.

Nightlife

Those who spend the night on Cabbage Key find little else to do but downshift into the natural tempo of proper island living. Night time is the quiet, flip side of the key's daytime bustle. About

4 P.M, most of the day-trippers are gone and it's time to do some serious reclining.

TABLE HOPPING

The Inn is the only place to eat on Cabbage Key. Because it is highly touted among boaters and tourists, and also because all ingredients must be shipped ashore, prices are high. Many will try to tell you, by the way, that this is home of the original Jimmy Buffett Cheeseburger in Paradise. But then many restaurants make that same claim. Seems anyplace from Jacksonville Beach to Barbados that can slap a slab of Velveeta atop a ground beef patty tries to claim inspiration rights.

Stone crab is available in season, and the Inn is also renowned for its key lime pie.

ISLAND LANDINGS

The Inn accommodates guests on an extended escape from reality with a handful of rustic rooms and cottages, each with its own old-island, inelegant personality. Rates are reasonable and attractive. Make reservations as far in advance as possible.

TOURIST TRAPS

If Cabbage Key didn't persist so stubbornly in old-island ways — resisting temptations to upgrade for tourists — it would almost be considered a tourist trap in itself. Fortunately, the owners are wise enough to realize that lack of air-conditioning, tour trams, and plushness make Cabbage Key the popular destination it is. Nonetheless, in season, when I prefer to skirt the crowds for a boater's luncheon, I will instead hit Barnacle Phil's on North Captiva.

 USEPPA ISLAND

QUICK TOUR

Come by boat or seaplane to this unbridged, shell-mound island. Hop ashore at the westside dock only if you are a guest, member of the Useppa Island Club, or part of an authorized tour. Follow the dock to the 1904-built reception center, the island's oldest building, to find your accommodations and any other information.

Feet are the principal mode of transportation. Yours will take you around the 100-acre island as you head south to the swimming pool and croquet and tennis courts. Amerindian archaeological sites lie near the pool and along paths to the south. They delve into the ancient shell mounds that give the island its unusual rolling terrain. A wooden walkover bisects the island and delivers residents and visitors to the front door of their Old Florida-style homes through jungle vegetation and a particularly interesting tree that forms an archway.

On the eastern face of the island, you will come to the old and historic Collier Inn, which has, besides a restaurant and bar, a museum display remembering the island's golden era of shining stars and the founding of the Izaak Walton Club for tarpon fishermen. Follow the historic Pink Promenade through the island's residential center to its north point and then loop around to return via the man-made beach.

BACKFLASH

Useppa rises between Cayo Costa and Pine Island like a mirage. You pass it on your way to Cabbage Key or Boca Grande, and blink a couple of times to make sure your eyes don't deceive you. You may be tempted to grab a pair of binoculars and take a closer look, expecting to glimpse Gatsbian men and parasoled ladies among tin roofs and airy verandahs. Useppa Island freezes a chunk of history under semitropical sun. All the buildings are constructed 1920s style, many of them renovated originals from the days when Barron Collier entertained the likes of Shirley Temple, Hedy Lamarr, Zane Grey, and Teddy Roosevelt. During the greater part of this century, the island has hosted wealthy escapists in a private club setting. In 1912, land magnate Collier established the Izaak Walton Club of Useppa Island, an organization devoted entirely to tarpon fishing.

But Useppa's past goes back much further than socialites and fishermen. Recent excavations on the island have established its importance as a B.C. Calusa Amerindian village. Once called Toempe, it was the largest of the Amerindian tribe's settlements, historians believe. It was also the site of bloody battles with Spanish explorers who tried to steal away this island gem from its rightful owners.

A couple of theories on how Useppa got its current name circulate. One, of course, involves pirate Gasparilla; the other, naturally, has to do with a fisherman. The José Gaspar version involves a beautiful princess named Josefa, treasure, love, scorn, and beheading. The more likely "fish tale" involves a different Jose, Jose Caldez, whose boat was perhaps named *Josefa*. In either case, *Josefa* got corrupted by non-Spanish tongues into Useppa, and so it remains today.

There seems to be some veracity to the treasure tale. As the legendaires tell it, shortly after Chicago millionaire John Roach bought the island in the 1890s, he was visited by sailors who dug up a treasure chest in the stealth of the night and left before their host had risen the next morning. (Stolen gems seem to be a recurrent affliction on Useppa.)

Islanders on Useppa in more modern times included counter-revolutionaries in training for the Cuban Bay of Pigs invasion. Gone are any traces of bygone belligerents. Useppa's entrenchment in the past is selective. Its time machine is stuck on the 20s and the good life. In 1976, Garfield Beckstead retrieved the little island so big on history from oblivion. He painstakingly restored and renovated Useppa's privileged heritage, returning its gracious architectural styles and carefree resort existence.

Historical Attractions

Most of the people who marched along Useppa's long dateline left behind structural reminders of their reign. The Calusa Amerindians left their shell burial and waste mounds; streetcar mogul John Roach contributed the island's reception center; Barron

Collier further developed Useppa style with the home that now serves as the Collier Inn and in the guest cottages he built for the rich R&R'ers. In the **Collier Inn**, a display of tarpon trophies and a signed guest book recalls the island's halcyon days.

THE NATURAL

Though much of Useppa Island's beauty relies on the man-made (including the beach) and the meticulously landscaped, a great deal of the island's pristine ecology remains intact, thanks to the fact that its marshy terrain is unbuildable. Peninsulas and narrowly bridged sub-islands skirt Useppa's western and southern edges in mangroves and grass flats that support a realm of wetland occupants.

AQUA-ADVENTURE

Touring

Nonguests can enjoy Useppa Island from arm's length by boating around the island, which lies roughly at Channel Marker 64. The island's lovely architecture is observable from offshore. Equally impressive is the fleet of million-dollar sailing yachts that weigh anchor in Oyster Bay at the island's southwest end. Collier Inn poses majestically leeside, framed picture-perfect in royal palms.

Besides the major destinations covered in this chapter, small shoals and island beaches, such as the one on Chino Key, provide venue for shelling, private sunbathing, and beachcombing. A club taxi boat carries guests to other nearby island landings.

A luncheon charter from South Seas Plantation Marina on Captiva Island carries 150 passengers aboard a double-decker, air-conditioned boat four times weekly. Call **Captiva Cruises** at 472-7549.

Fishing

The Izaak Walton Club still headquarters out of Useppa Island. It was founded by Barron Collier in 1912, when Useppa became the base for serious social-class anglers. The Club then awarded diamond buttons for tarpon catches over 150 pounds.

Snorkeling/Scuba

Gasparilla Island waters offer the area's best visibility — up to 15 feet at times. Bridges, defunct railroad trestles and phosphate docks, reefs, and jetties make homes for fish and off-the-beach exploration grounds for divers. Beware of strong currents in the south-end pass. The wreck of a 65-foot shrimp boat lies about five miles off the island's north end.

Boating, Sailing & Canoeing

Guests can rent boats from the marina on Useppa for island hopping in local waters.

ISLAND ADVENTURE

Hiking

Despite elevations of up to 35 feet, hiking Useppa Island is anything but strenuous. Four miles of path take you past manicured landscaping, homes old and new, picturesque gazebos, and even some wildlife.

Biking

Biking the island's path is allowed. Rentals are available at the Reception Center.

Shelling & Beachcombing

Useppa's beach came off a barge many years ago. The thought was nice, but you'll never see it listed under "Best Beaches."

Golfing

Barron Collier built the first golf course on Useppa circa 1912. The fourth tee was built on the deck of an old schooner. That golf course is now under renovation. There are three holes currently in play, plus a putting green.

Tennis

Two hard-surface tennis courts are found near the Collier Inn.

Other

Croquet, shuffleboard and outdoor chess courts provide unusual diversion in this ultracivilized island world.

CULTURE

The People

The permanent population of Useppa is approximately five. Most club members alight upon the island only in the winter months. They bought homes on Useppa for privacy and security. Because boaters approaching the dock are so thoroughly screened, islanders practice an open-door policy. Steep membership fees keep out the "wrong kind of people." What this all amounts to is a somewhat chilly atmosphere that could give the normally warm lover of islands frostbite. I recommend admiring Useppa from afar and lodging on North Captiva if you're looking to cut loose from the mainland for a spell.

Island Inspirations

Useppa lays claim to hosting a number of bygone luminati. Mystery novelist Mary Roberts Rinehart had a home on Useppa in the 1920s and built another one on nearby Cabbage Key for her son and his bride.

Architecture

When Garfield Beckstead, along with Mariner Properties, took over Useppa Island in 1976, they made it their goal to restore and maintain its historic style of indigenous architecture today termed Old Florida. Tin roofs; white clapboard siding; a square, no-nonsense design; and wide porches typify this style, to which modern, Victorian-style flourishes are added.

TABLE HOPPING

The **Tarpon Bar** at the Reception Center complex serves continental breakfast and deli lunch in a casual atmosphere. The **Collier Inn** is intimate and formal, with old-time appointments and lunch and dinner menus.

ISLAND LANDINGS

Some club members rent out their homes and townhouses when they are not using them. These range from basic furnished condo packages to fine family homes that accommodate up to six.

Prices match accordingly. For information, write or call the Useppa Island Club in advance at P.O. Box 2300, Pineland, FL 33945; 941-283-1061.

 CAYO COSTA

QUICK TOUR

The Intracoastal Waterway and Gulf of Mexico are the only way to Cayo Costa. Come ashore at the north end on either the gulf or bay side and walk or take the tram across the island. A long stretch of beach edges the Gulf front. Near the docks lie picnic and camping grounds. Where the campground is located was called Reservation Street in an earlier life, the main street for a community known simply as The Settlement.

The path across the island's northern end features a side trip to a pioneer cemetery. The observant may find other remnants of erstwhile habitation. Blooming cacti and other flora festoon the walk — which is sometimes a run when weather turns warm and uncontrolled mosquito populations come to remind us of the hardships of eras past. On the bayside, campers anchor their boats for the night in Pelican Bay. From the northernmost point, you can see Boca Grande and watch the tarpon fishermen at their summer ritual. Down island, boaters anchor offshore and wade in to enjoy a stretch of secluded beach. The long, stringy island narrows to stone's throw at some points.

BACKFLASH

Today an outpost of escape from the dizzying world of VCRs and Rolodexes, Cayo Costa has a history of harboring lamsters. Hispanic fishermen first settled the seven-mile-long island back in the mid-1800s. The island, originally named LaCosta, held two of the area's four productive fishing *ranchos* back then. They provided Cuban traders with salted mullet and roe. The camps were located at the southern and northern extremes of Cayo Costa's pulled-taffy skinnyness and employed mostly Spaniards, many running from the law or governmental oppression. The fishermen embraced the anonymity of life on the obscure island of Cayo Costa and relished its lack of law enforcement.

As ice-packing plants replaced the old method of salting, the fish market expanded to northern lands, and more fishermen were needed. Local fish companies recruited men from the Carolinas. Many from these ranks also sought shelter from the law. Eventually communities of fishermen and their families sprang up around the old ranchos. Schools, stores, and graveyards became part of the settlements.

Pirates played a role in Cayo Costa's lawless legacy, as they did for all the surrounding islands. Gasparilla is said to have built a fort on the island, which is strategically located at the mouth of Charlotte Harbor. Although the Gasparilla legend is doubted by serious historians, the belief that Cayo Costa served as a stopover for slavers, pirates, and other unsavory types goes undisputed.

During the Civil War years, the island furthered its reputation as a harbor for refugees by sheltering non-Confederates fleeing the harassment of self-appointed rebel vigilantes. Later, around 1904, it sheltered sick sailors at a quarantine station that operated on government property until 1925. At the same time, according to rumors, an island brothel served as a haven for lonely men from the Boca Grande naval base, located on nearby Gasparilla Island.

As Charlotte Harbor became hailed for its sports fishing, many Cayo Costa fishermen took up guiding to supplement their incomes. Exposure to the luxuries enjoyed by their clients led the fishermen to covet material goods. The simplistic lifestyle of Cayo Costa ended and many families moved off-island in search of a better, more comfortable life.

In 1959, the Federal Bureau of Land Management deeded much of Cayo Costa to Lee County for use as a public park. That facility later closed and the county handed over the property to the state, which had already purchased a sizable chunk of the 2,500-

acre island. The state now owns about 90 percent of Cayo Costa. After making improvements to a campground the county had built, the state reopened the park to visitors seeking modern-day escape — if not from the law then from the pressures and paces of daily life. With no electricity or drinking water, and only rustic cabins and primitive tent sites, Cayo Costa has not changed much since its days of harboring lawless refugees. Only a few private homes remain on the island. Most of them serve as weekend getaway lairs. The rest of the island is occupied by undisturbed wildlife.

Historical Attractions

The devoted artifact seeker may still find relics of the old fish camp settlements. A decade ago, people used to talk about stumbling upon smudge pots from the quarantine station. And die-hard Gasparilla believers swear you can find the foundations of a pirate fort.

No luck finding any artifacts on Cayo Costa? Try nearby neglected **Punta Blanco** island in Pelican Bay. Another settlement centered there at the turn of the century, and later Barron Collier built a boat works for his vessels and those of guests at his resort on nearby Useppa Island. The casual wanderer will be happy to find the cemetery where many of the old settlers are buried. Other remnants were destroyed when the county first built its park on the island.

THE NATURAL

What Cayo Costa lacks in reminders of human history, it overcompensates for with the persistence of natural history. Cayo Costa preserves the real Old Florida, the one that predates the tin-roofed and privileged vacationing eras. This is the Florida the Amerindians tried to protect against European invasion. Cold showers are as plush as it gets. All else is natural. Besides the wild hogs that survive on the island, egrets, white pelicans, raccoons, osprey, and blackwing skimmers frequent the area. Prehistoric loggerhead turtles lumber ashore to lay and bury their eggs — away from the lights and crowds of other area beaches. Fifty-six days later the baby turtles emerge and scurry to the sea before birds can snatch them up. It's nature at its best and most basic. Cayo Costa has almost a desolate feel, especially in the off-season, though its popularity increases every year, particularly during the winter months.

Natural Attractions

Cayo Costa State Park encompasses 2,225 acres of the island and preserves wildlife as it has existed since before humanity ventured into these waterways. The park spreads from Gulf to bay, and the park service operates a tram to transport visitors from one side to the other. Tent camping sites and rustic cabins with no electricity or drinking water keep human presence within the park at low impact.

AQUA-ADVENTURE

Touring

Cayo Costa offers water exploration possibilities galore. Boaters indulge Robinson Crusoe fantasies by finding their own stretch of unoccupied beach and anchoring offshore for a day's worth of beachcombing and sunning. Boaters can dock their crafts Gulf side or bay side off Intracoastal Channel Marker 65.

Fishing

Positioned at the edge of Boca Grande Pass, Cayo Costa presents the ideal fishing venue.

Snorkeling/Scuba

Though Gulf waters this far south normally cloud over, at certain times of the year snorkeling reveals mangrove and grass-flat sealife on the bayside and Gulf fauna in two to five feet of water on ledges offshore. Farther offshore, professional salvagers are tracking down Spanish wrecks reputed to hold pirate treasure.

ISLAND ADVENTURE

Hiking

Six trails cover five miles at Cayo Costa's wooded north end and provide even-keel hiking. One takes you to the old pioneer cemetery. Bring lots of bug repellent.

Shelling & Beachcombing

Cayo Costa's long beach hosts scores of seashells, especially around Johnson Shoals, a sandbar that juts out perpendicularly from the island's north end. Best pickings are at low tide. Sanddollars, scallops, lightning whelks, and fighting conchs are common finds. Live shelling is prohibited in the state park.

CULTURE

The People

Cayo Costa's full-time population includes two state park rangers. A handful of private homes serve as weekend getaways for local residents who do little to no mingling with visitors.

Nightlife

One of my best memories of island nightlife is drifting offshore in Pelican Bay with a full moon overhead.

TABLE HOPPING

Picnic lunching is a favorite activity on Cayo Costa. Otherwise, hop in the boat and go to Cabbage Key, Pine Island or North Captiva.

ISLAND LANDINGS

The state maintains 12 rustic cabins on the island's Gulf side. And I mean rustic: platform bunk beds, no electricity, no drinking water. There are cold showers. Regardless, the accommodations are popular. In season, they are reserved a year in advance. Tent sites are also available and more plentiful. Call 941-966-3954. Used to be you could camp anywhere on the island, but rangers are cracking down on that practice.

 PINE ISLAND

QUICK TOUR

For the motorist, Pine Island begins at Matlacha (mat-la-SHAY), although this fishing village actually lies at the center of the island's 17-mile length. It just happens to be where the bridge from the mainland probes. Matlacha proper begins on the mainland side of the Matlacha Bridge on Pine Island Road (Route 78). Restaurants, fruit stands, and bait shacks announce your arrival. You first cross onto Porpoise Point Island, where Matlacha huddles. Across the bridge, more saggy fish houses, motels and shops in old Cracker style continue to salt island flavor. Tiny stucco and clapboard structures painted in candy-store colors give the town an artistic flair. Matlacha is best explored by foot.

Pine Island Road bisects Matlacha and crosses the mangrove wetlands of Little Pine Island to meet Stringfellow Road, Route 767, at Pine Island Center. Go left here to reach St. James City, the island's most commercial and populated area, fingered by canals. The drive passes loblolly pine forests that give the island its name, and acres of undeveloped property.

A right turn off Pine Island Road onto Stringfellow will take you toward Phillips Park and the Museum of the Island on Sesame Drive. Turn left off Stringfellow onto Pineland Road to find a time-warped hamlet of charming old homes atop ancient Amerindian mounds in Pineland. Follow Waterfront Drive through Pineland to Caloosa Drive and Bokeelia Road. Turn left back onto Stringfellow and continue up to Bokeelia (bo-KEEL-ee-a), a throwback to the days when commercial fishing meant the area's livelihood. Farms make up the scenery along this drive — rare-palm nurseries, sugarcane fields, ground crop growers, exotic fruit farms, even a cattle pasture. Sunburst Tropical Fruits on Howard Street offers tours of its commercial rare fruit (principally mangoes) farm and processing facility.

Bokeelia is practically an island of its own, cut off from the rest of Pine Island by Jug Creek. Main Street is the locale of the little activity one finds in Bokeelia. There's not much in the way of sight-seeing in these parts. Bokeelia — and all of Pine Island — is the place to go for some hardcore fishing. That's the total preoccupation. A few slick condo developments make a stab at updating tempos, but all in all the island sits mired in a pace dictated by tides and spawning seasons. Lack of beaches keep tourism minimal and a sense of strong identity intact.

Not to say you shouldn't go to Pine Island. Make lunch at the unpretentious Crab Shack at island's end your goal, and explore old-island ways. Stop at a fruit stand to sample Pine Island's exotic commercial crops. Browse through Matlacha's artsy shops. Take home some fresh oysters or crab from a local fish market. Visit the historical museum. Enjoy the preponderance of historic buildings. Or just drive along and relish stretches of uncluttered island scenery.

BACKFLASH

When explorer Pedro Menéndez de Avilés visited these shores in 1565, searching for a son lost to shipwreck and a group of Spaniards being held captive by the Calusas, he built a fort at a spot called San Anton, believed to have been on Pine Island (though other historians pinpoint it at Mound Key to the south). Later the first Jesuit missionary was established there.

Pine Island's offshore Galt Island and its community of Pineland once held major Calusa Amerindian villages with elaborate canal systems, religious centers, and sizable mounds. In their wake settled Cuban immigrants who set up fishing camps and began a way of life that continues to this day.

Remote Bokeelia served as an ideal locale for pirates. Captain Bru Baker is said to have settled at Bokeelia in the days of Gasparilla, his ally. The area is replete with legends of buried treasure.

In more modern times, Pine Island has hidden away the sort of vacationer bent on seclusion and sports fishing. The San Carlos Hotel in St. James City attracted famous tarpon-seekers the likes of Henry Ford, Thomas Edison, and Teddy Roosevelt. It later burned to the ground. United Mine Workers Union leader of the 1940s, John L. Lewis, was another notable early Pine Island visitor. His Pineland fish shack was donated in recent years to a homeless local fisherman so that it could continue to serve its original purpose.

In 1927, the first bridge to Matlacha was completed. Electricity didn't cross over until nearly ten years later. Gladiolus, vegetable, and cattle farms comprised most of the island's acreage. A new bridge replaced the so-called "Fishingest Bridge in the World" in 1968.

Pine Island is one of the few Florida islands to have escaped the uprooting of heritage caused by seasonal population fluctuations and tourism. Today, as in centuries past, Pine Island is about Amerindian villages, fishing, and farming.

Historical Attractions

Occupying the old Pine Island library at Phillips Park, **Museum of the Islands** (5728 Sesame Drive, Pine Island Center; 941-283-1525) concentrates on the island's Calusa heritage. In 1992 the newest addition opened with the unveiling of a midden mound replica, constructed on the museum's lawn and modeled after one excavated on Galt Island.

THE NATURAL

Pine Island is committed to saving its natural heritage from the ravages of unchecked development. On the island and along its fringe of keys and shoals, bird life thrives. Hawks and bald eagles nest undisturbed. Waders and seabirds include the reddish egret, tricolored heron, wood stork, and blackwing skimmer.

Islanders claim that a few white-tailed deer survive on the island, and reports of a wild hog and Florida panther come in from time to time. More common are the otter, bobcat, marsh rabbit, opossum, and ubiquitous raccoon.

Pine Island's lack of beaches keeps away throngs of wildlife-disturbing tourists. The even better news is it attracts rich sealife to its mangrove inlets, canals, and mudflats. The blue-eyed bay scallop is at home here as is the blue crab and a wide variety of fin fish from the coveted snook to the humble catfish.

These backwaters offer a good venue for manatee spotting. Check out the bay behind Island Shell & Gifts, a popular seawatch site just before the Matlacha bridge. The dolphin population of Pine Island got noticed when local citizens took exception to the collection of specimens in their waters by northern zoologists.

Pine Island Sound Aquatic Preserve encompasses 54,000 acres of submerged land and shallow water where the web of life and interdependence of species is respected and protected.

Natural Attractions

The Pine Island National Wildlife Refuge can be seen only by boat. It lies off the island's west shores and comprises several keys, the principal one being Big Bird Rookery.

AQUA-ADVENTURE

Touring

Island Charters (941-283-1113), based at Pineland Marina, runs water taxis to North Captiva, Cayo Costa, and Cabbage Key. **Tropic Star** (941-283-0015) departs from Four Winds Marina (16501 Stringfellow Rd., Bokeelia) and returns at 4 P.M. **She-Mar Charters** (941-283-5836) takes six-hour, family-oriented groups fishing, shelling, and sightseeing.

Fishing

If you are truly serious about your fishing vacations — don't like them interrupted with all that beaching and sightseeing nonsense — Pine Island is the place for you. Bokeelia especially provides easy access to bay waters. Snook, tarpon, redfish, triple tail, shark, sheepshead, mackerel, and lady fish are favorite catches.

Captain Bill Cyzewski (941-283-0106) comes highly touted as a knowledgeable fishing guide, or try **Snook'R Charters** (941-283-0789).

Boating, Sailing & Canoeing

A public boat ramp is available at Matlacha Park. **Gulf Coast Kayak** (4882 Pine Island Rd., Matlacha; 941-283-1125) conducts day or overnight trips in the Matlacha Aquatic Preserve and other local natural areas, along with full moon and new moon astronomy ventures.

Other

Super Feat Para-Sailing & Water Skiing School serves Sanibel, Captiva, and Pine Island. Call 941-283-2020.

ISLAND ADVENTURE

Biking

A short, sporadic bike path/route travels through Bokeelia and St. James City at the island's southern end. Stringfellow Road is lightly enough traveled to provide safe, easy, and extensive on-road biking. Plans are in the works for a continuous bike path connecting St. James City, Bokeelia, and Matlacha for a 39-mile loop.

Swimming

Pine Island's dearth of natural beaches discourage sea bathing. A small, back-bay beach in St. James at the end of Tropical Point Drive is known more for its wildlife than its swimming. The public swimming pool at Phillips Parks is a more popular choice.

Golfing

Alden Pines Country Club at Pineland (14027 Clubhouse Dr.; 941-283-2179) is a semi-private club. The par-72 course has 18 holes in a natural setting.

Tennis

Two courts at **Phillips Park** are open to the public.

CULTURE

The People

When you get into a conversation with a Pine Islander, sooner or later the word fish comes up. For many of the local fishermen, commercial harvesting has been a family way of life for generations. For others, it's a hobby that can't be taken too seriously and precludes any chance of yuppiedom taking grip. As one Bokeelia man stated it: "You don't see any BMWs or Porsches here. We always say, 'If you can't pull a boat with it, why own it?'"

Pine Islanders (full-timers number about 6,800) are generally classified as stubborn and overprotective of their island. An admirable quality in islanders, indeed! They resist overdevelopment with the feisty struggle of a hooked tarpon. They remain attached to the sea like an oyster to a mangrove prop. They once demonstrated their devotion to their island and its wildlife by fighting zoologists who were collecting porpoises in Pine Island Sound. More recently, they cohered against the banning of net fishing in Florida.

Pine Islanders tend to be more earthy and natural than their neighboring island counterparts. I think of Birkenstocks and health foods when I picture the island's younger, arts-driven community.

Fairs & Festivals

Pine Island Seafood Festival takes place in March amid partying and fish-feasting.

Museums & Galleries

For locally produced art, visit **The Crossed Palms Gallery** at Bokeelia (8315 Main St., 941-283-2283).

Island Shopping

Mel Meo's (5509 Pine Island Rd., Pine Island Center; 941-283-9484) is an unusual shop that sells hand-painted clothing and other art, along with seafood and miscellany.

Architecture

Whole sections of Pine Island, along with several individual buildings, have been designated historic structures. Samples of Cracker architecture, a vernacular style typified by steep tin roofs and simple square lines, abound. Pineland's mound-squatting homes are prime examples, occasionally dressed up with latticework and vivid paint jobs.

On Bokeelia, the entire Main Street is designated historical. Notice especially the Captains House on Main Street, a fine example of slightly upscale folk housing of the early 1900s. It features French Provincial elements and a covered widow's walk. Turner

Mansion, nearby, represents a higher standard of living during that era and is reminiscent of New England styles, as are many of Old Florida's marine-themed structures.

Mobile homes make up a good share of the island's old residential areas. Newer developments crop up slowly and try, for the most part, to blend in.

TABLE HOPPING

Two culinary musts on Pine Island are the exotic fruits and the fresh *fruits de mer*. Mangoes are specifically associated with Pine Island, where they have been farmed for decades. These are in season in early summer. Dozens of varieties grow in configurations from small, red, round, and turpentine-y to melon-sized, liver-shaped, orange, and indescribably sweet. The most popular varieties include Kent, Haden, and Keitt. One grower on Pine Island produces a Valencia variety that you should look for in the fruit stands. Besides mangoes, you will find guavas, longans, carambolas (star fruit) and lychees. The only other place in Florida where these tropical fruits grow commercially lies on the east coast at a latitude some 90 miles south of Pine Island.

You can visit one of the farms, a small acreage known as **Sunburst Tropical Fruit Co.** (7113 Howard Street, Bokeelia; 941-283-1200). Owners Nita and Gary Grochowski sell their own fresh fruit, chutneys, sauces, dried fruits, spice plants, and a cookbook Nita wrote about tropical fruits, titled *Sunburst Tropical Fruit Co. Cookbook*. Its recipes use all varieties of Pine Island-grown fruits.

What makes Pine Island so nearly tropical? The warm waters of Charlotte Harbor run wide at the island's north end around Bokeelia. They insulate the land, warming cold air before it reaches fragile fruit groves and creating a pocket of microclimate. Fruit lovers from miles around pilgrimage to roadside stands along Pine Island Road throughout the summer and fall.

The island also attracts serious fish aficionados. Matlacha is home to several active fish houses, where fresh oysters, shrimp, blue crab, grouper, snapper, pompano, scallops, and sea trout are off-loaded for transshipment. Much of it stays in town to sate appetites of residents and visitors looking for the freshest, most full-flavored sea products available. Several seafood markets sell to the public.

Pine Island restaurants are generally stuck in a time before everything came julienned and sun-dried. Freshness was a premise on Pine Island long before "new American cuisine" chefs pretended to have invented it. Nothing fancy: raw oysters, steamed crab, fried grouper sandwiches, crab cakes — standard fish-house fare. One exception is a new development in Matlacha that emerged from a cluster of bayside Cracker shacks. **The Mad Hatter Tea Room** (4283 Pine Island Rd. NW; 941-283-3486) serves "flip-flop and shorts gourmet cookery." The tiny dining room spills out from a white, peely clapboard house into red, white and blue alfresco tables dockside. The view of stilted fish and bait houses jutting into the sound on the mainland side of the Matlacha bridge is purely Pine Island. Call ahead for by-water directions.

A favorite of mine also sits on the water and is reachable by boat, this one in St. James City. The **Waterfront Restaurant** (2131 Oleander St.; 941-283-0592) occupies an old one-room schoolhouse and serves seafood a step dressier than one expects on Pine Island. Eat sandwiches, baskets, or fine dinners on brown-paper tablecloths under paddle fans. Boat tie-ups are available. If the weather's right, ask for a seat outdoors dockside.

One of the oldest (and it looks it) local favorites slumps waterside in Bokeelia. **Crab Shack**'s (8031 Main St.; 941-283-2466) homemade goodness and just-off-the-boat freshness makes it a hard place to find a table at lunchtime. For dining by boat, pull into the **Bootlegger Restaurant** at Four Winds Marina (16501 Stringfellow Rd.; 941-283-4301).

Pine Island Seafood Festival Cookbook (available at Mel Meo's Shop; see *Island Shopping*) offers simple recipes for mullet, crab, shrimp, oysters, pompano, and other local seafood.

ISLAND LANDINGS

In Bokeelia, fancy marine-oriented complexes such as the

Bocilla Island Club (800-992-6168 or 941-283-5512) are trying to survive. At the other end of the scale, rustic **Jug Creek Cottages** are for rent through the Department of Natural Resources (941-964-0375). The small motels of downtown Matlacha and fishing lodges such as **Water's Edge** in St. James City (Oleander & Sanibel Blvd.; 941-283-0515) offer a taste of unvarnished Pine Island. A **KOA** in St. James City (5120 Stringfellow Rd., 941-283-2415) accommodates campers.

Sources & Resources

Visit or contact the **Greater Pine Island Chamber of Commerce** before the Matlacha bridge on Pine Island Road (P.O. Box 525, Pine Island, FL 33909, 941-283-0888). For current events reported in the leisurely manner of Pine Island, subscribe to the *Pine Island Eagle*. Write or call at 10700 Stringfellow Rd., Suite 60, Bokeelia FL 33922 (941-283-2260). **Calusa Land Trust & Nature Preserve** of Pine Island invites membership and contributions to assist in its protection of sensitive wetlands. Write P.O. Box 216, Bokeelia, FL 33922. For a complete history of the island, pick up a copy of Elaine Jordan's *The Forgotten Island* (available in local stores and the Museum of the Islands).

 NORTH CAPTIVA

QUICK TOUR

Referred to also as Upper Captiva, North Captiva treads water without benefit of a lifeline to shore. One must travel by boat or private plane to get there. For a day of beaching, anchor offshore on the over three-mile-long Gulf front and wade in. To dock, you must approach Safety Harbor on the island's northeastern side. This is not an easy feat, which is one reason the island remains so sparsely and blessedly uncrowded. Get good directions from the boat rental facility or call ahead.

At the mouth of the harbor struts a historic stilt fish house, relic of the turn-of-the-century commercial fishing era. One of about a dozen still standing where hundreds once served as homes for resident fishermen, the structure is listed on the National Register of Historic Places.

Depressurizing constitutes the primary activity on the island along long, shell-strewn strands where one can often roam without meeting another human. People travel inconspicuously by foot or golf cart along sandy cross-island pathways, where one can commune freely with pure nature. The island's low-key activity centers around Safety Harbor.

The most popular thing to do, especially for day-trippers, is eat at one of the island's fine restaurants in Safety Harbor. Most people who stay on North Captiva use it as a launching pad to more island exploration and water sports.

BACKFLASH

Once part of Captiva Island — little sister to mainland-tethered Sanibel — North Captiva broke away for a life of its own amid the hurricane of 1921. And we are all so much better because of it. For whereas Captiva is a beachy, quirky little island with character all its own, North Captiva affects an entirely separate, renegade personality with sparse settlement, a private airstrip, and state-protected beaches.

The island has been the site of such diverse activities as a tomato plantation, a commercial fishing enterprise, and now a community of mostly second-home retreats. Recent building on North Captiva began in the 1960s, more than 20 years before electricity reached the island. In 1975, the state of Florida acquired 500 of the island's 700 total acres and designated it as a barrier island preserve.

Historical Attractions

One of the area's best sights lies halfway across Pine Island Sound at a shoal known as Captiva Rocks. Here a colony of **fish shacks**, remnant of the area's turn-of-the-century commercial fishing operations, are maintained by private owners as weekend fishing getaways. One more such structure — this one an erstwhile ice house — stands at the entrance of Safety Harbor.

THE NATURAL

Under state guardianship, North Captiva holds on to its natural endowments. Birds ply its protected harbor and Gulf beaches in search of food. Shells are not as picked over as they are on the more inhabited barrier islands. Lizards, snakes, and raccoons chase each other around the food chain.

Natural Attractions

North Captiva State Recreation Area spreads over 500 acres at the island's southern end. Completely undeveloped, it provides refuge for waterfowl, shore birds, and migrating species.

AQUA-ADVENTURE

Touring

North Captiva docking lies off the Intracoastal Waterway at Channel Marker 46 in Safety Harbor. The approach is tricky to maneuver, so call ahead to the island for good directions.

Fishing

Think of the island as a big fishing boat. Go to any side and throw in your line. Redfish, tarpon, mangrove snapper, and sheepshead thrive in these waters.

Swimming

Besides offshore stretches of shallow water gradually deepening, a swimming pool at Safety Harbor is open to residents and guests.

ISLAND ADVENTURE

Hiking

Unless you rent a golf cart, hiking is your only on-island transportation option. Trails are informal, radiating out from Safety Harbor to the restaurants, residential areas, and beaches. I prefer to wander aimlessly and see where it takes me. North Captiva is that kind of place, that kind of pace.

Shelling & Beachcombing

You could perfect beach-bumming here. As a barrier island,

North Captiva attracts any number of seashell species. Beaches are often deserted. In some places you'll come across the ruins of sea-battered homes that make for fun exploring. The beach runs wide to skinny, and is typically fluffy and white.

CULTURE

The People

Most of the homeowners on North Captiva use the island as a second-home getaway. The permanent population numbers around 30, composed primarily of business owners and service staff. Residents walk or cart around with serene smiles on their faces, casually greeting visitors as gracefully as fellow islanders. Their placidity is nearly scary; their hospitality inspirational.

During the day, nonworking islanders are harder to spot than bald eagles — unless you rise early enough to catch them taking off in their boats. Not until Saturday night cocktail hour do you see them surface in their white slacks and windburns.

Architecture

With few exceptions, the buildings on North Captiva tend toward modern — some, on the Gulf side, unusually so. Most are stilted and demurely stained to blend in with nature. The necessity of barging in materials dictates simplicity, yet all is comfortable and appealing.

Nightlife

Nightlife starts with a cocktail-hour ritual around sunset in the clubhouse area. This should be followed by a walk on the beach in quest of the elusive green flash.

TABLE HOPPING

There are only three restaurants on North Captiva (soon to be four), but each merits mention. All prepare the Gulf's freshest offerings in a creative and resourceful style forced upon them by dint of the island's remoteness. All cluster in the vicinity of Safety Harbor.

Barnacle Phil's (4401 Point House Trail; 941-472-6394), which hides behind the mangroves near the harbor entrance, serves a casual selection of hamburgers, grouper sandwiches, and black beans 'n rice outside or at one of the few indoor tables at the breeze-cooled establishment. This is a local hangout as well as a mecca for boaters who shun the trendier bustle of Cabbage Key.

Less hidden, **Over the Waterfront** (941-472-6994) sits directly atop the bay at the spot where residents and visitors dock their boats, in the back of a general store. The tiny eatery serves a standard lunch daily and spectacular dinners whenever there are reservations. The dinner menu changes nightly and stars local catches.

Grady's (533 Rum Rd.; 941-395-1500) lies on a canal off Safety Harbor and is open for breakfast, lunch, and dinner. Local ingredients from pompano to prickly pear cactus get made into what is termed "barrier island cuisine."

ISLAND LANDINGS

Your only option for accommodations on North Captiva is a minimum three-day rental in a privately owned condo or home. Contact **Upper Captiva Property Management** (P.O. Box 476, Captiva Island, FL 33924; 941-472-9223) to reserve and receive information on taxi service for guests. For a house rental, contact **North Captiva Island Club** (P.O. Box 1000, Pineland, FL 33945, 800-576-7343 or 813-395-1001). Bring groceries and supplies with you, because the sparse selection of necessaries available for purchase on the island will cost you dearly.

Sources & Resources

Upper Captiva Property Management (P.O. Box 476, Captiva Island, FL 33924; 941-472-9223) is the best source for information about anything on the island.

 CAPTIVA ISLAND

QUICK TOUR

Captiva's sister island to the south, Sanibel, serves as its gateway. Blind Pass Bridge connects the two, separated by a flush of water that alternately opens and closes the pass. Captiva's remoteness from the mainland keeps the little island curiously eccentric.

Turner's Beach lies where the two islands meet and extends southward. Here is one of only two public beach accesses. Parking and entrance to Captiva Beach is found at the north end of Captiva Road, past the gate to South Seas Plantation.

The 5.5-mile drive between these two points is one of the greatest treats the skinny little island offers. A jungle of tropical vegetation overlayered with feathery casuarinas creates a lush tunnel effect, but with cathedral ceilings. Then quite suddenly the road takes a couple of serrated turns and spits you out into open sky, sea, and sand. It slices between Gulf and bay, past beach and old island homes edged in gargantuan agaves, blooming cacti, tangled sea grapes, and graceful coconut palms.

Another jerk-stop turn starts the road into "downtown Captiva," if there is such a thing. Quirky restaurants, a general store, confused side streets, saggy beach cottages, and trendy shops jumble helter-skelter along this Adam's apple swell in Captiva's throat.

It's fun to get lost on the side streets, swallowed up by Captiva's personality. Stop at the lovely Chapel-by-the-Sea, an interdenominational church popular for weddings and seaside meditation. Many of the island's early pioneers have been laid to rest in a cemetery beside the chapel.

Captiva is not the type of place one visits in search of fever-pitch beach partying or nonstop sightseeing. One sneaks off to Captiva without giving the office a definite destination. Activity here often requires a prone position (some say the gravitational pull on Captiva is stronger than anywhere else in Florida). Less than two miles across at its widest point, Captiva is but an exclamation mark in an expression of delight.

BACKFLASH

Captiva legend attributes its name to a bygone prison camp established there by pirate Gasparilla for comely kidnap victims. Whether or not the old sea tale holds water, it's a known fact that Captiva Island does indeed captivate.

Island worship.
(Chelle Koster Walton)

At various times in its past, Captiva has supported citrus and tomato farms, communities of fishermen and a coconut plantation. In the 1920s through the 1940s, well-to-do notables intent upon anonymity in the wilds made their way to Captiva. Most famous were Charles and Anne Lindbergh, who sneaked away to the island when the aviator's fame became too much to handle. Political cartoonist and conservation activist Jay Norwood "Ding" Darling gained Captiva and Sanibel islands national attention by fighting for their natural attributes during his regular visits there. Teddy Roosevelt also came to the island to cast a line.

Captiva upholds its reputation as a hideout today. South Seas Plantation, a gated resort that takes up a good one-third of the island, often hosts publicity-weary stars.

Historical Attractions

The **Captiva History House** (at South Seas Plantation; 941-472-5111) chronicles the island's days as a remote fishing community and coconut plantation with photos and artifacts.

THE NATURAL

Because tiny Captiva is still unincorporated, unlike sister Sanibel, few restraints hold back development. Only the exorbitant price of land on Captiva precludes its total plundering. The best examples of native fauna and flora are found in islanders' yards along Captiva Road, where the accepted look is wild and jungly.

The top-billed attraction on Captiva is, and always has been, the island's beaches. Islanders recently shelled out a lot of money to regain a hold on the sands that had shifted in time down to Sanibel shores. A renourishment project temporarily restored the wide expanses of shell-strewn beach.

Natural Attractions

Turner's Beach is the most popular of Captiva's two public beach accesses. Located where the islands begin to take a northerly heading, it's a great place to catch sunset. The beach is wide and comfy, but a strong riptide makes swimming dangerous. There are restrooms and some parking, but arrive early and don't park in the lot on the Sanibel side unless you have a resident sticker.

Parking is a major problem at Captiva's north end beach access, another good place to catch the sun as it does its curtain call. In between the two extremes, the beach is public, but you cannot park anywhere near it.

Buck Key is partially a protected refuge on Captiva Island's bay side. It holds many national champion trees, including a Jamaican Caper, Jamaican Dogwood, and False Mastic.

AQUA-ADVENTURE

Touring

Boats arriving at Captiva can find dockage at **South Seas Plantation** (ICW marker #39; 941-472-5111) or 'Tween Waters Inn (ICW marker #38; 941-472-5161). Advance reservations are recommended in high season. **Jensen's Twin Palm Marina** (15107 Captiva Dr.; 941-472-5800) runs water taxis to North Captiva, Cabbage Key, and Cayo Costa. The *Jean Nicolet*, a double-decker out of South Seas Plantation Marina (941-472-7549), visits Cabbage Key and Useppa Island for lunch.

Fishing

Several fishing, shelling and sightseeing charters depart from 'Tween Waters Marina (Captiva Rd.; 941-472-5161). **South Seas Plantation** (941-472-5111), though a private resort, offers a variety of charters to the public with advance reservation. Captiva sponsors two major fishing tournaments in May: the Tarpon Tide Tournament and the Caloosa Catch & Release Fishing Tournament.

Swimming

Signs at Turner's Beach prohibit swimming. Pay attention: Lives have been lost to the strong current. Elsewhere along the beach, swimming in the gentle waves is safe and carefree.

Snorkeling/Scuba

Pieces of Eight Dive Center (941-472-8383) operates out of South Seas Marina, taking snorkelers and divers into offshore waters to explore ledges and wrecks. The center teaches certification courses and rents out diving and underwater video equipment. Waters close to shore are generally too murky.

Boating, Sailing & Canoeing

The full-service marina at 'Tween Waters Inn (Captiva Rd.; 941-472-5161) rents motorboats, sailboats, canoes, kayaks, fishing equipment, bicycles, and aquabikes. A full complement of rental boats is stocked by **South Seas Plantation Marina** (941-472-5111), and a sailing school operates from the premises. **Jensen's Twin Palm Marina** (15107 Captiva Dr.; 941-472-5800) rents pontoon and other motorboats.

Offshore Sailing School (South Seas Plantation; 941-472-5111) teaches "rag boat" skills.

For **Sanibel Sea Kayak Wildlife Tours**, call the 'Tween Waters Marina (941-472-5161).

Sailboarding & Surfing

Holiday Ski School (941-472-5111, ext. 3459), one South Seas concession, specializes in waterskiing, parasailing and jet skiing.

Redfish Pass, which separates Captiva from North Captiva, is the site of brisk sport and competitive sailboarding.

ISLAND ADVENTURE

Biking

Bikers on Captiva vie with motor traffic on the serpentine road. In high season, this becomes tricky, if not dangerous. For family cycling, go to Sanibel, unless you stay at South Seas, where controlled traffic promises more safety. You can rent your bikes at some resorts or at **Jim's Bike Rental** (11534 Andy Rosse Ln.; 941-472-1296).

Shelling & Beachcombing

The island's north-end beach gathers the best shells. For collecting trips to the out-islands, contact **Capt. Mike Fuery's Shelling Charters** (941-472-1015) or **Duke Sells Shelling Charters** (941-472-5462).

CULTURE

The People

"Old money" forms the basis of Captiva's seasonal population, a gracious class that once occupied low-slung cottages and shunned development. They are a casual breed of the rich. This profile changes as family property falls into the hands of yuppie beneficiaries. Then there's an even deeper layer in the hierarchy of old islanders. A handful of Captiva homesteaders still live there, most notably an 80-something gentleman by the name of Uncle Joe Wightman (see sidebar). Because Captiva is unincorporated, only voter registration figures are available. Those numbered 604 in 1990, with a median age of 43.

Island Inspirations

Anne Morrow Lindbergh and **Robert Rauschenberg** are two names that have contributed to Captiva's reputation as an artist's haven. One a writer of the 1940s, the other a contemporary visual artist, both have nurtured their arts on Captiva.

Lindbergh visited often in the 1940s and is believed to have written her inspirational *Gift From the Sea* while on the island. Though she never mentions her secret hideaway in it nor in any of her published diaries, her famous aviator husband Charles does record their visits in his *Autobiography of Values*. Rauschenberg still calls Captiva home and has established an artist's commune on his Captiva acreage.

Back in the early days, another man absorbed the inspirational powers of Captiva Island, and in return left his own gifts. **Jay Norwood "Ding" Darling**, a Pulitzer Prize–winning political cartoonist, visited regularly for many years. He built a stilt fish house in the water with a drawbridge to land, where he could work undisturbed. He penned many cartoons to and for his Captiva friends. His most important island legacy, however, is the 4,900-acre wildlife sanctuary on Sanibel that bears his name.

Museums & Galleries

Wildlife is often the theme of art on Captiva. For remarkable wildlife paintings, sculptures and jewelry, visit **Jungle Drums Gallery** (11532 Andy Rosse Ln.; 941-395-2266).

Architecture

The old islanders still call their homes "beach shacks," no matter that they would sell in the millions. Only recently have some of these been sold out of the family and replaced with modern monstrosities more indicative of the wealth they represent. The old homes are simple, built for Florida living with high ceilings, cool terrazzo floors, and paddle fans everywhere.

Nightlife

'Tween Waters **Crow's Nest** (Captiva Rd, 941-472-5161) is famous locally for its nightlife. Visitors and residents on both Sanibel and Captiva flock there for the best of the islands' live music, in a range from reggae to jazz. At South Seas Plantation, steel drums often set the mood in **Chadwick's Lounge** (941-472-5111), which is open to the public.

TABLE HOPPING

Eventually you'll run into the **Mucky Duck Restaurant** (Andy Rosse Ln.; 941-472-3434). Practically every visitor to Captiva does. The bustling Gulf-side restaurant with its English pub theme is a favorite spot for lunch and dinner. You may have to wait for a table, but with a front-row seat at the sandpiper ballet — who cares?

ISLAND LANDINGS

The danger of staying at a place like **South Seas Plantation** (P.O. Box 194, Captiva Island, FL 33924; US 800-237-3102, FL 800-282-3402 or 941-472-5111) is that you are isolated in a contrived world where every little whim is sated. This means you miss out on local color. **'Tween Waters Inn** (Captiva Rd.; 941-472-5161), with its historic depth and handy marina, is a more involving choice. I like the beach cottages you find at **Jensen's Twin Palms Resort & Marina** (15107 Captiva Dr.; 941-472-5800). They are unpretentious and offer docking facilities.

Downtown Captiva's most famous signpost.
(Chelle Koster Walton)

TOURIST TRAPS

You'll hear and read a lot about the **Bubble Room Restaurant** (15001 Captiva Dr.; 941-472-5558), where reputation was built upon gimmickry. Knickknacks from the 1930s and 1940s congest the walls and spill out into the parking lot. The servers wear Boy Scout uniforms covered with "badges" expressing sentiments sometimes less than honorable. It's a fun place to experience once. The food is good, but not worth the prices. In season, the wait is long and the pace is rush, rush, rush.

Sources & Resources

Elinore Dormer's *Sea Shell Islands* (Rose, 1979) captures the factual history of both Sanibel and Captiva. In a more folksy style, reminiscent of Florida's own Marjorie Kinnan Rawlings, Ted Levering tells about early settlement of the islands in *The Other Side of the Bridge* (Willowmead, 1991). To submerge yourself in the mood of Captiva inspiration, take Anne Morrow Lindbergh's *Gift*

From the Sea (Pantheon, 1955) along to the beach. The Sanibel newspapers cover Captiva doings, but the island also has a weekly of its own, the *Captiva Current* (P.O. Box 549, Captiva Island, FL 33924; 941-482-6860).

SANIBEL ISLAND

QUICK TOUR

Although you will begin to see commercial enterprises using the Sanibel name well before, the city of Sanibel begins at the end of a three-mile county causeway ($3 toll for most vehicles without stickers) that skips across three man-made spoiler islands. Daytrippers and windsurfers favor the beaches along these islands. The Sanibel-Captiva Chamber of Commerce sits near the causeway's doorstep and is an excellent resource. At the four-way stop sign, turn left onto Periwinkle Way for a visit to the historic lighthouse. A wildlife trail and beach encompass it.

The other end of Periwinkle Way is a shopper's route. Along this road and adjacent Palm Ridge Road cluster most of the island's boutiques, galleries, and restaurants. Sanibel Community Center on Periwinkle is the focal point for fairs and various activities. Turn right off Palm Ridge onto Wooster Lane to Dunlop Road to visit the Island Historical Village, BIG Arts Center, and new library.

Return to Palm Ridge, which leads to Sanibel-Captiva Road and the island's natural personality. Sanibel-Captiva Conservation Center and the J. N. "Ding" Darling National Wildlife Refuge stretch jungle tentacles along the road. San-Cap Road is also the site of the Bailey-Matthews Shell Museum. The entrance to Bowman's Beach lies down the road. Sanibel officially ends at Blind Pass, where Captiva takes over across a bridge. Part of Turner's Beach curls around the island's end. This section of the island is referred to as Santiva.

Returning down-island, turn right on Rabbit Road to get to the island's Gulf face. Go left on Gulf Drive and follow its contortions past homes, resorts, and the turn-off to Gulfside Park beach (Algiers Road). Casa Ybel Road or Donax Road will return you to Periwinkle's business sections, or you can continue along East Gulf Drive, which eventually meets Periwinkle a few miles short of the lighthouse.

BACKFLASH

Sanibel's early history proceeded at the pace of the island's gopher tortoises. Human habitation, from the days of the Calusa Amerindians until the building of the causeway in 1963, remained sparse and rugged. It is believed that Ponce de León discovered the islands of Sanibel and Captiva in 1513. He and his followers' arrival led to eventual elimination of the island's aborigines by 1800.

A short-lived colony and later the establishment of a lighthouse reservation filled the gap between *conquistadores* and homesteaders, who settled Sanibel circa 1890. The lighthouse was built to service the brisk cattle trade between Fort Myers and Cuba.

Farming, fishing, and eventually serving tourists provided a meager livelihood. In 1926, a ferry service began transporting residents and tourists from mainland to island, with the last ferry of the day closing Sanibel down at 5:30 p.m. Islanders protested loudly when, in 1963, a proposal for a bridge meant the end of the island ferry and the privacy it afforded them. Hurricane damage contributed to the eventual demise of the island's tomato and citrus farms. Fishing later took a back seat to tourism.

Development threatened to overrun the island soon after the bridge was built, and the islanders decided to put on the brakes by incorporating. Strict restraints to building slowed development and kept it as environmentally compatible as possible, but powerful developers found ways to buck the system and exploit this natural gold mine. Rate-of-growth ordinances were discarded and real estate prices soared out of reality.

Today, Sanibel reigns as one of Florida's most popular resort islands. It is also one of the state's most important refuge islands. This plurality often results in contradictions and conflict between commercial and environmental factions. Thanks to the establishment of the J. N. "Ding" Darling National Wildlife Refuge on Sanibel in the 1960s, Sanibel's role as an environmental protector persists into posterity.

Historical Attractions

The Sanibel Island Historical Village (850 Dunlop Rd.; 941-472-4648) is a growing collection of vintage island structures that began with a Cracker-style pioneer abode that now houses the mainstay museum. Added in recent years: the original island post office which dates to the mid-1920s; the relocated Old Bailey Store remembering the island's pre-causeway days; and Miss Charlotta's Tea Room serving refreshment as it did when it stood at the ferry landing. More attractions are planned.

The hidden **Sanibel Cemetery** lies off the bike path and away from the road on Middle Gulf Drive. No signs direct you to it; just follow the path and you'll come across a fenced plot with wooden headstones announcing the names of early settlers.

Built in 1884, the **Sanibel Lighthouse** at the island's southeast end was one of its first permanent structures. Once vital to cattle transports from the mainland, it winks still as a beacon of warning and welcome. The lighthouse and Old Florida-style lightkeeper's cottage were renovated in 1991.

THE NATURAL

Sanibel and Captiva came into existence as a high ridge of sand stabilized, grew, and eventually split in two. Sanibel sands continue to win the island its greatest favor. Residents and visitors alike value Sanibel's trove of shell-strewn beaches — 15 miles in all. Sandy shoreline stretches from end to end, with public accesses placed at regular intervals. The island's east-west heading prevents beach erosion and enhances beachcombing finds. Sanibel is known as the Shelling Capital of the Western Hemisphere. Collectors come from around the world to search the fabled beaches. Bowman's Beach at mid-island is one of the shelling spots they favor most.

Sanibel beaches are also known for their protection of nesting loggerhead turtles. **Caretta Research Foundation**, which works to protect the endangered 300-pound creatures, was founded and is headquartered on Sanibel.

The island's protected wetlands, Sanibel's other treasure, attract flocks of bird watchers and nature lovers. It has changed considerably over the years due to the introduction of noxious exotic plants. Old-timers tell of a time when they could see the lighthouse from mid-island. The introduction of the Australian pine tree, or casuarina, around 1910, brought the island its first tall trees. Unfortunately, it and another bane to Florida landscaping, the Brazilian pepper, tend to overwhelm native vegetation. Sanibel works diligently to rid the island of these dictatorial plants. Many visitors (and some residents) vehemently protest the uprooting of the casuarinas which, despite their faults, do lend romance with their lacy foliage and whispering-winds special effects.

Cabbage palms, gumbo limbos, coffee plants, railroad vines, sea oats, sea grapes, sea hibiscus, and blue porterweed are some of the island's native plants. The rare and threatened **joewood**, a blossoming, shrubby tree, has been designated the island's official plant. With its near-tropical climate, the island is suitable for exotic fruit and flowering plant cultivation. You'll find yards redolent and chromatic with bougainvillea, hibiscus, mango, banana, key limes, papaya, avocado, gardenia, and poinsettia.

All wildlife is protected on Sanibel. The island's unofficial wildlife ambassador is the alligator. Sanibel was first to criminalize the feeding of the once-threatened creature. State laws later followed Sanibel's lead. In birddom, the osprey gets particular attention via the Sanibel-based **International Osprey Fund**. The Audubon Society also has a local chapter, and various other wildlife protection groups gather on environmentally conscious Sanibel. Audubon spotters have counted 114 species around Sanibel.

The Florida bobcat is occasionally spotted on Sanibel, and even the rare and endangered Florida panther, where development is light. Armadillos, raccoons, opossums, and otters more commonly populate the island's four-legged world.

Sanibel lighthouse.
(Lee County Visitor & Convention Bureau)

Natural Attractions

J. N. "Ding" Darling National Wildlife Refuge (941-472-1100) showcases the best of southern Florida's wildlife. Within its 4,900 acres, osprey, egrets, pelicans, roseate spoonbills, ibis, manatees, alligators, armadillos, and black snakes take refuge. Native plants flourish in this Everglades-like atmosphere: sea grapes, sabal palms, buttonwood, and gumbo limbo.

The Sanibel-Captiva Conservation Center (3333 Sanibel-Captiva Road, 941-472-2329) research and preservation facility encompasses 1,192 acres and is open to the public. A guided or self-guided tour introduces you to indigenous fauna, and indoor displays further educate, including a touch tank. Guest lecturers, seminars, and workshops address environmental issues during the winter season. The center hosts interpretative on-site programs, beach walks, wildlife cruises, and Children's Corners.

The Bailey-Matthews Shell Museum (941-395-2233) on Sanibel-Captiva Road, with its 1995 projected completion date, will underline Sanibel's shelling reputation with educational exhibits that tell the role of shells in natural and human history. The **C.R.O.W.** (Care and Rehabilitation of Wildlife) hospital complex duplicates natural habitat and attends to sick and injured wildlife. Visit by appointment; call 941-472-3644. **Aqua Trek and Sealife Learning Center** (2353 Periwinkle Way; 941-472-8680) gives kids and adults the opportunity to enjoy a 100-gallon touch tank and 15 aquariums and other sea animal displays that introduce life in the Gulf. The center serves as a marine laboratory and departure point for informative beach walks by a marine biologist.

AQUA-ADVENTURE

Touring

Half-day charters depart from **Sanibel Marina** (634 North Yachtsman Dr., 941-472-2723), which lies in the harbor near the lighthouse around ICW Marker 2. Docking is also available. Charters typically sightsee to the upper islands of Cayo Costa and Cabbage Key. Sanibel provides good access to the southern islands of Estero, Lover's Key, and Little Hickory Island as well.

Fishing

Several fishing guides operate out of **Sanibel Marina** (634 North Yachtsman Dr., 941-472-2723). All are excellent and have been around these waters for a very long time. **Crabby Chuck's Stone Crab Claws** (941-482-2214) offers unique opportunities to witness the life of local crabbers on "U-Pick" charters to harvest stone crab claws (in season mid-October to mid-May) from local traps. The charters are tailored to customers' needs and can do pick-ups from any feasible location on the island.

A T-shaped **fishing pier** extends into bay waters at the island's south end near the lighthouse and is open to the public. Captain Mike Fuery wrote the book on fishing in the area. And he ought to know. He's been working as a charter guide for decades and he's one of the best. (He took President Carter fly fishing recently.) Buy his *South Florida Bay and Coastal Fishing* (Sanibel Sanddollar Publications, 1987).

Swimming

The gentle Gulf and bay waters provide safe and warm swimming practically year-round. Be careful in summer months when rays burrow along the shore to lay eggs. They won't hurt you unless you step on them. To avoid this, shuffle your feet at water's edge. Do not swim off the shores of Turner's Beach where strong currents have taken the lives of even strong swimmers. The city of Sanibel owns and maintains an Olympic-size swimming pool at its **Recreation Complex** at the Sanibel Elementary School (3840 Sanibel-Captiva Road, 941-472-0345). It's a good place for lapping and training, but mostly too deep for kid's play.

Boating, Sailing & Canoeing

A free municipal boat ramp accommodates trailered craft near the causeway's landfall. **Sanibel Marina** (634 North Yachtsman Dr.; 941-472-2723) rents powerboats for half- and full-day trips in intracoastal waters only. Many resorts rent small sailboats, paddleboats, and other water toys. **Tarpon Bay Recreation** (900 Tarpon Bay Rd.;

941-472-8900) rents canoes and kayaks for use in the bay and through Ding Darling Refuge. For guided nature canoe tours, contact **Canoe Adventures** (941-472-4050).

Sailboarding & Surfing

Windsurfers flock to Sanibel's causeway for fun and competition.

ISLAND ADVENTURE

Hiking

The self-guided tour at **Sanibel-Captiva Conservation Center** covers four miles of easy trails with an observation tower in the middle. The Indigo Trail at **Ding Darling Refuge** penetrates into mangrove habitat with a five-mile loop.

Biking

Sanibel's 30 miles of bike path encourage unhurried sightseeing. Paved trails cover the island tip to tip — along the shopping district as well as into less automotive-competitive terrain. The best strip is behind Rabbit Road, connecting East Gulf Drive with Sanibel-Captiva Road. The paths that parallel Periwinkle Way can get dangerous in season when traffic is intense and motorists are impatient.

Sanibel's large resorts rent bikes. Otherwise, try the **Bike Route** (2330 Palm Ridge Rd.; 941-472-1955) or **Finnimore's Cycle Shop** (2343 Periwinkle Way; 941-472-5577).

Shelling & Beachcombing

Sanibel and seashells are practically synonymous. The classic bent-from- the-waist shelling stance, here in the Shelling Capital of the Western Hemisphere, even has its own name: The Sanibel Stoop. An eastward hook on the island's south end allows it to snag many of the shells the sea washes in its direction. Its fame as the third best shelling area in the world has made it a prime destination of serious conchologists and amateurs for decades. The rare junonia is the trademark shell prize of the island. Shellers who find them get their picture in the local paper. Resorts are sometimes accused of planting them on their beaches for publicity. Recently, a groundbreaking state law was passed prohibiting any live shelling on Sanibel.

The **Sanibel Public Library** (2401 Library Way; 941-472-2483) houses an identification collection of shells. For local shelling information, buy Margaret Greenberg's *The Sanibel Shell Guide* (Anna Publishing, 1982) or *Capt. Mike Fuery's Florida Shelling Guide*, featuring Sanibel and Captiva (Sanibel Sanddollar Publications, 1987).

Golfing

Two semi-private, 18-hole golf courses perforate island sands, the **Dunes Golf & Tennis Club** (949 Sandcastle Rd., 941-472-3355) and **Beachview Golf Course** (110 Par View Dr., 941-472-2626).

Tennis & Racquetball

Five lighted tennis courts are open to the public at the Sanibel Elementary School **City Recreation Complex** (3840 Sanibel-Captiva Road; 941-472-0345). **Signal Inn Resort** (1811 Olde Middle Gulf Dr.; 941-472-4690) has two racquetball courts for hire.

Other

The **Sanibel Recreation Complex** (3840 Sanibel-Captiva Road; 941-472-0345) has a multipurpose gymnasium, baseball fields, and a state-of-the-art playground. **Finnimore's Cycle Shop** (2343 Periwinkle Way; 941-472-5577) rents in-line skates by the hour. Skaters can use the island's bike path.

CULTURE

The People

Most Sanibelians grabbed onto the island as their salvation from northern climes. Longtime islanders share an attitude more committed than many feel toward their birthplace. They cohere on one cause: the protection of their adopted homeland from rampant development. Their guardianship nurtures an overprotected child they try to shelter from corrupting influences and modern paces.

A recent illustration of how islanders actively fight overdevelopment is the issue of a new causeway, which was finally petitioned for referendum. Against the wishes of the city council and Lee County (which owns the bridge), islanders voted to delay construction until further studies could be completed. Islanders protested the building of the bridge in the first place, back in 1963. Although they lost that battle, they continued their vigilance against condo build-up. Sanibelians incorporated into their own city in 1974 in an attempt to take control of their fate and protect the island's natural treasures.

The island's newer population is more diverse and less cohesive. Part-time or absentee owners possess much of the property. As real estate prices and property taxes soared, many of the "old breed" were forced off-island, replaced by a younger, professional population of commuters and, still, many retirees, albeit wealthier than those who left. Current full-time population these day counts around 5,500.

Island Inspirations

Creative inspiration floods the islands like new-moon tide; imaginations effortlessly take flight with the pelicans and roseate spoonbills.

The beauty of Sanibel begs to be rhapsodized, poeticized, and immortalized. The island, consequently, claims more than its share of published authors — both resident and visiting. Poet **Edna St. Vincent Millay** was one of the earliest literary artists to visit Sanibel. Her 1936 stay was marked more by destruction than by creativity when the original manuscript of her *Conversations at Midnight* burned in a hotel fire.

A longtime fishing guide on Sanibel, **Randy White**, is making a name for himself on a national level as author of murder mysteries in the setting of the islands. His "Doc Ford" promises to be the Travis McGee of Sanibel. The sly sleuth made his debut in White's first novel, *Sanibel Flats* (St. Martin's Press, 1990), and returns in two more recent mysteries. Despite the fact that Sanibel has seen only one murder in recent history, it seems to be a popular setting for whodunits. Resident Bill Hallstead, writing under the name William Beechcroft, has penned several mystery novels, including *Chain of Vengeance* (out of print), which climaxes on Sanibel. *Piano*

Bird (Random House, 1984) by Lucille Kallen, too, brings dastard-ly deeds to the pure white sands of Sanibel.

Visual artists abound. Internationally acclaimed **Ikki Matsumoto**, an Oriental stylist, is best known for his whimsical capturings of island wildlife. Photographer **Charlie McCullough** creates dramatic portraits of Sanibel life. Other authors and artists form the Barrier Island Group for the Arts (BIG Arts), an organization with its own facility (900 Dunlop Rd; 941-395-0900) that sponsors showings, readings, art fairs, and other cultural events. **The Sanibel/Captiva Art League** (941-472-4594) sponsors workshops and exhibits.

Fairs & Festivals

The Sanibel Shell Fair takes place at the Sanibel Community Center (2173 Periwinkle Way; 941-472-2155) early each March. Exhibitors from around the world display their prize specimens and shell art. **The BIG Arts Fair** occupies Thanksgiving weekend at the Sanibel Community Center. Throughout the season, arts and crafts fairs are scheduled practically every weekend at that location and at the Sanibel Elementary School.

Museums & Galleries

Sanibel's plethora of art galleries attests to the island's artistic temperament. They specialize in everything from wildlife watercolors to African art. One of the island's oldest, **Schoolhouse Gallery** (520 Tarpon Bay Rd; 941-472-1193), saved a historic building from demise. Here, as the name implies, pioneer island children once received their education. **Matsumoto Gallery** (751 Tarpon Bay Rd.; 941-472-6686) occupies another renovated structure, an old beach house redone in Caribbean motif. It features the work of Ikki Matsumoto and other local artists.

A Touch of Sanibel Pottery (1544 Periwinkle Way; 472-4330) displays the works of local clay artists David and Barbara Hoggatt. **Whale & the Bird Nature Gallery** (1560 Periwinkle Way : 941-472-8333) concentrates on Sanibel's natural gifts.

Architecture

Side trips down shell-named streets such as Coquina Drive, Golden Olive Court, and Shell Basket Lane take you into Sanibel's residential areas, where architectural styles range from renovated Cracker cottages to stately Victorian mansions. Even Art Deco dwellings are popping up in neighborhoods, despite islanders' attempt to keep out what they call incompatible styles. Recently, they went so far as to legislate maximum home sizes.

Theater

Professional and community theater at **Pirate Playhouse** (2200 Periwinkle Way; 941-472-0006) and **Old Schoolhouse Theater** (1905 Periwinkle Way; 941-472-6862), and stage shows and readings at the **BIG Arts Center** (900 Dunlop Rd; 941-395-0900) demonstrate islanders' sea-inspired creativity and appreciation thereof.

Music

Beethoven to Buffett finds favor among island residents. The annual **Sanibel Festival and Bach on the Beach** celebrate their love of classical music throughout March. The Dunes Golf & Tennis Club hosts **Jazz on the Green**, featuring major artists, each October. In the nightclubs, reggae, rock, jazz, steel drum, and Jimmy Buffett-style folk music find favor. Resident **Danny Morgan** blends all into what he calls indigenous Sanibel-Captiva music. He performs locally and has recorded a couple of albums.

Nightlife

Nightlife on Sanibel is low-key: Street lights are taboo, and clubs give last call at midnight. **The Jacaranda** (1223 Periwinkle Way; 941-472-1771) often hosts live local bands.

TABLE HOPPING

Restaurants proliferate. Dress is always casual. Gulf shrimp, stone crab, grouper, and piña coladas are the main fare at the island's bevy of seafood restaurants. Most popular of these are **McT's Shrimp House** (1523 Periwinkle Way; 941-472-3161) and

Schoolhouse turned theater on Sanibel.
(Chelle Koster Walton)

Tarwinkles Seafood Emporium (Periwinkle Way & Tarpon Bay Rd.; 941-472-1366). Locals flock to **The Lazy Flamingos** (6520 Pine Ave.; 941-472-5353 and 1036 Periwinkle Way; 941-472-6939) for Key West-type atmosphere and casual bites. For a taste of authentic island style, **Island Inn** (3111 W. Gulf Dr.; 941-472-1561) is a vintage Sanibel institution.

    Gramma Dot's (634 N. Yachtsman; 941-472-8138) at the Sanibel Marina is the island's one dock-and-dine restaurant.

    Our favorite island chef, Danny Mellman, owns and creates magic at the **Greenhouse Grill** (2407 Periwinkle Way; 941-472-6882), using fresh local products and clever experimental style. For a sampling of island cuisine, attend **Taste of the Islands,** an annual event held at the Dunes Golf & Tennis Club in December.

    A banquet of cookbooks feeds the appetites of local cuisine connoisseurs. Look for *The Sanibel-Captiva Cookbook*, published for the benefit of Children's Center of the Islands. It features some local restaurant recipes as well as islander contributions. *The Best of Sanibel-Captiva Islands*, published by the local Chamber of Commerce (and available at the Chamber and local bookstores), also contains restaurant recipes. *Accidental Hostess* is a fun book, filled with light-hearted pointers on how to survive the inevitable onslaught of winter guests plus easy, breezy recipes. It's put together by four island women. A local caterer has compiled seafood recipes designed to keep the kitchen cool via microwave and barbecue in her *Fish Fare*.

ISLAND LANDINGS

The island's major resorts lie along a jagged road known as Gulf Drive. **Sundial Beach and Tennis Resort** (1451 Middle Gulf Dr., Sanibel Island, FL 33957; 941-472-4252) is Sanibel's largest. **Gulf Breeze Cottages** (1081 Shell Basket Ln., Sanibel Island, FL 33957; 941-472-1626) offer more intimate accommodations, and a host of others fall somewhere between the two in ambience and price. In off-season, many resorts offer affordable packages.

The **Island Inn** (P.O. Box 659, Sanibel Island, FL 33957; 941-472-1561) brandishes the refinement of Florida's great old inns and hotels, but without any snobbery. It has the same congenial and relaxed atmosphere Granny Matthews, a Sanibel matriarch of renown, elicited at the turn of the century when she entertained the whole island — even guests from other resorts — at Saturday night barbecues. During the winter season, November 15 to April 30, it's an American-plan resort; off-season it's a B&B. The innkeepers don't pretend to furnish extravagantly; all is done in uncontrived old island style, trimmed in white lattice and graciousness.

The **Castaways** (6460 Sanibel-Captiva Rd., Sanibel Island, FL 33957; 941-472-1252) has its own marina, and spans bay to Gulf with unfancy cottages. Camping is permitted only at **Periwinkle Trailer Park** (Periwinkle Way; 941-472-1433). Guests and visitors alike are treated to the owner's exotic aviary garden.

Sources & Resources

For a comprehensive tour guide of the islands, pick up *The Trolley Guide to Sanibel & Captiva Islands*. No one knows the ins and outs of the islands better than Betty Anholt, who operates the trolleys on the islands with her husband. For more musings and irreverent insights into local island life, buy my *Sanibel Island Eyes and Other Island Afflictions & Addictions* (P.O. Box 243, Sanibel, FL 33951).

If you wish to remember the islands in pictures, there are two primarily photographic albums from which to choose. Richard N. Campen's *Sanibel and Captiva, Enchanting Islands* (West Summit Press, 1977) freeze-frames the islands the way they were 15 years ago, while Lynn Stone's images in *Sanibel Island* (Voyageur Press, 1991) reflect his impressions — primarily of the wildlife — as a contemporary visitor.

Two weeklies are published on Sanibel Island: *The Islander* (2407 Periwinkle Way; 941-472-5185) and the *Island Reporter* (2340 Periwinkle Way; 941-472-1587). The *Reporter* is less fluff, more news.

The Historical Preservation Committee of Sanibel provides background information about the island. Write or call the City of Sanibel Museum Fund, 800 Dunlop Rd., Sanibel FL 33957; 941-472-4648. **The Sanibel-Captiva Chamber of Commerce** is located at the island's doorstep on Causeway Road; call 941-472-1080, or write P.O. Box 166, Sanibel, FL 33957.

 ESTERO ISLAND

QUICK TOUR

The High Bridge on San Carlos Parkway skips first across San Carlos Island and then onto Estero Island, descending upon the city of Fort Myers Beach, or "The Beach," as local shorthand has it. San Carlos Island is home port for the FunKruz, a half-day gambling excursion out of Palm Grove Marina. Watch for the signs. You will also find the island's shrimp industry and its 100-some trawlers headquartered in the same neighborhood.

From the High Bridge, you get a preview of Estero Island's offerings: elbow-to-elbow resort shops, condos and motels, youthful bars, and glorious sands. Times Square is the center of activity at the island's approach. North of this intersection on Estero Boulevard cluster beach-food bastions, surf shops, and municipal parking — seemingly always full — for the beach. Continuing on, the bustle gives way to a few low-key resorts and mom-pop hotels as the island slims down to walking distance between Gulf and bay and ends at Bowditch Park (no parking; must take trolley from below the bridge).

South of Times Square, heavy road and sidewalk traffic give the city a free-and-easy attitude bordering on bedlam at times (especially during spring break). More T-shirt shops, bars, restaurants, and a tattoo studio. Eventually, the crowds thin out as you head down-island to more secluded sands and classier resorts and restaurants.

What's there to see and do on Fort Myers Beach? The question is answered in one word: beach. The beach is the center of activity, social encountering, recreation and culture. Above all, you'll find the beach's peculiar branc of theater thriving here: people watching. Bring your dark shades and binocs.

BACKFLASH

Estero Island's early Calusa inhabitants prevented Spanish colonization in 1569 when they attacked the fort and its settlement of 36 buildings. That left the island open to vagrants and freebooters. Estero's favorite pirate tale involves the dashing Captain "Calico Jack" Rackham and lady pirate Anne Bonny. The two reportedly honeymooned on Estero following ship's damage sustained in battle near Cuba, circa 1720.

Like a puzzle piece, the jagged island fit neatly into Lee island coast's history of commercial fishing and tourism. Shrimping particularly sustained early islanders, as it does today. Estero's long stretch of breezy, swimmable beach and its close proximity to land brought early and uncontrolled vacation development. An antithesis to Lee Island vacationing, a visit to Fort Myers Beach more closely resembles the rowdiness of Daytona Beach.

THE NATURAL

Much of Estero Island is overdeveloped. The beach itself, at 7.5 miles long, is the most natural thing the island has going for it, and quite often its appeal and wildlife flee with the noise of jet skis, boat traffic, and parasail concessions.

There's the 40-acre bayside **Matanzas Preserve**, but it's not really accessible to the public.

Head south to uncover the natural beauty that once was Estero Island. Estuarine wildlife remains relatively unscathed in the backwaters between Estero and Big Hickory Island.

AQUA-ADVENTURE

Touring

Want beach involvement without the crowds? Do what the locals do. Get in a boat and buzz the beach. Throw in the anchor where you hear good music emanating from a beach party and enjoy the ambience hassle-free. At some places you can get within swimming distance of the beach. Another favorite boating activity is scooting through Matanzas Pass between San Carlos and Estero islands and bar- or restaurant-hopping among the many bay establishments with dockage. This is also where you'll find marinas with facilities.

Several tour boats leave out of Fort Myers Beach area, the grandest of which is the **Europa FunKruz,** docked at Palm Grove Marina (2500 Main St.; 941-463-7333). Night, day, and Sunday brunch cruises are escorted by a seagull entourage. For reservations call 800-688-7529. Smaller-scale tours run out of **Pink Shell Resort** (275 Estero Blvd.; 941-463-6181) to Big Hickory Island. **Island Tall Ship Cruises** (645 San Carlos Blvd., 941-765-7447) take you to see in a romantic red-sailed yacht.

Fishing

Like many west coast islands, Estero is anchored to the sea and the fishing life. Fleets of "party boats," otherwise known as "head boats," depart from local marinas to deep waters for grouper, tuna, pompano, and tarpon. Check with **Getaway Marina** (18400 San

Tall ship sailing off Estero Island.
(Lee County Visitor & Convention Bureau)

Carlos Blvd.; 941-466-3600).

A free fishing pier juts out from land at Lynn Hall Memorial Park near Times Square. Bait shops and other concessions can be found there.

Swimming

The greatest danger of swimming at Fort Myers Beach comes from jet ski and boat traffic. Keep visible and stay close to shore.

Snorkeling/Scuba

Fort Myers Beach environs hold some nice diving spots, most

of them seven to 25 miles offshore. The include rock formations, a mine sweeper wreck, artificial reef, and soft coral gardens.

Other

Paradise Parasail & Water Skiing operates out of Fort Myers Beach. Call 941-463-7272.

ISLAND ADVENTURE

Biking

The **Caloosa Riders Bicycle Club** has members throughout Lee County. One of its favorite on-road rides follows Estero Boulevard across the bridges to Lover's Key and Bonita Beach. They do it early weekend mornings when traffic is light. For more information on the club, call 941-482-3137. **Beach Cycle and Repair** (1901 Estero Blvd., 941-463-8844) rents bicycles.

Shelling & Beachcombing

Though not as widely touted as is the shelling on Sanibel, beachcombing at Estero's secluded southern tip reaps great benefits.

Golfing

The public is welcome at the **Bay Beach Golf Club** (7401 Estero Blvd.; 941-463-2064). Miniature golf courses are more Estero's style and you'll find a few in the area.

Tennis

The Bay Beach Racquet Club (7401 Estero Blvd.; 941-463-4473) has courts open to the public.

CULTURE

The People

Fort Myers Beach is home to about 12,000 people. The segment of population that often pops into mind first when visualizing Fort Myers Beach is the shrimpers, a rowdy and party-loving group when in port during the winter and spring. In summer, they migrate to Texas.

Many other islanders work in the tourist service industry. The town has its share of retirees (53.8 percent are not in the work force) and commuters as well, folks generally fascinated with boats, beaches or fishing. They like to think of themselves as friendlier, less snobby than islanders from, say, Sanibel or Captiva. More than half of them are married with no children. Despite that fact, the Chamber recently turned to promoting Estero as the The Family Island in an attempt to change its sybaritic reputation. Suddenly, playgrounds appeared on the beaches; but the spring breakers continue to crash here en masse.

ISLAND INSPIRATIONS

The **Beach Art Association** sponsors several shows and rotating exhibits each year at the **Fort Myers Beach Public Library** (145 Bay Rd.; 941-463-9691). Classes are offered to members.

Fairs & Festivals

Incredible as it seems — once you've witnessed its uncontained revelry, that is — the annual **Fort Myers Shrimp Festival** began as a religious ceremony. It still kicks off every March with the Blessing of the Fleet. A celebration of the island's main industry follows with a parade, partying, and lots of shrimp consumption. A **sandsculpting contest** takes place on the beach every November.

Architecture

Between a lot of concrete and anonymous high rises, you will find sandwiched a good many cottages with beach personality, styled after New England counterparts.

Music

The Fort Myers Beach scene rocketed one local musical group to national attention in recent years: a band by the name of **Blackfish**.

Nightlife

Nightlife happens all day long on Fort Myers Beach. Bars along the beach start serving at noon, and live bands often strike up in the afternoons in season. Music is loud and high-energy stuff produced by local groups.

Lani Kai Island Resort (1400 Estero Blvd.; 941-463-3111) has always been the cornerstone of Fort Myers Beach party, with bashes on the beach and roof. Other popular spots: **Pier One** (1000-A Estero Blvd.; 941-463-4242), **The Reef** (2601 Estero Blvd.; 941-463-4181), and **Top O'Mast Lounge** (1028 Estero Blvd.; 941-463-9424). Off the beach, on San Carlos Island, try **The Hard Dock Cafe** at **The Bridge Restaurant** (708 Fisherman's Wharf; 941-765-0050) for something slightly tamer and mores bluesy or jazzy.

TABLE HOPPING

Gulf shrimp reigns symbolic of Lee County gastronomy, with the local shrimp capital centered in Fort Myers Beach. The shrimp are graded by size and assigned all sorts of vague measurements — jumbo, large, medium-sized, boat grade, and so on. The surest way to know what size shrimp you are ordering is to ask for the count-per-pound designation. This will be something like 21-25s, meaning there are 21 to 25 shrimp per pound. "Boat grade" usually designates a mixture of sizes, usually small.

Shrimp wind up on practically every restaurant menu on San Carlos and Estero islands; seafood of all sorts is the focus. **The Fishmonger Restaurant** on San Carlos (19030 San Carlos Blvd.; 941-765-5544) uses underutilized local seafood species such as the rock shrimp, a hard-shelled and sweet-fleshed cousin, and triggerfish. **The Gulf Shore Restaurant** (1270 Estero Blvd.; 941-463-9551) has survived decades as a symbol of beach dining in a vintage setting. It's a great place for breakfast with a view.

Docking is available at **Channel Mark Restaurant** (19001 San Carlos Blvd.; 941-463-9127), which features outdoor seating and dressier seafood dishes than The Beach norm. Quality, however, fluctuates. Another boat-in favorite: **Snug Harbor** (645 San Carlos Blvd.; 941-463-4343).

ISLAND LANDINGS

The Beach provides every variety of ambience for an island vacation, from high-rise to low-rent. The **Pink Shell Beach & Bay Resort** (275 Estero Blvd.; 941-463-6181), at Estero's northern end, is a family favorite, offering a variety of options out of the main flow of traffic. Docking is also available, along with a marina and store.

There are a number of RV parks and campgrounds in the vicinity, along with cellblock-looking accommodations with the spring breaker in mind, all of which will save you money if you come off-season or reserve early for the winter months. These mostly center around Times Square.

For something quieter, classier, and more costly, head to the island's south end.

TOURIST TRAPS

Beware where you park in Fort Myers Beach. Make sure there are no "No Parking" signs. Otherwise your car will be towed to parts unknown and it will cost you a small fortune to retrieve it because of a scam reportedly perpetrated by towing companies and some local businesses.

Sources & Resources

The **Fort Myers Beach Chamber of Commerce** distributes information at 17200 San Carlos Blvd., Fort Myers Beach, FL 33931; 941-454-7500.

 BONITA BEACH AREA ISLANDS

QUICK TOUR

When Estero Boulevard, Route 865, crosses the bridge from Estero Island to Black Island it becomes Hickory Boulevard. Not only does the name change, but the mood as well. Drastically. Marshy backwaters take over the scenery. Resorts, nightlife, and restaurants disappear. Nature reigns.

The cluster of protected islands that fall between Fort Myers Beach and Bonita Beach are all vaguely known as Lover's Key, although the road never actually touches Lover's Key. First you

come to Black Island. If you disembark at Lover's Key Recreation
Area or Carl E. Johnson Park (which are soon to be merged), you
will cross Inner Key and mangrove estuaries before you reach
Lover's Key and its secluded Gulf beach.

Mound Key, one of Estero Bay's 150-plus unbridged islets, is
named for its Calusa Amerindian shell deposits and is explorable by
boat. It and Big Hickory Island make for a worthwhile sightseeing
expedition.

A short hop over another island and you enter Bonita Beach,
which occupies Little Hickory Island. Bonita Beach starts out mild-
ly commercial, with a few high rises and its share of seafood houses, fishing charters, and traffic. Enterprises thin out to low-key, low-
profile types before they give way completely to residential. Bonita
Beach is much less hyped than its neighbor Estero. A string of homes
interspersed with public beach accesses leads gently into more development again at Little Hickory's south end. Barefoot Beach Preserve
tips the island with a return to nature as it used to be. To get there,
you must turn right off Bonita Beach Road in what looks like a
private housing development, complete with security gate. Pass
through the gate and follow the slow speed-bumpy road past dense
condo building to beach parking. Bonita Beach Road exits the island
and leads to the mainland at Bonita Springs.

BACKFLASH

The Calusa Indians left heaped-big reminders of their residency on many of the area's islands and shores. Some believe Mound
Key to have been the local Calusa capital and site of the area's first
fort and missionary. These islands remained sparsely settled by
stout-hearted farmers and fisherfolk after the Calusa reign. In the
1920s, commercial fishing enterprises began taking advantage of the
Gulf's bounty. Fishermen occupied palmetto huts with sand floors.
Competition grew so fierce that feuds would break out over claims
to fishing rights.

The out-islands of Bonita Beach inspired their share of folk-
tales, especially Black Island, home of retired pirate Black Augustus.

When he died, Black Augustus left his island to Mollie Johnson of nearby Mound Key. "Grandma" Johnson has been called the first lady of Bonita and was loved for her kindheartedness and healing abilities. Legend has it she once harbored and nursed outlaw Ed Watson, who was being sought for the murder of James Gang heroine Belle Starr.

At one time, dozens of little islands lay between Little Hickory Island's southern end and the mainland, but were dredged in to create solid land, circa 1940, by a wheeler-dealer who hoped to extend his claim to mainland property. Bonita Beach remained a quiet spot until linkage to Estero opened the floodgates to tourism.

THE NATURAL

Start with the beaches — all 10-plus miles of lightly trod sands. Bonita area beaches are a refreshing pause between the more crowded and commercial areas to the north and south. You will feel the difference the moment you cross the Bonita Beach/Fort Myers Beach bridge onto state-owned Black Island and the northernmost beaches. On Little Hickory Island, accesses every 500 feet or so allow public entrance onto a shelly, natural beach.

Bayside, nature may not be as glamorous, but it is rich indeed. Between the mainland's spongy shores and the islands' mottled profile you'll find thriving estuarine wildlife. Manatees, dolphin, herons, roseate spoonbills, ospreys, hawks, egrets, and eagles come to feed among the grass flats and mangroves of this aqualife nursery known as the **Estero Bay Aquatic Preserve.**

Citizens watch over the little islands and their wildlife via the Adopt-An-Island program initiated by Estero Bay Boat Tours. To adopt, care for, and name your own island, call 941-992-2200.

NATURAL ATTRACTIONS

As romantic as its name, Lover's Key is home to **Lover's Key State Recreation Area** and **Carl E. Johnson Park.** You can't drive to the beach at Johnson Park; you can walk or you can take the minitram. The ride winds through ancient mangrove ecosystems to a beach and picnic grounds that few tourists ever find. Facilities include restrooms, picnic tables, showers, and some concessions during the season.

Bonita Public Beach at the end of Hickory Boulevard is a favorite destination for those who relish its fun-loving spirit and don't mind the crowds it attracts. Don't like the throngs? Park instead at one of the island's many beach accesses for more peace, privacy, and shells. Or head south to the unknown 342-acre **Barefoot Beach Preserve** with its 8,200 feet of beach and low sand dunes.

AQUA-ADVENTURE

Touring

Bonita Beach enjoys an enviable springboard position to both the glamour islands to the north and the natural serenity of Ten Thousand Islands to the south. Besides that, bay waters and emptying rivers make for fascinating exploration. It helps to know the area. Mound Key, as an ancient Amerindian settlement and home to early pioneers, provides an offbeat boating destination.

The best sightseeing tour of Mound Key and Big Hickory Island departs from the mainland at **Weeks Fish Camp** (Coconut Road, Bonita Springs). Call **Estero Bay Boat Tours** at 941-992-2200. Charlie Weeks and his staff know (and treat) these islands and waters like family. Tours from Fort Myers Beach to Big Hickory Island run out of **Pink Shell Resort**. Call Island Water Tours at 941-463-6181. To approach Bonita Beach by sea, enter Estero Bay at San Carlos Pass north of Little Hickory Island.

Fishing

Once a fishing community, Bonita Beach retains its old-time character with a variety of marinas and fishing charters to take you to where the big ones are biting. Although Bonita Beach is known as the coast's Snook Capital, mackerel, trout, tarpon, grouper, sheepshead, and redfish are just as plentiful offshore and in the back bays and rivers. **Snook** (a.k.a. robalo), by the way, are the prized catch of local fishermen. A game fish, they are nonetheless exquisite in taste, but unavailable commercially. Seasonal restrictions apply.

Swimming

Warm waters bottomed with gradually sloping sands surpass the standards of the area's swimming with their secluded and hidden feel. Gulf temperatures range from an average of 66 to 87 degrees.

Boating, Sailing & Canoeing

Half- and whole-day motorboat rentals are available at **Bonita Beach Resort Motel** (26395 Hickory Boulevard; 941-992-2137). **Lover's Key Recreation Area** provides boat-ramping facilities free of charge.

ISLAND ADVENTURE

Hiking

In the area of Lover's Key and Black Island, both of which are protected and lightly developed, trails lead from parking areas to beachfront.

Shelling & Beachcombing

Here shellers find abundant prizes typical of the area: lightning whelks, conchs, olives, cones, tulips, worm shells, top shells, and scallops. Because fewer people find the beaches on Lover's Key and Black Island, shellers find more to stoop for. Some will tell you that Big Hickory Island hoards the best shells in these parts.

CULTURE

The People

For decades, Bonita Beach remained a folksy place populated by fishermen and winter residents in unpretentious beach homes. In the past few years, with the arrival of grand golfing communities on the mainland nearby, the community is making an attempt to upgrade its image. What results is a rather wide split between down-home and friendly, and snobbish and sophisticated. The island's unaffected personality dominates.

The love of locals for their pristine environment is demonstrated by their Adopt-An-Island program. The brainchild of two charter captains, it keeps the 150-some mangrove islands and sandbars clear of monofilament line and other debris detrimental to wildlife. Capt. Charlie Weeks and Carl Johnson run the program from Weeks Camp, and keep it operating with their own out-of-pocket funding.

Nightlife

Doc's Beach House (27908 Hickory Blvd; 941-992-6444) collects lively crowds of locals and beach types at its no-frills location at Barefoot Beach.

TABLE HOPPING

Ambience runs the spectrum from come-as-you-are beach joints to dressy dining rooms trimmed in lattice and linen (though there's more of the former). Views of sailboats against the sunset or trolling mullet fishermen serve up a sense of place as a side dish to Bonita Beach's brand of come-and-get-it hospitality.

Stop and have a burger and beer upstairs at **Doc's Beach House** (27908 Hickory Blvd; 941-992-6444), a perfect perspective for beach-gazing. For dinner or Sunday brunch, **McCully's Rooftop Restaurant** (Hickory Blvd., 941-597-4445), at the island's northern end, serves great seafood along with stunning views, with available docking.

My favorite restaurant in these parts is **Big Hickory Fishing Nook** (26107 Hickory Blvd. SW., 941-992-0991), which accommodates boaters as well as landlubbers. It caters to unusual appetites with gator, quail, buffalo burgers, and natural foods. Seating indoors and out, marina-side.

ISLAND LANDINGS

Bonita Beach attracts sun-loving vacationers and their families, furnishing them with several options. Luxury condominiums with sky-high rooms book-end more casual beach cottages at the island's extremes. On back bays, rivers, and canals, fishing motels and camps cater to the sportsmen who find the area so alluring.

Bonita Beach Resort Motel (26395 Hickory Boulevard; (813)

992-2137) spreads 20 units between the main road and the bay, with lots of customer docking, a boat ramp, pontoon rentals, and a playground for the kids. Nothing plush or fancy about the room furnishings, it's meant for the fishing-devoted.

Sources & Resources

The Bonita Springs Area Chamber of Commerce has jurisdiction over Bonita Beach and its upper islands. For more information, contact it at P.O. Box 1240, Bonita Springs, FL 33959; 800-226-2943 or 813-992-2943.

ISLAND PROFILE: CAPTIVA'S UNCLE JOE

The drive through Captiva Island makes for a twisty, rollicking trip. Exploring the island's past with Captiva's "Uncle Joe" Wightman rides much the same way: Here the story takes an unexpected turn; there time and tides leave their gaps. Both trips delight and entertain, and eventually converge. For Captiva history lives through Uncle Joe Wightman, just as the short, barrel-chested octagenarian himself embodies the tiny island's robust past.

With his bare feet and a white beard almost half his size, Joe represents the old Captiva way of life. He came to the island in 1917 at the age of nine. Seventy-odd years later he scurries along Wightman Lane in his motorized cart, and speaks fondly and factually of Captiva yesteryear.

"The story I tell does not bring in all the legends of the area. I try to keep hearsay out, because there's no way of proving or disproving some of these stories," he begins his meandering tour down the island's historical backroads. The bumpy journey through time begins in Captiva's homesteading era. The Wightman family moved to the islands from Washington State because of a brochure Joe's father had read touting Sanibel as "the garden spot of the world." Grapefruit trees populated the island in those days. Joe and his brothers worked the groves for 10 cents an hour. They went to school in a building which now partially houses Chapel-by-the-Sea, a popular wedding spot on Captiva. They ate purloo — a raccoon and turnip stew — and nursed themselves when they got sick ("we had to either outlive it [the sickness] or die"). In their spare time, they swatted mosquitoes and fished.

"I'd never been where there were that many mosquitoes and sand fleas before. The first thing I knew my skin was raw from them biting," he remembers. From the natives, the Wightman's learned to burn smudge pots of strangler fig wood to discourage the insects, he recalls. For many years, after a hurricane wiped out much of the citrus crop, Joe made his living from the sea. Many farmers were forced to sell out because they could not pay taxes. When Prohibition hit, some of the local fishermen turned to a new occupation.

"This was bootleggers' headquarters in a way," said Joe. "Cuban fish boats — we called 'em 'smacks'— would leave down there with hulls full of whiskey, six bottles to a case, wrapped in sackcloth so they could be put underwater. They were two-masted schooners with live bait wells in the center where they put the whiskey. The fishermen here would row out to meet the Cubans. Many bootleggers posed as fishermen or guides at that time."

Uncle Joe studied electrical and diesel engineering through correspondence courses when he gave up fishing for a living. After serving in World War II, Joe moved to Virginia to string electric lines.

"I left the island a couple of times with the intention of not coming back. But I always came back."

This time frost skidded him on home to Captiva's balmy, palmy shores. Now in his 40s and too old to climb poles, he set to work as a contractor in Captiva homes. Barefoot once again, Joe began upgrading electrical systems so islanders could hook up stoves and refrigerators. That was about the time folks started calling him "Uncle Joe."

"In the deep-down South, that's an honorary name, like in Uncle Tom. I took my electrician's job very seriously. Someone couldn't have biscuits for dinner if they had no stove. So they called me. I would go any time of the day or night, and worked 12-hour days if that's what it took. And when I got caught up, I'd go fishing. I was a dependable electrician, and folks appreciated it." Since those days, Uncle Joe has become somewhat of a legend himself on Captiva, perhaps a character he'd leave out of his own stories, if he weren't for sure certain he was fact. A framed page from a magazine hangs on his porch. The title of the article reads "The Barefoot Historian."

"I think they were more interested in my feet than in history," he shrugs it off.

There's a touch of sadness in the animated face full of white beard when Joe talks of land value increases chasing out the old breed of Captivan. "These islands were settled by farmers and fishermen who depended on what they raised for their livelihood," he says. He mourns the loss of that simple, secluded Captiva lifestyle. Pioneer attitudes of self-sufficiency and independence still rule Uncle Joe's life, softened by a quick wit and a twinkling eye. As the armchair tour ends, he says good-bye with an invitation back to his humble cottage.

"I'll always be here. When I die, I guess they'll take me out of here feet first."

Bare feet first?

"May as well take me barefoot," he chuckles. "I don't think the earthworms care if you have shoes on or not."

CHAPTER VI

MARCO &

TEN THOUSAND ISLANDS

Back in the pioneering days of what is today known as Collier County, things were no less wild than in the Wild West. Then, the land belonged to either Lee County to the north or Monroe County, home of the Florida Keys. Naples is the county seat of Collier County today. From its mainland, Gulf-side perch it serves as gateway to the Everglades, the last vestige of civilization before the intriguing wilderness of this vast land of swamps and mangrove islands.

Off Naples's southern, moneyed shores lies **Key Island**, where two eras of Florida bygones mesh at the boundaries of the Keewaydin Island Club. Half private resort, half environmentally protected, it makes an apt transition from the elite air of Naples to the unruly nature of the Ten Thousand Islands. **Cannon Island** in

282

Rookery Bay is known for its oak hammocks, air plants, and wild orchids, and is a popular place for canoeists and hikers.

Marco Island officially heads the 90-mile stretch of key-clotted waters known as Ten Thousand Islands. A cluster of uninhabited mangrove islands fill the gap between Key and Marco, forming a barrier for Rookery and Johnson Bays.

Coconut Island and **Little Marco Island** lie at the mouth of Big Marco Pass. Coconut is known for its abundant beachcombing booty. Off Marco's northern shores, four small islands form the **Isles of Capri** development, created in 1955. Cradled between shorelines in the Intracoastal Waterway, a succession of mangrove islands shelter wildlife. Three national wildlife preserve islands right offshore Marco's midsection, known popularly as the A B C Islands, make nesting sights for pelicans, frigates, and other local birds.

Marco Island itself encompasses two other communities: Marco, a highly developed resort town that feels like an extension of Naples, and Goodland, which still belongs to the fishing, slightly behind-the-times aura of Ten Thousand Islands.

Like pieces of a puzzle that's been flung apart, islands and keys of all shapes, sizes, and personalities mottle the shoreline south of Marco. **Cape Romano** and environs tease with bleached white, natural, deserted beaches, but these are difficult to reach without grounding your boat and cutting up your feet on rocky, coral-like bottom. **Panther Key** is a popular boater's beach stop. Tour operators capitalize on its legend of "Panther Key John Gomez," the self-proclaimed cabin boy to pirate Gasparilla. He died a hermit in 1900 at the age of 120-something. Once occupied by a clam cannery which has left dock pilings as its only reminder, Panther Key's perimeters draw deep water.

South of Fakahatchee Pass begins the realm overseen by the National Park Service. On **Indian Key**, naturalist John James Audubon camped, studied, and drew birds. It guards Indian Key Pass into Chokoloskee Bay along with **Kingston Key**, a popular destination for beachers looking for shells and secluded sands. **Picnic**

Key, between **Tiger** and **Stop Keys**, earns its name with its sandy beach. Shifting **Pavilion Key** is another anchorage point. The sands of **Mormon Key** are strewn with clam and conch shells left over from the days when shellfish were plentiful throughout the area. No one's sure why they died out. One of the coast's commercial fish houses occupied **Turkey Key** in earlier days. **Wood Key** was once home to a relatively large community.

Everglades City, the original county seat of Collier, ties Ten Thousand Islands' western region to civilization. Since 1957, **Chokoloskee Island** has been tethered to the frontier town by a two-mile-long causeway. Today it is the only island within Everglades National Park that is still inhabited, except for an island fish house or two that managed to legally survive the government's burning of all buildings when it took over in 1947.

From Chokoloskee, by boat is the only way to reach the keys and islands that stand between the Gulf and the Everglades' so-called River of Grass. The islands vary in size from map specks to great land masses such as **Cape Sable** and **Lopez Place**. Some float free of land, others are thinly separated by brackish, jungle-clogged creeks. Some boast secluded sandy beaches, others sequestered bird colonies along the Wilderness Waterway.

For the purpose of this book, our exploration of west coast islands ends here at Cape Sable, east of which the makeup of the islands begins to resemble more that of the Florida Keys, which contain them from the Atlantic Ocean.

THE NITTY-GRITTY

Land Routes

Naples Municipal Airport is the closest facility receiving national and regional carriers, with daily flights from Tampa, Orlando, and Miami by American Eagle. Major airline flights are limited, and many opt to fly into Fort Myers's Southwest International Airport, an hour's drive from Marco. Marco Island Airport on Route 951, six miles from Marco Island, offers charter air service.

Highway 41 is the lifeline through the Everglades. Also called Tamiami Trail, the story of its construction is riddled with tall tales of taming the wetlands of the Everglades. Recently, Interstate 75 was completed to parallel to the north its 'tween-coasts run. It is devoid of the flavor Tamiami Trail delivers.

KEY ISLAND: To reach Key Island, water transport is necessary. A Keewaydin Island Club ferry takes lodging and dining guests with reservations to the island from a landing at the end of Gordon Drive in Naples. From Highway 41, take Fifth Avenue South to Gulf Shore Boulevard, turn left, and continue until it becomes Gordon Drive, which dead-ends near the sign for the Keewaydin dock. Once ashore, feet are your means of transportation. A golf-cart tram known as the club limo carries baggage for Keewaydin resort guests.

For transportation from the Fort Myers or Naples airport to the Keewaydin landing, call **Affordable Limousine Service** (800-245-6007 or 941-455-6007), **Naples Shuttle** (941-262-8982), or **Naples Taxi** (941-775-0505).

MARCO ISLAND AND ISLES OF CAPRI: Route 951 exits off of Highway 41 and Interstate 75 (Exit 15). Follow it south to Marco Island. Split off on Route 952 to get to Isles of Capri. To enter Marco Island from Highway 41 headed west, take Route 92 to the Goodland end of the island.

Marco Island University Limousine Service (800-642-5207 or 941-642-5207) shuttles up to six in a stretch limo, up to 20 in a tour bus, from as far away as West Palm Beach. The **Marco Island Trolley Tour** (941-394-1600) makes stops throughout the town of Marco and issues passes for one-day reboarding.

CHOKOLOSKEE ISLAND: From Highway 41 or Interstate 75, take Route 29 south through Everglades City and across the causeway to Chokoloskee Island.

Island Life

Marco Island and Key Island huddle around the 26-degree north latitude mark; Chokoloskee Island, at the southern extreme, is found at latitude 25 degrees 50 minutes north.

Marco Island temperatures range from an average low of 51 degrees in January to an average high of 95 in September. Average rainfall is 56 inches a year. Gulf water ranges from an average of 63 to 86 degrees.

Winter, naturally, is the preferred season for fair-weather islanders. Year-rounders put up with the humid heat and its inevitable mosquitoes. Some Chokoloskee islanders call 'em "swamp angels," but most islanders have less-heavenly names for them. (In those parts, natives seem little bothered by this natural part of island living.) Since mosquitoes breed best in standing, brackish water, you can imagine how they love Ten Thousand Islands. Late October through mid-December you get some reprieve, from both insects and crowds. Fall is the islander time of year. It may seem like summer to the unhabituated. But islanders feel the crisping up of the air that means the humidity has dropped somewhat below its customary 80 to 100 percent.

Winters can bring a chill to the air even this far south — enough to give you goose bumps on the beach. You'll see the locals dragging out the winter jackets and heavy sweaters they rarely get a chance to wear. That's why islanders look so out of date in wintertime; we've had those warm clothes forever — since we moved down South, perhaps, or at least since we took that last skiing vacation. For local weather conditions, call 941-591-1234 or 941-263-0101.

 KEY ISLAND

QUICK TOUR

Key Island measures seven miles long by less than a mile wide. The Key Island experience begins at the Naples landing where the *Kokomis*, Keewaydin's original circa-1935 ferryboat, chugs you across five minutes of water at Gordon Pass to the chickee landing on the island. Only overnight or meal guests are allowed to board. The club's "limo," a stretch golf cart, delivers you and your luggage to your cottage.

Only steps from the landing sits the club lodge, which calls for a tour to acquaint yourself with the feel and history of the place. It will effectively transport you back to the 1930s while instilling the proper mood of relaxed gentility.

From the lodge, the beach beckons. On the way, you'll pass the shuffleboard court, tennis courts, basketball court, cottages, pool bar and grill, swimming pool, and beach chickee. Seven miles of untainted beach — four of which lie within resort boundaries — skirt the Gulf of Mexico.

A system of paths draws you off the waterfront and into the island's highly acclaimed bird habitat on its bayside. You can get a map from the front desk to find gopher tortoises, osprey nests, a lake, and other treasures.

BACKFLASH

The modern-day history of Key Island begins in 1935, when Chestman Kittridge, Jr., a member of the board of directors for the system of Keewaydin Camps across the Eastern United States and

Keewaydin Island Club dock.

(Chelle Koster Walton)

Canada, envisioned the island as a southern satellite for the children of wealthy winterers. Two open structures were built for the "Upper School" and "Lower School." A pecky cypress lodge was also constructed as the heart of the resort, along with some guest cottages. A ferry named *Kokomis* made the five-minute crossing from the mainland to the island, filled with visitors and supplies. The name Keewaydin comes from Longfellow's "Song of Hiawatha," meaning "homeward bound wind."

Kittridge died upon the completion of the educational resort's first season, in May, 1936, but other members of the Keewaydin Camp organization carried on his work. At certain times during the period between 1936 and the closing of the school in 1942, the ferry brought children from Naples to the island in an effort to make the endeavor work. World War II dealt the Southwest Florida Keewaydin Club a hard blow. Blackout orders along the Gulf and scarcity of gas and supplies brought operations to a close during the 1944-45 season.

The club was saved from demise when, in the spring of 1946, a couple from Illinois purchased it. They and their daughter ran the club until 1989 when it was jointly acquired by Bolton and Lu Drackett and John and Jackie Remington, all previous visitors. Today the Dracketts have sole ownership of the club. In 1987, its lodge was listed on the National Register of Historic Places. In 1992, a gradual renovation program was mounted. Local conservation agencies and the state own all but 60 acres of the island, which effectively preserves the undeveloped portion of the island from commercial exploitation.

Historical Attractions

The Keewaydin Club Lodge is listed on the National Register of Historic Places. Built in 1935 of pecky cypress and Florida pine, it exudes the warmth of a gracious old sportsman's club. Coral stone fireplaces, 30-foot ceilings, and French doors opening to Gulf views are some of the building's best features. It also holds three dining rooms, a library/game room, and a cognac parlor.

THE NATURAL

Key Island's natural gifts first attracted guests in 1935, and continue to do so. One must be a lover of the wilds to appreciate the rustic island style of living still prevalent at Keewaydin.

More than 150 subtropical plants grow on the island. Though exotic casuarinas still exist there and hibiscus brighten up the landscaping, most vegetation is native. It is said that Mrs. Thomas Edison introduced night-blooming cereus to the island. Mangroves, slash pines, palmetto, and sabal palms prevail.

The birdlife is legendary; even the disinterested become birdwatchers after only a short stay. It's the island's best entertainment, and the island tempo allows the most compulsive to slow down and eye the ospreys. The exotic roseate spoonbill is the club's mascot, gracing its logo. Great horned owls, pileated woodpeckers, towhees, kingfishers, bald eagles, wood storks, and herons can also be sighted on the island and in the vicinity of Rookery Bay. The Naples Conservancy conducts loggerhead turtle research from a station on the island. Rumor has it that bobcats and deer make occasional cameo appearances, along with the island's more common raccoons and armadillos.

Each room comes with a Rookery Bay Estuarine Sanctuary Guide for you to use during your visit.

Natural Attractions

Rookery Bay Estuarine Reserve (941-775-8569), the Gulf Coast's largest and most pristine wildlife sanctuary, occupies more than 8,000 acres at the gateway to Ten Thousand Islands. The reserve's visitor's center is located on the mainland near Marco Island and sponsors various canoe trips to explore the backwaters and beaches of Key Island.

AQUA-ADVENTURE

Touring

Deep water off Key Island's Gulf front makes for easy offshore anchoring. If you wish to explore Key Island separately from the club, and do not own a boat, you can rent one or hire a charter out of Naples or Marco Island. Lodging or dining guests can dock at the club's slips with prior reservation. The island is easily accessible from the Gulf via Gordon Pass, right at its backdoor.

Captain Pat Kirk conducts bird-watching tours from the resort on an in-demand basis. The trips last two to three hours aboard *Kelly's Kat*. Other boat cruises and charters can be arranged through the front desk.

Fishing

Fishing doesn't get much better than in these parts. Rookery Bay is the destination of serious fishermen from everywhere. Keewaydin's Dollar Bay yields la crème de la crème: snook, redfish, tarpon, sheepshead, mackerel. Guests are encouraged to release their catch.

Swimming

During a winter visit we were told the pool was heated. I'd guess otherwise. It is beautifully tiled, though, and has a view of the Gulf.

ISLAND ADVENTURE

Hiking

Get a map from the front office (guests get one in their room) to explore the more than five miles of nature trails of Keewaydin. Burma Road bisects the island and takes you into its midsection for a view of wildlife. It branches off into the Sea Breeze (beach and cacti), Sawgrass, Osprey, and Sanctuary trails. The more difficult Lake Trail requires sturdy shoes and long pants and sleeves. The outcome can make it worth the effort, however, if you're one of the privileged to spot a deer sipping at the lake.

Shelling & Beachcombing

Key Island provides the best shelling in the Collier County region, simply by nature of its seclusion. Empty shells wash ashore in abundance; throw back live shells. Common finds: scallops, cockles, clams, and murex. A showcase of more than 200 shells collected on the island is displayed in the main lodge so guests can identify their finds. Shelling books are also available in the library.

Tennis

Keewaydin Club has one Har-Tru court.

Other

The resort offers boule and two shuffleboard courts.

CULTURE

The People

Few actually live full-time at Keewaydin Club. Most of the staff commute from Naples. Guests come, for the most part, from the Midwest during the winter season; from other parts of Florida in summer.

Architecture

Eight of Keewaydin's buildings are original, including the lodge. Pecten and Flamingo cottages once served as Keewaydin Camp's schoolhouses. Junonia, Palmetto, Poinsettia, Everglades, and Scotch Bonnet were the first guest cottages. These reflect the simplicity of old Florida Cracker style. Newer cottages are stilted and trimmed in crosshatch lattice.

The 8,000-square-foot lodge is a work of art in native materials: coral stone fireplace mantels against cypress walls reaching to pine ceiling beams. Tarpon fish scales, loggerhead turtle shells, and

Key Island hammock.
(Chelle Koster Walton)

mounted fish adorn the walls. Shades of Western decor (wagon-wheel chandeliers) and native Amerindian artifacts connect with the area's frontier past.

Music

A grand piano graces the lodge's Great Room. The pianist is versatile and talented. We enjoyed sitting before a fire on Saturday evening and listening to his medley of jazz, Grand Marnier in hand.

Nightlife

Unless you count walking on the beach, there is none. There is, however, evidently quite a bit up-river. Our cottage was poised at the mouth of the pass. This was lovely during the daytime, when we could watch the admirable boat traffic draining out of Naples Bay. When the bars let out around midnight, however, we sadly had to close our windows to sea breezes and noise.

TABLE HOPPING

Dining (except for beverages) is inclusive for guests at Keewaydin. Nonguests can make reservations for breakfast, lunch, or dinner. The food is wonderful and priced high-end.

Lunch and dinner menus change daily, sometimes with a theme. Dinner etiquette requires men to wear jackets. It's a many-coursed affair done up in the tiny portions and artistic presentation telltale of nouveau. The breakfasts remain more or less constant, and truly delightful. Service is impeccable. Views are of the Gulf or islandy murals, some old, some new.

ISLAND LANDINGS

Do not expect luxury. New management is upgrading, yet hopefully will retain the ungussied appeal that lets you know you're staying on an island with no bridge to mainland realities. Hammocks swing outside almost every cottage. It comes close to a religious retreat. Our cottage, for example, held a dying Chinese palm, and even though the cottage had been newly renovated, it was quite simple. Wicker prevailed, sassily ignoring Mobil's new mandate to trade it in for four stars. We were thankful for a small fridge and an outdoor shower. What else did we need?

Fourteen cottages hold 45 units, all with water views, none with telephones or televisions. For information or reservations, contact **Keewaydin Island Club**, 260 Bay Rd., Naples FL 33940; 800-688-1935 or 941-262-4149.

MARCO & THE GULF ISLANDS

QUICK TOUR

Route 952, or Capri Boulevard, makes the trip through Isles of Capri development, which straddles four connected islands. Stringing along the route are modest and majestic homes, marinas, bait shops, condos, restaurants, and side streets with exotic names. Though radically developed, the area has more of a quiet fishing community feel than next-door Marco, with its upscale homes and upshooting condo buildings. Most of the commercial enterprise clusters at an S in the road. This amounts to a restaurant, an antique shop, the community center, and, straight ahead at the stop sign on Kon Tiki Drive, a seafood market. Back on Capri Boulevard, you'll pass a general store, a marina, real estate offices, another marina, and seaside restaurants before you head back into a residential area.

A road map of Marco Island, which measures about 24 square miles (6.5 miles by 5 at its widest), looks like three islands loosely divided by three main east-west roads, filled in with fingers of canal-pocked land.

From the north, a high arching bridge on Route 951, Collier Boulevard, drops you into the lap of Marco's residential and commercial development. Turn right on Bald Eagle Drive to visit Old Marco. Named for the island's emblematic claim to environmental fame, the road escapes the rat race for a brief respite into the island's Ten Thousand Island personality and bygone memories. Marinas line the bayside, which bustles with the activity of fishing boats and charters. Waterfront restaurants have a salty, laid-back flavor. At the end of the road, a couple of vintage houses and the Olde Marco Inn mark historical flavor among newer resorts and shopping centers.

Back on Collier Boulevard, get to Tigertail Beach, the main public access, by going right on Tigertail Court, then left on Hernando Drive. North of here is a private development, so head back to Collier, which begins its travels along the golden resort beach for which the island is famous. Unfortunately, you can't see the beach for the forest of condos. A beach access for residents only lies at the north end, another public access without parking at the very southern end.

San Marco Drive intersects the island midway and takes you most directly to Goodland. Winterberry Drive is less traveled. If you turn right on Barfield Drive, you'll find yourself among the island's priciest homes in the Estates Area. You'll notice a bit more elevation in these parts, and if you make your way to Indian Hill, you almost get the feel of driving San Francisco streets. Head back north on Barfield and turn right on San Marco, or Route 92. Just before the south-end bridge, you'll see the turnoff to Goodland. This tiny village, only a mile in circumference, lies at the end of a twisty, mangrove-fringed road. On the bay along Goodland Drive and Harbour Place is where you'll find most of the fun and flavor, amid stacks of crab traps. Visit one of the popular seafood restaurants and the Village Place local crafts shop. The rest of the town is mostly mobile home resort, marinas, and modern resort, interspersed with old crackerbox homes. Route 92 takes you off-island into Everglades fringes.

By-boat forays to the south lead through mangrove islands and beachy barrier islands between Marco and the boundaries of Everglades National Park at Fakahatchee Bay.

BACKFLASH

The Calusas were Goodland's earliest settlers, as was the case on most of the islands south of Sarasota. Goodland is believed to have been an important and sizable settlement, with towering shell mounds still standing as proof. Some reach 50 feet high.

Ponce de León landed at Caxambas Pass in 1513. The dunes then lining the Gulf front led the explorer to judge Florida as a mountainous land. Subsequent Spanish *conquistadores* discovered two artesian wells at Caxambas (meaning freshwater) Pass, making it a routine stopover for sailors in years to come. Spanish explorers later named the island San Marco after Saint Mark, which got shortened to Key Marco, then changed to Marco Island.

The name Goodland indicates the area's earliest reputation for good farmland. It is said to have been one of the continent's first named places. Henry Pettit, Goodland's original pioneer, grew avocados at the turn of the century.

Meanwhile, at the island's north-end village, clam canning made islanders a living. James Barfield discovered the profitability of the local clam beds and built a factory. Pioneer Captain Bill Collier revolutionized the industry with his invention of an automated clam dredge. A railroad was built through today's Isles of Capri, and the enterprise flourished into the 1940s on Fredericks Bay until killed off by a blight. In so-called Smokehouse Bay, mullet fishing and curing was the day's business. Where palatial mansions of the Estates Area flourish today, pineapples once grew. The enterprise lasted only 25 years, ruined by Hawaiian competition and the high mineral content of Marco's soil.

Collier, who had settled wild Marco in 1896, built a home, which later developed into a hotel for visiting sportsmen. Besides making a living charging guests $2 a night for a room in the Olde Marco Inn, he hunted for skins and fished.

In 1950, developer Barron Collier (no relation to Capt. Bill) moved 150-some villagers from Caxambas to Goodland, with plans to develop the north end. He also relocated the grocery store, post office, fish house, church, and 15 to 20 small cottages built by the Burnham and Doxsee clam factories. Collier's plans never reached fruition in his lifetime. Marco remained mired in a frontier era of lawlessness and sparse population until 1955, when Barron Collier's descendants began developing the island as a resort. Touted as one of the largest excavation jobs in the history of the U.S., it undertook the building of 100 miles of canal and 200 of seawall. In the 1960s, during the Cuban missile crisis, a tracking station was built on Marco's south-end beach.

Isles of Capri was born in 1955 when L. L. (Doc) Loach created a fishermen's retreat out of 700 acres of four mangrove islands. He dredged in causeways and built a road to connect the four.

Historical Attractions

The best way to learn about Marco Island and its past is via the guided **Marco Island Trolley Tour** (941-394-1600). You can simulate this one-hour-45-minute ride and save yourself $10 by picking up a booklet at the Chamber of Commerce and following the self-guided historical tour. But the guided tour is fraught with humor and old-time lore worth the price of admission.

Among other bits of information, you'll learn about the shell mounds of **Indian Hill**, the highest point in Southwest Florida at 58 feet. On Addison Court you'll see the remains of a wall built entirely out of conch shells. In Old Marco, the **Olde Marco Inn**, a National Historic Register site, and **Collier House** remember the island's earliest settlement, circa 1882.

Marco's **shell mounds** brought archaeologist Frank Hamilton Cushing to the island in 1896 to uncover one of the richest finds in North America.

THE NATURAL

Cruising the resort strip along the beach, it may be hard to place Marco in the realm of the natural Ten Thousand Islands. Nonetheless, it heads this vast archipelago. That side of its character is most evident in the bay waters of the Intracoastal Waterway.

Marco's neighboring Rookery Bay Sanctuary harbors birds, dolphins, fish, and manatees enough to fulfill any naturalist's dreams. It is easily accessible through Johnson Bay, which provides pristine passage to Key Island's leeward side. Even on the island's most developed stretch of beach, loggerhead turtles still lumber up on Marco Island to lay their eggs in the same sand where they were born. The island's crescent-shaped beach is one of the few natural occurrences of its kind throughout the world. Nests of the bald eagle, Marco's symbol of ecological survival, are interspersed throughout the island. At last count, there were nine pair in evidence. I've been told that panthers and wild boars also live on the island.

Southward, through Big Marco Pass, mangrove islands clump between island and shoreline. Frigates, pelicans, and other birds nest on three islands just south of the bridge, a designated wildlife conservation area. South of the Goodland bridge, the true tenor of the Ten Thousand Islands sounds in the clusters of beach-fringed islands vegetated with a few telltale signs of erstwhile human occupation, lots of seagrape trees, and cabbage palms. The invasive Australian pine (casuarina) is less prevalent.

Natural Attractions

Tigertail Beach has an offshore sandbar known as Sanddollar Island. Between it and the beaches, tidal pools fill with fish and the shorebirds that feed upon them. Behind the beach, a restricted bird nesting area assures good bird-watching. The lake at Mackle Park off Heathwood Drive hosts a host of birds, including bald eagles from time to time. One nest nearby has been recently vacated.

The canal end on Scott Drive and Inlet Drive is a good place to spot manatees in spring.

AQUA-ADVENTURE

Touring

Deep waters offshore allow boats to get close to the Gulf beaches of Marco Island. From the Gulf, boats can enter Marco Bay through Capri Pass. From Naples Bay, an intracoastal waterway (not part of the official West Coast ICW) trickles down to Dollar Bay, Rookery Bay, and Johnson Bay, off of which you'll find one of Isles of Capri's marinas. Another is trickier to reach, via Big Marco Pass and Tarpon Bay. Big Marco Pass accesses the marinas and waterfront restaurants of Factory Bay, Marco River (around Marker 15), and Goodland. To get to Goodland's marinas and restaurants, look west of marker 6. Shallow Caxambas Pass separates south

Marco from Kice Island, Cape Romano, and the area's south-lying keys.

The three Marco Island communities' major marinas provide transient docking, gas, and other supplies. They include **Misfits Marina** (231 Capri Blvd., Isles of Capri; 941-642-9666), **Williams Capri Marina** (250 Capri Blvd., Isles of Capri; 941-394-5643), **Marco River Marina** (951 Bald Eagle Dr., Marco; 941-394-2502), **Factory Bay Marina** (1079 Bald Eagle Dr., Marco; 941-642-6717), and **Goodland Bay Marina** (604 Palm Ave.; 941-394-2797).

Cruising tour charters are abundant in Marco Island's marinas. **Capt. Sandy's Manatee Express** (941-642-5773) in Goodland travels by pontoon, with an emphasis on spotting sea cows (a.k.a. manatees). **Sunshine Tours** out of Marco River Marina (642-5415) uses custom cruise boats to take 12 to 125 passengers fishing, beaching, nature-watching, lunching in Goodland, or partying. The longest running tour boat is **Rosie** (1083 Bald Eagle Dr., Marco; 941-394-7673), a paddlewheel double-decker that goes on lunch, dinner, and sightseeing excursions.

Fishing

Fishing charters concentrate on the fecund waters of Marco Island's many bays and inlets. Rookery Bay is a favorite, especially in winter. Gordon and Caxambas Passes have a reputation as hot summer fishing spots.

Try **Fishing Charters of Marco** (941-394-6000) for offshore, inshore, shelling, and sightseeing tours. **Sunshine Tours** (Marco River Marina, 951 Bald Eagle Dr., Marco; 941-642-5415) takes fishermen aboard the *Miss Louise*, a 32-foot boat with bathroom. For up-to-date local fishing information, call its Fishing Hotline (941-642-8888). **Capt. Russ Gober** (221 W. Goodland Dr., Goodland; 941-394-3041) has been doing it for a long time. Son of Stan, of Stan's Idle Hour fame, he can offer customers cook-up services.

Snorkeling/Scuba

Contact **Aqua Adventures** (1079 Bald Eagle Dr., Marco; 941-

394-3483) about their dive trips, instructions, and equipment rentals and sales. They go off-shore to ledges and wrecks.

Boating, Sailing & Canoeing

Two marinas on Isles of Capri rent boats: **Misfits Marina** (231 Capri Blvd.; 941-642-9666) and **Williams Capri Marina** (250 Capri Blvd.; 941-394-5643). Try **Horizon Excursions** at Misfits Marina (231 Capri Rd.; 941-394-9226) for sailboat rentals, lessons and yacht charters. The *Sweet Liberty* (941-793-3525) catamaran sails also from Misfits.

Marco Island's only public boat ramp, on Roberts Bay at the island's south end, is accessible from **Caxambas Park** (S. Collier Ct.). Restrooms, bait, and fuel are available.

Marco River Marina (951 Bald Eagle Dr., Marco; 941-394-2502) rents center consoles and pontoons. **Factory Bay Marina** (1079 Bald Eagle Dr., Marco; 941-642-6717) rents pontoons, center consoles, and Boston Whalers, and conducts airboat tours into Ten Thousand Islands. **Ship Ahoy Marina** (Route 92, Goodland; 941-642-7772) rents pontoons. Call **Beach Sports Windsurf & Tackle** (571 S. Collier Blvd., Marco; 941-642-4282) about ocean kayak trips.

Sailboarding & Surfing

Beach Sports Windsurf & Tackle (571 S. Collier Blvd., Marco; 941-642-4282) rents windsurfers and wakeboards.

Other

Marco Island Jet Ski & Water Sports (Marriott's Marco Island Resort, 400 S. Collier Blvd., Marco; 941-394-4344) offers guided waverunner excursions through the Everglades, parasailing, and other rentals.

ISLAND ADVENTURE

Biking

On two wheels is a great way to explore the island. Bike paths line all of the major roads, but sometimes end without notice. Rent single-speed to hybrids and touring bikes at **Scootertown** (845 Bald

Eagle Dr., Marco; 941-394-8400), which delivers free with a $30 minimum rental. Beach cruisers are for rent, as well as in-line skates and mountain bikes, at **Island Cyclery** (842 Bald Eagle Dr., Marco; 941-394-8400).

Hiking

There are nature trails at **Mackle Park** (1361 Andalusia Terrace, Marco).

Shelling & Beachcombing

Marco touts its shelling along 3.5 miles of crescent beach. Try Coconut Island or some of the nearby Ten Thousand Islands (such as Shell Island) for less picked-over pickings. Most charter services offer shelling excursions to Coconut or Key Islands.

Golfing

Public courses are all off-island. The best you can do is practice at the **Marco Island YMCA Driving Range** (101 Sandhill St.; 941-394-3144).

Tennis

You'll find two lighted public tennis courts at **Tommie Barfield Elementary School** (Trinidad and Kirkwood). **Collier County Racquet Club** (1275 San Marco Rd., Marco; 941-394-5454) has tennis and racquetball courts.

Other

Mackle Park (1361 Andalusia Terrace, Marco) has basketball, football, shuffleboard, and other recreational facilities. Scootertown (845 Bald Eagle Dr., Marco; 941-394-8400), rents in-line skates. So does **Beach Sports Windsurf & Tackle** (571 S. Collier Blvd., Marco; 941-642-4282).

CULTURE

The People

Isles of Capri folks are retired or serving the retirees. In both cases, they're low-key and sea-loving, which keeps the community's streets quiet.

Marco Island's year-round population census of about 13,000 is based on property ownership. Visitors and seasonal residents from all over the world add another 30,000 to the population each winter. Residents consist of hotel workers, business owners, retired corporate heads, major sports figures, and fame-names such as Alan Jackson and Tom Cruise. The variety is rich. There are social activities, centers, and restaurants for Jewish, Italian-American, Greek-American, and German-American residents.

Marco itself is "more like a suburban island," according to Jeffrey Barlow, owner of The Dining Room restaurant and transplant from Montreal and England. "We liked the laid-back quality of it, until we tried to do business, of course, and get the restaurant going and wanted to get everything done quickly. You got into the habit of accepting the speed of things. The people *are* nice, kind. The absence of crime makes you more relaxed. There are young people. You don't see them as much because they work. The retirees are always around so you see them more."

The people have an affinity for fishing and boating. It's said there are more boats than cars on the island. A love of partying seems also prevalent, especially bayside, away from the tourist facade. In Goodland, a mix of natives and transplants cherish the laid-back quiet. Fiercely independent and chauvinistic about their island, they work as mullet fishermen, guides, and in the town's popular fish houses. Close-knit and community-minded, they strive to clean up the town and keep it development- free.

Island Inspirations

In Goodland, a recluse named **Albert Seeley** has left his paintings and a legend.

Fairs & Festivals

The **Art League of Marco Island** hosts four outdoor fine arts and crafts shows at the League's grounds (1010 Winterberry Dr., Marco; 941-394-2178) in January, February, March, and December. Gaining in notoriety, the **Mullet Festival** (221 W. Goodland Dr., Goodland; 941-394-3041), held the weekend before the Super Bowl at Stan's Idle Hour Restaurant and Bar, features barbecue ribs, smoked mullet, Seminole and Miccosukee tacos and crafts, a kid's carnival, mullet-cleaning contests, and crowning of the Queen: She who does the best rendition of the Stan's trademark Buzzard Lope dance gets to wear a buzzard-feather crown and mullet-net robe.

Museums & Galleries

Dick Kramer Studio (601 Elkcam Circle, Marco; 941-642-8589) carries original works, portraits, limited editions and signed lithographs, by appointment only.

The Art League of Marco Island (1010 Winterberry Dr., Marco; 941-394-4221) holds classes and shows, and sells members' works in its Gallery Gift Shop.

Island Shopping

The General Store (Capri Blvd.) in Isles of Capri is a charming throwback to island resourcefulness. Fresh fruit and tomatoes are sold outside; inside, everything from bacon to bait buckets. You can buy a hot cup of coffee and sandwich and sit on a porch overlooking a canal while enjoying them.

For a wealth of Florida novels and nonfiction, visit the **Book End** (Heritage Square, 1000 N. Collier Blvd., Marco; 941-394-5343). It also stocks mainstream literature. Buy or rent books and music on cassette at **All Ears** (Mission de San Marco Plaza, Marco; 941-642-2296). At the **Conch Shelf** (400 S. Collier Blvd., Marco; 941-394-2511), you'll find Florida specialty gifts — hand-carved herons, fish, and dolphins, and exclusive lines of crystal and glass. **The Village Place** (213 Harbor Place, Goodland; 941-394-1990), a nonprofit shop to benefit the town's school children, sells handcrafts and homemade local preserves (sea grape, cocoplum, etc.) in a vintage cottage setting.

Architecture

Isles of Capri spans the history of modern Florida island housing styles, with a preponderance of 1970s-type concrete block houses, plus more stylish evolutions. One style trademark of the entire Ten Thousand Island area occurs with frequency around commercial buildings and dockside. Chickee huts, a contribution of the Seminoles and Miccosukees of the Everglades, are thatched-roof structures popularly used for "tiki" bars and, in Isles of Capri, for screen-sided restaurants.

On Marco Island, the **Olde Marco Inn**, upgraded from a sportsmen's dorm to a classy continental restaurant, is one of the island's most precious remnants of yesteryear, dressed up through the years in Victorian trappings. Old homes in the inn's neighborhood, known as Old Marco, serve as shops and restaurants. The oldest is **Bill Collier's home,** dated 1882 and recently restored to perky prettiness.

In the Estates Area, architecture attains epic proportions — beautiful mansions, most of them swaying Mediterranean. One unusual Deco-style home on Eubanks Court was used in "Miami Vice" filming.

Some of the relocated Caxambas structures survive in Goodland: boxy cottages built from shipwreck wood. The **Baptist Church's community building** was once the Caxambas grocery store. The old **Goodland Theater** holds a store at Mar-Good resort.

Theater

J. T. Smith's Broadway Baby Grand Theatre (Mission San Marco Plaza, 599 S. Collier Blvd. #315, Marco; 941-642-7469) is an offshoot of the Olde Schoolhouse Theatre on Sanibel Island. The style is revue, the quality New York professional. **Marco Island Players** (941-394-5171) perform community theater in various venues.

Music

Country music is the sound of these islands. Though trendier establishments may try to align Marco with the islands of the Caribbean and South Seas, the island is "good old boy" Florida at its heart. The **Key Lime Band** plays at the Snook Inn. Other times there's a country crooner. At Stan's Idle Hour in Goodland, **Stan Gober** himself has recorded a tape of local-color songs. **Johnny Angel** is a another local celebrity and recording star, famous for his Marco Island rap tunes.

Nightlife

The Marco Movie Theater (Mission de San Marco Plaza, 599 S. Collier Blvd., Marco; 941-642-1111) offers first-run shows and waitress service for dinners, beer, and wine. Many of the restaurants and resort lounges feature live music regularly, from country bands to piano.

TABLE HOPPING

Stone crab claws are the trademark delicacy of Ten Thousand Island restaurants. This prized catch ("almost as rare as nightingales' tongues," Florida author Marjorie Kinnan Rawlings once described their taste) comes in a rock-hard package, thus its name. What I like almost best about stone crab (next to what it does to the tastebuds) is the fact that its gustatory pleasure comes guilt-free. Since only the claws of the shellfish are taken, and regenerated in time, no stone crab is asked to give its life to our seafood-gluttonous cause. Stone crabs are in season October 15 through May 15.

In Isles of Capri, buy 'em at **Capri Fisheries** (218 Kon Tiki Dr., 800-741-5569 or 941-394-3149). The market will mail stone crabs. It also sells shrimp and fish.

Isles of Capri's restaurants all charm the piscean diner with water views and docking nearby. **Blue Heron Inn** (387 Capri Blvd.; 941-394-6248) puts out white linens and a five-course spread for fine diners. **Bub's Sunset Bar & Grill** (231 Capri Blvd.; 941-394-8767) is a screened chickee at Misfits Marina, serving burgers, seafood, raw-bar items and casual fare. **Alexander's Shrimp Boat Restaurant** (203 Capri Blvd.; 941-394-0252) has a Bavarian specialties section on its otherwise Florida seafood menu.

For fresh fish and stone crab, the name to know is **Doxsee** (1165 Bald Eagle Dr., Marco; 941-394-6999). With more than 100 restaurants on the island, Marco covers every genre of cuisine. Its most trademark would have to be its old-Florida style of no-nonsense, trend-resistant seafood preparation. German cuisine also surfaces frequently.

The Snook Inn (1215 Bald Eagle Dr., Marco; 941-394-3313) fronts the Marco River, with boat docking and an outdoor chickee bar that's lively and fun. The restaurant is scenic. Those who don't sit by a window get a view of aquarium life. The food is typical old-Florida style, but not exactly the selling point. **Olde Marco Inn** (Old Marco, Marco; 941-394-3131/3132) is the old village's vestige of pioneer days. Once you were required to provide your own meat. Today you are pampered in refined surroundings with fine continental cuisine, emphasis on German. One other departure from fish-house cuisine is found at the Radisson's **Mango Leoni's** (Radisson Suite Beach Resort, 600 S. Collier Blvd., Marco; 941-394-4100). Its so-called Floribbean cookery represents the new in Florida style — a blend of tropic tastes that borrows heavily from Key West and the Caribbean.

Little Bar (205 Harbor Dr., Goodland; 394-5663) exceeds its humble name with lots of dining space, some on a screened porch dockside, some in a room decorated with the remains of a historic boat, some in rooms uniquely decorated with oak pipe-organ pieces. Friendly to a fault. The cuisine stretches to new tropic styles. I like to have lunch at a dockside table at **Stan's Idle Hour** (221 W. Goodland Dr., Goodland; 941-394-3041). The backbay view of the mullet fishing industry and local-colorful surroundings go well with the Southern fried specialties.

Treasured Recipes, published by the San Marco Catholic Church, is a collection of local food how-to. Call 941-394-5181.

ISLAND LANDINGS

The big three on Marco are the **Hilton,** the **Marriott,** and the **Radisson,** all three posing sky high along Marco's luxuriously white beach. The Hilton serves the luxury market, the Marriott with its sprawling facilities caters to the business clientele, and the Radisson concentrates on families with roomy kitchen suites and a demonstrated commitment to introducing children to the environment.

For accommodations with docking, look to the bayside. **The Boat House** (1180 Edington Place, Marco Island, FL 33937; 941-642-2400) is an inexpensive option with nice, modern, one- or two-bedroom condos, and a swimming pool. **The Pavilion** (1170 Edington Place, Marco Island, FL 33937; 941-394-3345) offers more seclusion on its waterfront. You have your choice of one-bedroom, two-bedroom, or villa, all modern facilities with a property swimming pool.

Mar-Good RV Park, Campground and Cottages (321 Peartree Ave., Goodland, FL 33933; 941-394-6383) takes up much of the town. Its air-conditioned cottages have one or two bedrooms and kitchenettes. Docking is available with gas, plus a deli, store, and tackle-bait shop. Some of the amenities occupy the old Goodland Theater. The fish camp is owned by two retired circus veterans, Reckless Rex and Reckless Ruby.

TOURIST TRAPS

Many nature-elitist islanders and island-lovers find Marco Island an atrocity for diminishing its green space in favor of concrete. To some degree I am one of them, but parts of the island tug at my heart and keep Marco Island from falling completely out of my favor. Keep to Old Marco's bayfront and Goodland, and you'll find true island spirit alive and well here.

Sources & Resources

Marco Island Area Chamber of Commerce, 1102 N. Collier Blvd., Marco Island, FL 33937; 941-394-3061. **Marco Island & The Everglades Convention & Visitors Bureau,** 1102 N. Collier Blvd., Marco Island, FL 33937; 800-788-6272 or 941-394-3061.

Marco Island Eagle (P.O. Box 579, Marco Island, FL 33969; 941-394-7592) is a 25-year-old weekly covering community news. *Naples Daily News' The Marco Island* (941-262-3161) even has a Society column with tidbits of gossip. It's distributed free on the island.

For a taste of recent history and controversy, pick up a copy of The Last Paradise: *The Building of Marco Island* by Douglas Waitley, which covers the island's development by Barron Collier's descendants, a.k.a. Deltona Corporation. Marion Spjut Gilliland wrote two books on the subject of Marco's early Amerindian settlements, *Key Marco's Buried Treasure* (University of Florida Press, 1989) and *The Material Culture of Key Marco*, Florida (University Presses of Florida, 1975).

CHOKOLOSKEE & TEN THOUSAND ISLANDS

QUICK TOUR

Highway 29 probes 147-acre Chokoloskee Island from Everglades City on the mainland, crossing bay waters via a two-mile, mangrove-fringed causeway backdropped by the shimmering waters of Chokoloskee Bay. Housing and RV resort developments first greet you island-side. On the right, the "Chokoloskee Mall" signifies the island sense of humor: It is an unglorified grouping of grocery store, tackle shop, and post office.

At the four-way stop, go right on Chokoloskee Drive through modest home and trailer communities. Turn left on Mamie Street and follow the narrow road to its south end at the bay. There the red, stilted Smallwood Museum hangs over the water, a hangover from another era. Backtrack on Mamie until you get to Hamilton Lane. The general store and Chokoloskee Island Park (a trailer encampment) take opposite corners. Go left to buy fresh-from-the-source seafood at Hamilton Stone Crabs. After that you'll have seen about all there is to see of the island (most of the attraction is on the water). Mamie will turn into Demere Lane and return you to Highway 29. You'll have traveled about two miles around the island.

For a quick introductory tour of the immediate vicinity of Ten Thousand Islands, board an Everglades Park tour in Everglades City. There are scores of other sightseeing charters available from local marinas. Or bring or rent your own craft and set out to explore. Some of the area's islands still hold remnants of times past. Lopez Place, today one of several designated campgrounds for overnight canoeists on the Wilderness Waterway, harbors the remains of a cistern, now boarded up. Names etched into the cistern's cement date back to 1887. The Watson Place, a 35-plus-acre island on the Chatham River, marks the turn-of-the-century homestead of a locally infamous outlaw believed to have been part of the James Gang (the gunfighters, not the musicians). Other mangrove islands have decks, chickees, and restrooms for recreational users.

Mostly what you'll find in this vast maze of backwater keys is quiet. Only frolicking dolphins, low alligator profiles, an occasional pair of wood storks, a roseate spoonbill now and then, and flurries of white ibises and egrets punctuate the eerie, harmonious   infinity.

BACKFLASH

The Everglades and Ten Thousand Islands have traditionally served as home to Florida's Amerindians, who plied their watery highways in dugout canoes and built up low-lying islands by dredging and piling oyster shell fill. The largest shell island was named Chokoloskee, a Seminole word for "old home."

As do most islands, this area claims a Ponce de León incident. Legend says he stopped at Cape Romano, which he called Manataca, for a brief layover — brief because the in-residence Calusa Indians threatened. In the end, the natives retreated out of fear of artillery.

At the close of the Seminole Wars, natives who wished to escape being shipped out West went into hiding in the mysterious, impenetrable land of the Everglades. For years it remained their territory. Captain Richard Bushrod Turner, a U.S. veteran of the Seminole Wars, retired in the late 1870s to a large island near Chokoloskee that now bears his name. Others — many escaping something or other — settled smaller islands where they lived a life safe from the eye of the law.

In the early days of white Everglades settlement, circa 1880, islanders made a living fishing for mullet, turtles, and clams, hunting egret plumes, trading firewood, and growing vegetables, fruit, and sugarcane. Produce went to New York by way of Key West.

Living arrangements were the most rudimentary, making use of palm fronds and whatever materials the locals could obtain by trade.

Charles G. McKinney, known variously as The Sage and "the man who put the chuckle in Chokoloskee," was one of the island's first settlers, along with a family called Santini. McKinney started the island's first post office, school, and church. His humorous musings were published in the *American Eagle*, a weekly newspaper in Estero, for nearly 20 years.

From the early days of poaching bird feathers, surviving in the 'Glades often meant skirting the law, later by hunting alligators and by smuggling. Chokoloskee history grew to legendary proportions when Ed Watson moved to the area in the 1890s. Linked with the James Gang and the murder of Belle Starr, his own murder at the Smallwood Store in 1910 became the subject of a recent best-selling novel by Peter Matthiessen (*Killing Mr. Watson*, Random House, 1990).

In 1947, the National Park Service took control of the Everglades and Ten Thousand Islands, restoring law and order and striving to return all things to their natural state. In 1957, the first bridge connected Chokoloskee to the mainland at Everglades City.

Historical Attractions

Where Seminole Amerindians once traded with the white settlers of Chokoloskee Island, **Smallwood's Store** (360 Mamie St.; 941-695-2989) still stands today as a museum and monument to a bygone way of life. The stilted wooden building on the bay has withstood hurricanes and witnessed the slaughter of a famous outlaw. Today it dwells in utter quietude. Inside, dusty shelves are lined with bottles, cans, farming equipment, and other general store memorabilia from the era when it opened, circa 1900.

THE NATURAL

Ten Thousand Islands make up the largest mangrove forest in the world. The mangrove, that leggy lover of salt water, fringes all the islands, taking hold wherever one of its bobbing seeds drops roots to build yet another key out of a sandbar. Native author Loren "Totch" Brown tells how he built his own Totch Key when at age 11 he stuck a ring of "bobs" into an oyster bar. Today, at age 74, he has mixed feelings about the mangroves. He claims that, left uncontrolled, the prolific plant is ruining fishing in the islands by overtaking oyster bars where fish once fed. He favors controlled burning.

Besides red, black, and white mangroves, other native vegetation such as cabbage palms and palmettos proliferates. A couple of exotic fruit trees here and there survive as reminders of a time when people lived on these islands, growing avocados, mangoes, tamarinds, and sugarcane to eat and trade.

The mangroves support a chain of animal life that begins with the tiniest fish and barnacles. They feed off its roots and the massive tonnage of leaves it drops each year. Birds roost in its wiry branches, among them the platypus-billed roseate spoonbill, mangrove cuckoos, black-whiskered vireos, herons, ospreys, pelicans, and wood storks. White ibises, known to old-timers as Chokoloskee chickens and a tasty dinner, and egrets abound. I've boated through on an occasion when the outboard scared up such huge flocks of birds that they practically blotted out the sun.

The 'Glades' most symbolic creature is the American alligator, whose snorts resound in the springtime when romance is in the air. A few crocodiles keep the 'gator population company. The islands are home to some unique and rare creatures, including the snail (formerly Everglades) kite, the manatee, and the golden Florida panther, all endangered. One local told me of boating through a vegetation-canopied creek and witnessing a panther jump over the boat from tree to tree. Panthers, however, are not usually that visible.

Natural Attractions

Ten Thousand Islands is a natural attraction that few really get into. Mosquitoes and limited accessibility weed out the less than enthusiastic. There are various ways to explore. Powerboating and sailing require a sharp eye and knowledge of channel markers. Tours extract the available sense of aloneness, an endangered species itself. Canoeing, for the energetic, is the most involving mode of exploration. Remember, collecting any living plant or animal is prohibited. You may pick up driftwood only for fuel, and collect one quart of empty (nonliving) seashells per person per day.

AQUA-ADVENTURE

Touring

Get an official nautical chart before attempting to find your way around this labyrinth of look-alike islands. You may be best off hiring a charter or joining a tour. Even the most experienced boaters complain that the charts are inaccurate in pinpointing the channels through tricky waters. Pontoon boats work best in these shallow waters. No matter how you go, wear long sleeves and pants, and take mosquito repellent.

Popular destinations include the Barron River for lunch at the historic Rod & Gun Club in Everglades City, or winding up on a deserted Gulf-side island beach. From Chokoloskee, Goodland is within easy motoring distance for lunch on Buzzard Bay.

Fishing

Chokoloskee is a major home port for commercial and sports fishermen. You'll have no problem finding fishing charters at the island's marinas. Within park limits, commercial fishing is prohibited, as is the use and possession of spear guns and poles. It's against the law to take live lobster and queen conch. (Conch collecting is illegal throughout Florida.)

Says Captain Russ Gober of Goodland: "The best thing about fishing the Ten Thousand Islands area is you can see a lot of nice wildlife. So you can do two things at once — fishing and sightseeing — as opposed to the Gulf, where you just see water — and that's pretty — but here you see birds and you see where they live. It's neat!" Gober favors Fakahatchee and Pumpkin Bays. Depending upon where you cast your line, you can fish from fresh and salt water in the rivers and bays of Ten Thousand Islands.

Capt. Viron Bender at Chokoloskee Island Park (941-695-

3584) has long years of experience in local waters. **Capt. John Carlisle's Tackle Box** (941-695-2244) sells bait, tackle, and charters.

Snorkeling/Scuba

Underwater enthusiasts recommend the northern tip of Indian Key for snorkeling.

Boating, Sailing & Canoeing

Chokoloskee Island Park & Marina (Hamilton Ln.; 941-695-2414) has a boat ramp, gas, bait, ice, dockage, and sites for trailers and tents.

A wilderness canoeist's dream, the designated **Wilderness Waterway** of Ten Thousand Islands weaves through 100 miles of backwater. The park service has designed trips ranging in duration from two-hours to eight days. Maps point out several designated free overnight camp spots. Canoeists must register in advance with the Ranger Station in Everglades City. The best time to avoid bugs and filled-up campsites is late October through February. Canoe rentals and shuttles are available out of Everglades City. Call FL 800-445-7724 or 941-695-2591. Contact Everglades National Park, 40001 State Rd. 9336, Homestead, FL 33034; 305-242-7700.

ISLAND ADVENTURE

Biking

A bike path crosses the causeway between Everglades City and Chokoloskee Island. It ends at the island, but there's little traffic to compete against for road space. **Chokoloskee Island Park** (Hamilton Ln.; 941-695-2414) rents bikes.

Shelling & Beachcombing

Some of the inner islands and keys have beaches where settlers once cleared away the mangroves. You'll find lots of shells in the landfill the ancient Amerindians once built, mostly oysters. More likely finds would be natural and historic artifacts. Laws limit empty shell collection to one quart per person per day. Collection of live shells, and driftwood for other than campfires, is prohibited.

Other

Waterskiing and personal watercraft, such as jet skis, are prohibited within park boundaries.

CULTURE

The People

The Ten Thousand Islands have always attracted the rugged individual: folks looking to be left alone for one reason or another. Local lore is rife with characters: strong-willed Seminoles, a man named Darwin who claimed relation to the evolution theorist, a hermit/former pirate named Panther Key John Gomez.

In the beginning on Chokoloskee, everyone — almost everyone — farmed for a living. Then they fished, and did a few illegal things — plume plucking, 'gator hunting, and pot smuggling — to supplement the bad-market times. Then came sportsmen with their tempting dollars and need for guides. They were followed by restrictions against commercial fishing and more tourists and yet more restrictions. Now, the islanders mostly cater to tourism. "We're an opportunistic population here," is how one local put it. They're also a resourceful, unpretentious bunch more characteristic of the kind of longtime Floridians you find inland than along coastal islands. A palpable frontier personality and survival instincts linger.

Before the causeway, 135 lived on the island. Today, there are around 600. "Us natives still have something together," says Totch Brown. "If something tragic were to happen, we'd pull together. We still stick together, not like the old days when we were one big happy family."

ISLAND INSPIRATIONS

Artists since the time of **John James Audubon** have been moved to immortalize the beauty of the Ten Thousand Islands and its creatures on canvas.

The mystique and intrigue of Ten Thousand Islands have inspired a few to record its aura of Wild West lawlessness. **Peter Matthiessen** in 1990 wrote about Chokoloskee's most famous outlaw in *Killing Mister Watson* (Random House, 1990). One source for Matthiessen's research for the book was an old-timer named **Totch Brown,** who in 1994 published his own colloquial, nonfictional account of times past, *Totch: A Life in the Everglades* (University Presses of Florida, 1993). He's also made videos about the islands' history for educational and trade sale.

Fairs & Festivals

February's **Seafood Festival** (more than 20 years old) in Everglades City packs the island with campers. It features country music, Seminole crafts and food, and of course seafood.

Island Shopping

Island Grill N Grocery (238 Mamie St.; 941-695-3633) embodies the spirit of Chokoloskee: it's friendly and resourceful, sells stone crab and rotisserie chicken, and is well-stocked with fishing supplies. It's the closest thing to a restaurant on Chokoloskee.

Architecture

The **Smallwood's Store Museum** is the most interesting island structure, preserving old island Cracker style. Most other homes and buildings are small, concrete or mobile homes, many run-down.

TABLE HOPPING

Chokoloskee Island is the major supplier of stone crab for the famous Joe's Stone Crab restaurant in Miami. According to Totch Brown, he and his uncle invented America's appetite for the local delicacy. One of the biggest operations is **Ernest Hamilton's Stone Crabs** (Hamilton Ln.; 941-695-2771), a wholesaler that caters to individual buyers as well.

ISLAND LANDINGS

Ten Thousand Islands are not about comfortable lodging. They're about roughing it. What accommodations you choose depends upon how rough you want to get. At the "luxury" end of the scale is the old **Parkway Motel & Marina** (Chokoloskee Island, FL 33925; 941-695-3261). (Nearby Everglades City has an inn, B&B and other accommodations.) At the roughest extreme, try tent camping under one of the chickee roofs along the canoe waterway. Bring lots of repellent — and a sense of adventure.

Chokoloskee best accommodates RV-traveling visitors with a hankering to spend their days casting a line. **Outdoor Resorts** (P.O. Box 429, Chokoloskee, FL 33925; US 800-237-8247 or FL 800-282-9028) is the most modern and well-kept facility, with tennis courts, boat rentals, fishing guides, and motel rooms. **Chokoloskee Island Park** (P.O. Box 430, Chokoloskee, FL 33925; 941-695-2414) is a full-service travel-trailer resort and marina. It accepts tenters.

Sources & Resources

The Everglades Echo (2301 CR 951, Suite C, Naples, FL 33999; 941-353-0444) covers Chokoloskee and other nearby communities.

Charlton W. Tebeau's *The Story of the Chokoloskee Bay Country* (University of Miami Press, 1955; Banyan, 1976) is a good source for local history. The Bible of Everglades conservationism, a book that made the U.S. Government sit up and take notice of this national treasure in the 1940s, is the classic *The Everglades: River of Grass* by Marjory Stoneman Douglas (Pineapple Press, 1988 rev. ed.).

Everglades Area Chamber of Commerce, P.O. Box 130, Everglades City, FL 33929; 941-695-3941. Stop in on your way to the island; it's located at the corner of Highway 41 and Route 29. **Marco Island & The Everglades Convention & Visitors Bureau,** 1102 N. Collier Blvd., Marco Island, FL 33937; 800-788-6272 or 941-394-3061.

ISLAND PROFILE: LOREN "TOTCH" BROWN

"The first man who came here — whether Neanderthal or whatever — done what I would've done: fill the islands. Oyster shells were the only thing to fill with. The Calusas was the last to do it, except for my family."

Totch Brown.
(Chelle Koster Walton)

Loren G. "Totch" Brown is my guide through his native homeland, Ten Thousand Islands. Born here in 1920, his history and that of the islands are as intertwined as the prop roots of the red mangroves along the shoreline. He points out Need Help Key. Totch's grandfather, Charles G. McKinney, named it so because the soil was depleted. McKinney, known as "The Sage," was one of the region's first settlers. He built the first post office on Chokoloskee Island, where the Smallwood Store later made history as the stage for murderer Edward J. Watson's finale.

Totch points out the spot where the fiasco took place. At the boat ramp rails west of the store-turned-museum, Watson was gunned down by locals, as Totch tells it, unable to defend himself because a recent hurricane had dampened his ammunition.

"My mother, then a girl of seventeen, was on the beach nearby and saw everything that happened," writes Totch.

On Liquor Still Key, Totch's daddy used oyster shell fill to raise an island for his copper moonshine still. Most vestiges of civilization were burned when the islands became part of the Everglades National Park in 1947, says Totch. Nature later erased the beach landings, inland prairies, and farmsteads of earlier days. But with Totch at the helm, you can still see — or at least imagine — the way it was.

The old Lopez Place harbors the remains of a cistern. Totch's dad used to come here to get fresh water for his "'shine." Next to the cistern grows the tamarind tree that young Totch used to climb. "My mom made tamarind-ade from it," Totch recalls. "It was shy on sugar, and there weren't no ice, but it tasted better to me probably than milk shakes do to kids today."

The Watson Place, a 35-acre island on the Chatham River, marks the turn-of-the-century homestead of outlaw Watson. Totch's family moved to Watson Place when he was 12. "Without a doubt, some of the best of my years were right here," he says as he finds the ruins of Watson's sugar mill, the rock furnace that his father built underneath Watson's cast-iron syrup kettle, and the cistern where Totch conducted studies on alligator behavior.

Like most of Ten Thousand Islands' early residents, Totch hunted for food and money. He developed his career as an alligator poacher by learning his prey's habits. In later years, when a bad heart limited physical activity, Totch turned to pot smuggling, which eventually landed him in jail (technically, on tax-evasion charges), but ultimately led to his latest profession as a writer. Seems no one was interested in hearing his life's story until he got to the part where he hauled marijuana from Grand Bahama and Colombia to the impenetrable cover of the Everglades.

Since Totch has started telling tales of criminal adventure, he's perked up the ears of book publishers, moviemakers, and news reporters across the country. The success of his book, *Totch: A Life in the Everglades*, has led to videos, TV interviews, and near hero-worship by the press. But he takes little pride in his lawless ways of yore. Out in the Gulf, Turkey Key, once the site of a commercial fish house, sparks memories of better times. Totch sold fish to run boats back when he harvested pompano from these waters with his wife Estelle and their three youngsters.

As the five-hour tour draws to an end, and we come full circle back to Chokoloskee Island, Totch grows quieter, the stories briefer. At 74, after a quadruple bypass and other health problems, Totch needs his rest. He would like to prescribe the same for his beloved homeland, that inextricable part of his persona that could also use a break.

"Time run out for us. Time run out for the quiet Everglades," he told me, flat on his back. "I don't think it will ever be restored. People like to play too much and they don't care about tomorrow."

ABC Islands 283
Aborigines 8, 253
Alligators 13, 67, 255, 257, 308, 313, 317
Amberjacks 21, 45, 51, 79, 132
Amerindians 8, 9-10, 19, 21, 41, 47, 55, 69, 75, 77, 78, 84, 87, 90, 104, 112, 116, 136, 146, 150, 153, 167, 173, 185, 217, 221, 222, 228, 231, 232, 233, 253, 267, 274, 275, 294, 302, 303, 308, 309, 313, 314, 316
Anansco, Juan 168
Anclote Key 103, 105, 110-111
Anclote Key Lighthouse 110
Anclote Key State Preserve 111
Anna Maria (town of) 155, 159-166
Anna Maria Island 22, 146, 155, 156, 157-158, 159-166, 167, 168, 180
Anna Maria Island Museum 160, 161
Ants 14
Apache Amerindians 41, 75
Apalachicola 30, 31, 32, 55, 76, 82, 83
Arbogast, E.M. 179
Archibald Memorial Park 122
Armadillos 13, 113, 257, 289
Atsena (Atseena) Otie 87, 90, 91, 93
Audubon Island 67
Audubon, John James 283, 313
Audubon Society 67, 255, 255
Avocados 21, 255, 295, 310
Bailey-Matthews Shell Museum 252, 257
Baker, Bru 10, 232
Bald eagles 14, 75, 75, 79, 110, 218, 233, 242, 275, 289, 297
Bananas 12, 48, 56, 255
Bank blink 33
Barefoot Beach Preserve 274, 276, 278
Barfield, James 295
Barron River 311
Bass 58, 76
Bean, George Emerson 161

Beasley County Park 47, 48
Beckstead, Garfield 222, 225
Beer Can Beach (*see* Greer Island)
Belleair Beach 121, 125, 126
Belleair Shores 106, 122, 126
Big Hickory Island 202, 268, 274, 275, 276
Big Lagoon 36
Big Lagoon State Recreation Area 36
Big Marco Pass 283, 297
Big Sarasota Pass 175
Billfish 58, 132
Bird Key
    Cedar Keys 87, 91
    Sarasota 157, 158, 173, 174, 180
Black Augustus 275
Black bears 12
Black bucks 75
Black Island 202, 273, 274, 275, 276
Black snakes 14
Black widows 15
Black's Island 69
Blackwing skimmers 67, 79, 151, 161, 228, 233
Blind Pass 243, 252
Blind Pass Beach 195, 197
Blue Mountain Beach 54
Boars (wild hogs) 12, 76, 228, 233, 297
Bobcats 12, 233, 257, 289
Boca Ciega Bay 124
Boca Grande 10, 22, 201, 203-204, 206-217, 221, 226, 227
Boca Grande Bayou 210, 212
Boca Grande Isle 210
Boca Grande Pass 208, 211, 213, 228
Boca Lighthouse 207, 208, 211, 212
Bokeelia 204, 231-239
Bonita Beach 201-202, 204-205, 270, 273, 279
Bonita Public Beach 276
Bonita Springs 205, 274
Bonne Fortune 146
Bonny, Anne 9, 267
Bowditch Park Beach 267
Bowles, William Augustus (Billy

Bowlegs) 9, 47, 61, 69, 78, 90
Bowman's Beach 252
Box tortoises 14, 41
Bradenton 146, 153, 155, 157, 168, 189
Bradenton Beach 155, 160-166
Brohard Park 157, 189, 194
Brown, Loren G. "Totch" 310, 313, 314, 316-318
Brown recluses 15
Browne, Dik 19, 170
Buck Key 247
Buffett, Jimmy 26, 51, 95, 220
Buttonwood trees 257
Buzzard Bay 311
Cabbage Key
    Lee County 8, 198, 202, 203-4, 212, 217-220, 221, 225, 230, 234, 243, 247, 258
    Pinellas County 142
Cabbage Key Inn 217, 218-219, 220
Cabbage palms 21, 48, 92. 97, 113, 150, 198, 218, 255, 297, 310 (*see also* Sabal palms)
Caladesi Island 14, 26, 103, 106, 111-115, 117
Caladesi Island State Park 113, 114, 115
Calusa Amerindians 8, 167, 173, 217, 222, 232, 233, 253, 267, 274, 294, 308, 316
Cannon Island 282
Cape Haze 203
Cape Romano 103, 283, 298, 308
Cape Sable 284
Cape St. George Lighthouse 77, 78
Cape San Blas 30, 31, 32, 33, 68-74
Cape San Blas Lighthouse 69, 70
Capone, Al 136
Capri Pass 297
Captiva Beach 244
Captiva History House 246
Captiva Island 2, 11, 17, 198, 202, 204, 223, 234, 240, 243-252, 253, 254, 260, 271, 279-281
Carambolas (star fruit) 21, 237
Cardinals 14
Carl E. Johnson Park 274, 275-276
Carrabelle 32, 84

Casey, John 185
Casey Key 11, 156-157, 159, 180, 184-188
Casino Beach 40, 42
Casperson Beach 157, 158, 189, 190, 191
Castor, Henry 150
Catlin, George 44
Caxambas 295, 298, 303
Caxambas Park 299
Cayo Costa 10, 198, 202, 203, 208, 212, 221, 226-230, 234, 247, 258
Cayo Costa State Park 228, 229
Cayo Pelau 202, 210, 214
Cedar Key 10, 12, 19, 20, 21, 22, 67, 86-101
Cedar Key Historical Society Museum 88, 92
Cedar Key State Museum 89, 91-92, 93
Cedar Key Wildlife Refuge 14, 87, 92
Chadwick Park 195
Chafer, Prudence 116
Chaise's Key (see Casey Key)
Charlotte Harbor 8, 207, 227, 237
Charlotte Harbor & Northern Railway 10, 208
Chatham River 317
Chickee huts 286, 287, 303, 304, 308, 315
Chino Key 223
Chokoloskee Bay 283, 307
Chokoloskee Island 284, 285, 307-318
Choctawatchee Bay 47, 57
Chowtaw Amerindian 55
Circus 11, 156, 168, 189
City Island 158, 172-178
Civil War 10, 41, 44, 46, 47, 66, 70, 91, 150, 168, 227
Clams 72, 73, 91, 97, 283, 284, 290, 295, 309
Clearwater 12, 26, 87, 102, 105, 109, 116-119
Clearwater Beach 17, 103, 106, 116-121
Clearwater Marine Science Aquarium Center 116, 117
Cleveland, President Grover 110
Clinton, President Bill 143
Cobia 16, 21, 58, 132
Cockroaches 14

Coconut Island 283, 300
Coconuts 12, 21, 156, 244, 246
Collier, Barron 221, 222, 223, 224, 228, 295-296, 306
Collier, Bill 295
Collier House 296, 303
Collier Inn 221, 223, 224, 225
Conch 230, 284, 296, 311
Coon Key 158
Coquina Beach 160
Coral snakes 14
Cortez 161, 162
Cottonmouth snakes 14, 92
Cormorants 14, 113
Cowhunters 21
Crab Island 47
Crabs 51, 82, 97, 129, 142, 237
  blue 83, 45, 233, 237
  ghost 41, 59, 69, 70, 73, 79
  (see also Stone crabs)
Crackers, Florida 21, 88, 96, 127, 141, 214, 231, 236, 254, 263, 291, 314
Crayfish (Crawfish) 21, 73
Creek Amerindians 9, 47, 75, 77, 78, 87
Crescent Beach 178, 181
Crooked Island 67
Cunningham Key 144
Cushing, Frank Hamilton 296
Darling, Jay Norwood "Ding" 246, 249
Darrow, Clarence 136
Davis, Jim 170
Davis, Robert 55
De Aury, Louis 110
De Luna, Tristan 40, 41
De Narváez, Pánfilo 9, 47
De Soto, Hernando 8, 146, 167
Deadman's Key 87, 91
Deal, Babs 187
Deal, Borden 187
Deer 289
  (see also White-tailed deer and Sambar deer)
Depot Key 10, 87, 90
Depression, the Great 11, 136, 143, 168
Destin 31, 47, 48, 52, 53-63, 65, 79
Destin Captain Len 55
Destin Fishing Museum 56
Destin Harbor 49, 53, 63
"Ding" Darling Wildlife Refuge (see J.N. "Ding" Darling

National Wildlife Refuge)
Dollar Bay 290, 297
Dolphins (Porpoises) 15, 42, 48, 52, 117, 137, 175, 234, 236, 275, 296, 308
Dolphinfish 16
Dog Island 30, 32, 84-85
Don Pedro Island 202, 203, 210, 212
Don Pedro Island State Recreation Area 212
Don CeSar Hotel 10, 104, 136-139, 143
Dona Bay 190
Dune Allen Beach 54
Dunedin 103, 115, 118
DuPont, Henry Francis 211
Dutchman Key 111
East Beach 146
Eastpoint 77, 83
Edison, Mrs. Thomas 289
Edison, Thomas 232
Eglin Air Force Base 40, 46-47, 50, 69
Egmont Key 10, 14, 104, 105, 108, 124, 146, 148, 150-152, 162
Egmont Key Lighthouse 150, 151
Egrets 13, 23, 92, 113, 228, 233, 257, 308, 309, 310
Emerald Coast 29, 33, 48, 53, 56
Emerson, Ralph Waldo 2
Englewood 155, 195, 197, 216
Englewood Beach 157, 158, 195-200
Ernst, Jimmy 19, 186-187
Estero Island 201-202, 204, 258, 266-273, 274, 275, 309
Euchee Amerindians 55
Everglades National Park 9, 10, 186, 257, 282, 284, 285, 294, 299, 303, 307-318
Everglades City 284, 285, 307, 309, 311, 312, 315
Factory Bay 297
Fakahatchee Bay 294, 312
Fakahatchee Pass 283
Fisherman's Park 137
Fishing licenses 16
Fitzgerald, F. Scott 10, 139, 143
Flounder 79, 83, 162
Florida Advisory Council on Environmental Education 15, 27

Florida islands
  number of 7
  formation of 8
  population of 6, 19-20
Ford, Henry 232
Fort Dade 151
Fort de Soto 2, 104, 105, 146-149
Fort de Soto County Park 26, 104, 145-149
Fort Island 86
Fort McRee 34, 35, 41
Fort Myers 11, 203-205, 253, 284, 285
Fort Myers Beach 201, 266-273, 275, 276
Fort Pickens 39-40, 41, 44, 45, 46
Fort Pickens National Park 39-44
Fort Walton Beach 29, 31, 40, 46-53, 55, 62, 65
Forts 10, 34, 35, 39-40, 41, 42, 44, 104, 147, 151, 162, 267
Frangista Beach 53
Fredericks Bay 295
Frigate birds 283, 297
Gainesville 87, 91
Galt Island 232, 233
Gaspar, José (Gasparilla) 9, 207, 210, 222, 227, 228, 232, 244-246, 283
Gasparilla Inn 10, 22, 206, 208, 210, 216
Gasparilla Island 11, 15, 17, 197, 198, 200, 201, 202, 203, 206-217, 224, 227
Gasparilla Island State Recreation Area 211, 212
Geckos 14
Gehrig, Lou 10, 136, 143
Geronimo 41
Gibbs, Bessie 98
Golden orb spiders 15
Gomez, John (Panther Key John) 283, 313
Goodland 283, 285, 294-307
Gopher tortoises 14, 113, 149, 151, 287
Gordon Pass 286, 290, 298
Grayton Beach 54, 55, 59-64
Grayton Beach State Recreation Area 54, 57, 58, 59, 65
Green flash 109, 242
Greer Island 167, 169

Grey, Zane 221
Groupers 16, 20, 21, 22, 45, 73, 83, 97, 125, 132, 142, 171, 173, 174, 198, 215, 237-238, 243, 263, 276
Grove City 203
Grunts 58
Guava 12, 237
Gulf Beaches Historical Museum 135, 136
Gulf Breeze 31, 39, 41
Gulf Islands National Seashore 29, 34, 35-36, 37, 39, 40, 41, 42, 47, 49
Gulfarium 47, 48, 52
Gulfside Park 253
Gumbo-limbo trees 12, 255, 257
Hatch, George 75
Hawks 14, 124, 233
Hearts of palm 21, 22, 97, 98 (see also Swamp cabbage)
Hellman, Lillian 182
Henderson Beach State Recreation Area 53, 57, 64
Hepburn, Audrey 170
Hermit Key 131
Herons 3, 13, 48, 113, 161, 218, 233, 275, 289, 310
Heron Lagoon 180
Higel, Harry L. 179, 189
Hodges, Quitman 100-101
Hog Island (see Honeymoon Island)
Hogs, feral (see Boars)
Holiday Isle 53
Holmes Beach 155, 160-166
Holocaust Memorial Museum 124
Honeymoon Island 12, 103, 106, 111-115
Honeymoon Island State Recreation Area 111, 115
Hoover, President Herbert 91
Horse and Chaise (see Venice)
Housekeeper spiders 15
Hummock Island 67
Hurricane Island 67
Hurricane Pass 112, 113
Hurricanes 24, 25, 70, 90, 91, 101, 103, 112, 113, 150, 253
Ibises 13, 92, 257, 308, 310
Indian Hill 294, 296
Indian Key 283, 312
Indian Key Pass 283,

Indian Pass 76
Indian Rocks Historical Museum 124
Indian Rocks Beach 103, 122, 124, 126, 127, 128
Indian Shores 106, 122, 124, 126
Inner Key 274
Intracoastal Waterway (ICW) 5, 32, 42, 87, 120, 129, 158, 162, 180, 187, 188, 190, 191, 195, 205, 210, 212, 218, 226, 241, 283, 296
Isla del Sol 144
Island Hotel 22, 98, 99
Island Inn 22, 264, 265
Isles of Capri 283, 285, 293-307
Izaak Walton Club 221, 223
Jacksonville 10
Jessup, Richard 187
J. N. "Ding" Darling National Wildlife Refuge 252, 254, 257, 259
James Gang 275
Jewfish 162, 174
Jewfish Key 167
Joewood 255
Johann Fust Community Library 206, 211
John's Pass 108, 123, 125, 127, 128, 130
Johnson, Don 170
Johnson, Mollie 275
Johnson Bay 283, 296, 297
Johnson Shoals 230
Jordan, Rufus 168
Jug Creek 231
Kantor, MacKinlay 182
Keewaydin Island Club 282, 285, 286-293
Kentucky Military Institute 189, 190, 192
Key Island 282, 283, 285, 286-293, 296, 300
Key limes 22, 129, 220, 255
Key Marco (see Marco Island)
Key West 10, 120, 150, 179, 208, 305, 309
Kice Island 298
Kingfish 132
Kingfish Wharf 130, 134
Kingston Key 283
Kipling, Rudyard 117
Kittridge, Jr., Chestman 287-288
Knight, Damon 127

LaCosta Island (*see* Cayo Costa)
Lafitte, Jean 9, 168
Lamarr, Hedy 11, 221
Langdon Beach 39
Lee, Robert E. 66, 147
Lefitt's Island 168
Lemon Bay 196, 197, 198, 216
Levique Juan (John) 123, 127
Lewis, John L. 233
Lido Key 156, 158, 169, 172-178
Lighthouses 10, 21, 69, 70, 71,
    76, 90-91, 92, 110, 150-
    151, 162, 207, 208, 211,
    212, 253, 254, 256, 258
Lindbergh, Anne Morrow 1, 2,
    19, 246, 249, 252
Lindbergh, Charles 2, 11 246,
    249
Lippincott, Joseph E. 187
Liquor Still Key 316
Little Bird Key 104, 144
Little Gasparilla Island 202, 203,
    210
Little Hickory Island 201-202,
    204-205, 238, 273-379
Little Marco Island 283
Little Pine Island 231
Little St. George Island 30, 32,
    77-84
Little Sarasota Bay 180, 185
Live oaks 92, 112, 185
Loach, L. L. 296
Lobsters 16, 21, 58, 73, 110,
    129, 311
Loggerhead turtles 48, 75, 84,
    117, 161, 196, 228-229, 255,
    289, 292, 296-297
Long Beach (village of) 167, 168
Long Key 104, 108, 134-143
Longans 237
Longboat Key 9, 156, 158, 166-
    172
Lopez Place 284, 308, 317
Love bugs 14-15
Lover's Key 202, 204, 258, 270,
    274, 276
Lover's Key State Recreation
    Area 274, 275, 277
Lubber grasshoppers 15
Lychees 237
Lynn Hall Memorial Park 269
MacDonald, John D. 11, 19, 95,
    179, 182, 187
Mackerel 16, 51, 79, 88, 171,
    198, 234, 276, 290

Mackle Park 297, 300
Madeira Beach 103, 108, 122,
    126, 127, 128
Madelaine Key 146, 148
Madira Bickel Indian Mound 153
Mahi-mahi (*see* Dolphinfish)
Manasota Beach 158, 195, 197,
    198
Manasota Beach Club 196, 200
Manasota Key 157, 158, 159,
    191, 195-200
Manatee County Public Beach
    160
Manatees 13, 175, 196-197, 234,
    257, 275, 296, 297, 298, 310
Mangos 12, 172, 231, 237, 255,
    310
Mangroves 12, 114, 117, 149,
    218, 231, 233, 234, 242,
    282, 283, 289, 294, 296,
    297, 307, 309-310, 312
Mann, Thomas 168
Marco (town of) 283, 284, 293-
    307
Marco Island 283, 284, 285, 286,
    289, 290, 293-307
Marco Bay 297
Marco River 297, 305
Marlin 29, 58
Matanzas Pass 268
Matanzas Preserve 268
Matlacha 231, 232-239
Matthiessen, Peter 309, 314
McKinney, Charles G. 309, 316
Mexico Beach 73
Miccosukee Amerindians 19,
    302, 303
Middle Beach (*see* Blind Pass
    Beach)
Midnight Pass 180, 181, 185
Millet, Edna St. Vincent 261
Miramar Beach 53
Mites 15
Monarch butterflies 33, 56, 61,
    71
Monkfish 21
Morgan, J. P. 10, 208
Mormon Key 284
Mosquitoes 14, 26, 33, 147, 167,
    205, 226, 276, 277, 310
Mote Marine Laboratory and
    Aquarium 173, 174, 178
Mound Key 202, 232, 274, 275
Muir, John 95
Mullet 15, 16, 51, 97, 171, 208,
    226, 238, 295, 301, 302,

305, 309
Mullet Key 102, 104, 147, 148,
    151
Museum of the Island 231, 232,
    233, 239
Museum of the Sea and Indian 56
Naples 11, 206, 282, 285, 288,
    291
Naples Bay 292, 297
Naples Conservancy 289
Navarre Beach 40, 42
Need Help Hey 316
Neville Wildlife Preserve 180
New Pass 169, 174, 175
Nokomis 189
Nokomis Beach 157, 184-188
No-see-ums 14, 26, 33, 205
North Captiva Island 198, 202,
    203-204, 220, 221, 230,
    234, 239-243, 246, 248
North Captiva State Recreation
    Area 241
North Key 87, 91
North Redington Beach 122, 127,
    128
Oaks (see Live oaks)
Okaloosa Island 29, 31, 40, 46-
    53, 57
Okaloosa Island Park 47
Okaloosa/Walton Peninsula 29,
    31, 53-65
Old Destin Post Office Museum
    56
Old Salt Works 69, 70, 74
Olde Marco Inn 294, 295, 296,
    303
Opossums 233, 257
Ospreys 13, 79, 92, 113, 114,
    218, 228, 255, 257, 287,
    289, 310
Otter Key 174
Oyster Bay 223
Oysters 45, 73, 79, 82-83, 97,
    129, 236, 237, 238, 308,
    310, 316
Palm Island 198, 202, 203, 210,
    216 (*see also* Longboat Key)
Palm trees 11, 12, 56, 223 (*see
    also* Cabbage palms, Sabal
    palms, and Coconuts)
Palmettos 12, 289, 310
Palmetto bugs 14
Panama City 29, 30, 32, 66, 67
Panama City Beach 29, 31, 43,
    65, 66, 67, 68

Panthers, Florida 12, 223, 257, 297, 310
Panther Key 283
Paradise Island 131
Pardee Key 104, 144
Passage Key 161, 162
Pass-A-Grille 104, 135-143
Pass-A-Grille Park 135, 139
Pavilion Key 283
Pelican Bay 226, 228, 230
Pelican Man's Bird Sanctuary 173, 175
Pelicans 48, 67, 71, 92, 94, 114, 124, 146, 173, 211, 228, 257, 283, 297, 310
Pensacola 10, 32, 39, 41, 46, 55, 72
Pensacola Bay 41, 42, 44
Pensacola Beach 39-40, 43, 44, 46
Pensacola Pass 41, 42, 44
Perdido Bay 35, 36
Perdido Key 29, 31, 34-38, 42
Perdido Key State Recreation Area 34, 36
Peregrine falcons 76
Perico Island 161
Peters, Mike 182
Pettit, Henry 295
Picnic Key 283-4
Pierce, C. W. 75
Piers, fishing 42, 47, 49, 107, 116, 118, 122, 125, 135, 146, 148, 160, 161, 162, 175, 181, 189, 190, 191, 194, 213, 258
Pine Island (Brooksville) 86
Pine Island (Lee County) 20, 202, 203-204, 221, 230, 231-239
Pine Island National Wildlife Refuge 234
Pine Island Sound 236
Pine Key 104, 144
Pineapples 12, 295
Pineland 231-239
Pirates 9-10, 35, 66, 118, 130, 133, 150, 207,210, 214, 222, 227, 228, 232, 244, 267, 275, 283
Plant, Henry 91, 136, 141
Pompano 16, 79, 83, 174, 237, 238, 243, 317
Ponce de León, Juan 8, 146, 160, 253, 295, 308

Porpoise Point Island 231
Porpoises (see Dolphins)
Port Charlotte 203
Port Charlotte State Recreation Area 195, 197, 199
Port Richey 87
Port St. Joe 31, 33, 71, 73
Preston, Evander 140-141
Pumpkin Bay 312
Punta Blanco 228
Punta Gorda 204, 208
Punta Rassa 21
Quietwater Beach 39, 44
Rabbits 233
Raccoons 13, 59, 79, 113, 228, 233, 241, 257, 276, 289
Rackham, "Calico" Jack 9
Railroad Depot 211
Railroads 10, 91, 208, 211, 213, 295
Rattlesnakes 14, 29, 92, 113, 151
Rauschenberg, Robert 19, 249
Rays 48, 258
Redfish 15, 16, 58, 79, 162, 234, 241, 290
Redfish Pass 248
Redington Beach 122, 127
Redington Shores 122, 126
Rinehart, Mary Roberts 217, 225
Ringling, John 11, 156, 168, 173, 174
Roach, John 222
Roberts Bay 190, 299
Roberts, Louis 179
Robins 13
Rookery Bay 283, 289, 297, 298
Rookery Bay Estuarine Reserve 289-290, 296
Roosevelt, Teddy 11, 221, 232, 246
Roseate spoonbills 13
Rum-running 102
Sabal palms 12, 257, 289 (see also Cabbage palms)
Safety Harbor 239-243
St. Amand, Charles 174
St. Andrews Bay 66, 67
St. Andrews State Park 31, 67, 68
St. Armands Circle 156, 172-178
St. Armands Key 156, 157, 158, 171, 172-178
St. Augustine 41
St. Christopher Key 147
St. George Island 30, 32, 77, 79-84

St. George Island State Park 77-80, 83
St. James City 231-239
St. Jean Key 147
St. Joseph Bay 70, 71
St. Joseph Peninsula State Park 69, 70, 71, 74
St. Pete Beach 10, 103, 104, 105, 108, 131, 135-143, 151, 159 (see also St. Petersburg Beach)
St. Petersburg 9, 11, 26, 102, 105, 108, 109, 117, 136, 149
St. Petersburg Beach 104, 138 (see also St. Pete Beach)
St. Vincent Island 12, 30, 31, 74-76
Salinas Park 33, 69
Sambar deer 12, 75, 76
San Carlos Island 204, 266, 268, 272
San Carlos Pass 276
San Marcos Movie House 211
Sand Island 67, 112
Sand Key 103, 106, 116, 121-130, 131
Sand Key Park 121, 129
Sanddollar Island 297
Sandestin 53, 55, 59, 60, 64-65
Sandhill cranes 13, 124
Sandpipers 14
Sanibel-Captiva Conservation Foundation 252, 257, 259
Sanibel Island 15, 17, 19, 21, 22, 70, 199, 202, 204, 235, 243, 246, 250, 251, 252-266, 270, 271, 276, 303
Sanibel Island Historical Village 252, 254
Sanibel Lighthouse 70, 252, 254, 258
Santa Rosa Area Seashore (Santa Rosa Day-Use Area) 40, 42
Santa Rosa Beach 54, 57
Santa Rosa Island 29, 31, 32, 39-46
Santa Rosa Sound 31, 39, 42, 46
Sapodillas 12, 21
Sapotes 12
Sarasota 19, 117, 155, 156, 157, 168, 169, 180, 182, 189, 192, 294
Sarasota Bay Walk 173, 174
Sarasota Big Pass 180

Sarasota Key (see Lido Key)
Scallops 73, 233, 237
Scharrer, Henry 112
Sea grapes 12, 21, 113, 244, 257, 297, 302
Sea oats 12, 28, 113, 255
Sea turtles 42, 56, 79, 117 (see also Loggerhead turtles)
Seagulls 14, 48, 67
Seahorse Key 87, 90-93
Seahorse Key Lighthouse 90-91, 92
Seashells 15, 18, 28, 37, 50, 56, 68, 72, 80, 94, 115, 118, 126, 149, 150, 164, 181, 199, 211, 214, 230, 248, 255, 257, 259-260, 270, 276, 283, 290, 300, 311, 312
Seaside 54, 55, 56, 59, 61, 62, 63, 64, 65
Seaside Institute 61, 63
Seminole Amerindians 10, 19, 21, 75, 185, 302, 303, 308, 309, 313, 314
Seminole Wars 10, 19, 21, 75, 308
Shell Island
  Pinellas County 29, 31, 65-68
  Ten Thousand Islands 300
Shell Key 104, 108 124, 137, 144, 149-152
Sharks 16, 56, 117, 132, 162, 173, 174, 190, 191, 192, 194, 195, 214, 234
Sheepsheads 16, 58, 79, 107, 198, 234, 241, 276
Shrimp 16, 20, 21, 22, 45, 51, 64, 73, 83, 97, 142, 237, 238, 263, 272, 304
Siesta Key 11, 156, 158, 159, 178-184, 189
Siesta Public Beach 182
Sister Keys 167
Skinks 14
Silva, Joe 124
Skinner, L. B. 117
Slash pines 48, 56, 113, 114, 289
Smallwood's Store Museum 307, 309, 314, 316
Smokehouse Bay 295
Snail (Everglades) kite 310
Snake Key 87, 90, 91
Snappers 16, 21, 58, 79, 83, 132, 174, 198, 237, 241

Snook 16, 162, 174, 233, 234, 276-277, 290
South Beach 214
South Lido Beach 173, 175
Spanish-American War 10, 147-148, 151
Spanish moss 12
Sponges 58, 117
Spring break 6, 29, 43
Star fruit (see Carambola)
Starr, Belle 275, 309
Steele, Augustus 90
Stewart, Rod 143
Stone crabs 16, 21, 98, 220, 263, 304, 314
Stop Key 283
Suncoast Seabird Sanctuary 122, 123, 124
Sunset Beach 104, 131, 133, 134
Sunshine Skyway 11, 162
Swamp cabbage 21 (see also Hearts of palm)
Tampa 87, 91, 102, 105, 136, 149, 150
Tampa Bay 11, 105, 124, 136, 147, 150, 160, 161, 162
Tarpon 15, 17, 79, 198, 208, 209, 210, 211, 212-213, 221, 223, 226, 234, 236, 241, 247, 290, 292
Tarpon Springs 106, 110, 111, 117
Tate, Ernest 116
Tate Island (see Clearwater Beach)
Temple, Shirley 11, 221
Ten Thousand Islands 9, 11, 17, 19, 27, 103, 205, 275, 282, 283, 284, 286, 289, 293, 296, 297, 299, 300, 303, 307-318
Terra Ceia 104, 108, 153
Tierra Verde 104, 108, 143-145, 146
Tiger Key 283
Tiger Tail 150
Tigertail Beach 294, 297
Timucuan Amerindians 8, 136, 167, 173
Tocabaga Amerindians 8, 104, 147, 173
Tornadoes 24, 25
Triggerf0000ish 21, 51, 58
Triple tails 16, 234

Treasure, buried 9, 131, 232
Treasure Island 6, 9, 104, 108, 123, 130-134
Trout 58, 79, 237, 276
Tupelo honey 73
Turkey Key 284, 317
Turkeys 75
Turner, Captain Richard Bushrod 308
Turner's Beach 244, 246, 247, 252, 258
Turtle Beach 179, 181
University of Florida 91
Upper Captiva (see North Captiva)
Useppa Island 8, 15, 202, 203-204, 220-226, 247
Venice (town of) 155, 157, 188-195
Venice Beach 157, 158, 185, 188-195, 199, 200
Venice Inlet 190
Vina Del Mar Island (Mud Key) 135
Wahoo 58
Watson, Edgar J. (Ed) 275, 309, 316, 317
Watson Place 308, 317
Waterspouts 24, 25
Way Key 26, 86, 90, 91
Wewahitchka 74
White flies 15
White-tailed deer 75, 76, 92, 233
Whitman, St. Clair 94
Wightman, (Uncle) Joe 249, 279-281
Wild hogs (see Boars)
Wildlife refuges 5, 14, 71, 74-77, 87, 92, 151, 180, 234, 252, 254, 257, 259
Wilderness Waterway 284, 308, 312, 315
Wolf Key 174
Wood Key 284
Wood storks 13, 76, 124, 161, 289, 308, 310
Woodpeckers 14, 110, 124, 248, 151, 289
World War I 41, 151
World War II 41, 55, 70, 71, 78, 84, 113, 136, 148, 151, 276, 288